the social worker's guide
to Child and Adolescent Mental Health

the social worker's guide

to Child and Adolescent Mental Health

Steven Walker
Foreword by Stephen Briggs

Jessica Kingsley *Publishers*
London and Philadelphia

First published in 2011
by Jessica Kingsley Publishers
116 Pentonville Road
London N1 9JB, UK
and
400 Market Street, Suite 400
Philadelphia, PA 19106, USA
www.jkp.com

Library of Congress Cataloging in Publication Data
Walker, Steven, 1954-
The social worker's guide to child and adolescent mental
health / Steven Walker ; foreword by Stephen Briggs.
p. cm.
Includes bibliographical references and index.
ISBN 978-1-84905-122-4 (alk. paper)
1. Child mental health. 2. Teenagers--Mental health. I. Title.
BF721.W225 2010
362.2083--dc22
2010004966

British Library Cataloguing in Publication Data
A CIP catalogue record for this book is available from the British Library

ISBN 978 1 84905 122 4

Printed and bound in Great Britain by
MPG Books Group

To Steve Herington

Acknowledgements

My sincere thanks to all those children and young people, parents, carers, colleagues and students I have known and worked with over the past 30 years, and from whom I have gained considerable inspiration, knowledge and learning. In particular I am indebted to the huge numbers of writers, researchers, academics and professional staff whose work I have drawn upon to improve and enhance the learning opportunities within this text. Any omissions are not deliberate and detailed references have been provided to enable the reader to investigate source material further in areas of particular or specialist interest. Copyright permissions have been sought where necessary but any missing should be brought to the attention of the author and publishers. Finally a special thanks to all at Jessica Kingsley Publishers, in particular Stephen Jones, Claire Cooper and Helen Kemp, whose support and forbearance has been deeply appreciated.

Steven Walker

Contents

List of Tables and Figures 8

Foreword by Stephen Briggs 9

Introduction 13

Part I Social Work Assessment and Intervention

Chapter 1   The Social Work Role in CAMHS 21

Chapter 2   Child Development and Attachment 47

Chapter 3   Mental Health Problems 69

Part II Applying the Skills of Social Work

Chapter 4   Social Work Skills and Methods 105

Chapter 5   Multi-disciplinary and Interprofessional Working 135

Chapter 6   Family and Community Support 159

Part III The Context of Social Work with Children and Young People

Chapter 7   The Organisational and Legal Framework 183

Chapter 8   Culture, Ethnicity and Diversity 205

Chapter 9   Understanding Spirituality and Religion 231

Conclusion 253

References 265

Subject Index 279

Author Index 286

List of Tables and Figures

Table Intro.1 Vulnerable groups in UK with mental health disorder   14

Table 2.1 Mental health problems, disorders and illnesses   49

Table 2.2 Domains assessed by the Child Health Questionnaire (CHQ)   53

Table 2.3 Prevalence of mental disorders   55

Table 2.4 Summary of developmental concepts   57

Table 2.5 Attachment behaviours and patterns in children and adolescents   59

Table 3.1 Mental health problems assessed by the Child Behaviour Checklist   72

Table 3.2 Common assessment tools   99

Table 4.1 Recommended treatments for children and young people's mental health disorders   116

Table 5.1 Health of the Nation (HoNOSCA) Scales   145

Table 7.1 CAMHS tiered framework   186

Table 7.2 Agency responses to the same presenting problem   192

Table 9.1 Fowler's stages of children's faith development   241

Figure 1.1 Tiers of CAMHS   34

Figure 5.1 Scale of collaboration, co-operation and co-ordination   139

Figure 5.2 Experience of Service Questionnaire (ESQ)   147

Figure 6.1 Method, model and focus   171

Figure 7.1 CAMHS service provider guidelines   184

Foreword

Social work faces challenges in relation to childhood mental health, in which it occupies a marginalised position in practice whilst having as a key theoretical underpinning the importance of children's emotional and psychological needs. It is more than 50 years since John Bowlby pointed out that psychological well-being is as important for childhood development as physical nourishment. We have now integrated this concept into our everyday assumptions and thinking; it has become embedded in our cultures that children need attention to their emotional and mental lives if they are to experience development during childhood and attain a healthy adulthood. We know that children require security of attachment, the availability of responsive and sensitive carers and opportunities for expression through play and learning and relationships. We know also that children who do not have these essentials are vulnerable and that attention paid to emotional and relational difficulties as they arise during childhood has the capacity to increase opportunities for recovery from difficulties and foster optimal development and resilience.

Recent government legislation has recognised the importance of mental health in childhood and the need to focus on providing this for children and young people who are in difficulties. The aim of developing a comprehensive child and adolescent mental health service is based on the central importance of mental health difficulties for the most vulnerable groups of children, groups that are routinely the preoccupation of social work, including children in care, refugee children, victims of child abuse, young offenders, those with learning difficulties and those with a parent who has a mental health problem, to name some of the key categories. Broadening the Child and Adolescent Mental Health Services (CAMHS) agenda in the quest for comprehensiveness has both released this work from its historically narrow professional base, usually within a medical model, and also revealed the extent of the difficulties services have in reaching and engaging with the large numbers of children and young people who have identifiable mental health issues and needs. The recent CAMHS review (Department for Children, Schools and Families [DCSF] 2008) confirms that children and adolescents have unacceptable waiting times for services and that the services they receive across the country are unequal. In making children's mental health 'everyone's business' (Lindsey 2005), this policy has generated a laudable aim and simultaneously some key questions in order to establish how services should go about meeting these needs.

To this question Steven Walker shows that social work has a particularly important contribution to make to the aimed-for comprehensive CAMHS. In demonstrating the relevance and advantages of the psychosocial approach applied in community settings, Walker shows that social work is best placed to make sense of the complex factors — internal and psychological, on the one hand, and environmental or societal on the other hand — that must be understood in order to address effectively the causes of mental health difficulties for each child. At its best, social work has this capacity, to connect internal and external and thus to get beyond more limited or one-dimensional approaches to understanding mental health; at times there is a cost to bear for this aspect of social work professional identity, but it provides opportunities too. As Walker shows, we have now to transcend the narrow, restrictive conflict of the 'nature versus nurture' debate that prevailed during the last century; we have to engage with diversity and use this capacity to move beyond the restrictive prejudiced practices of the past to generate practice which is socially inclusive and positions the service user as making an active contribution to services rather than being only a passive recipient. To do this social work needs to be able to make use of approaches that are based on theoretical inclusiveness and make for a practical, robust psychosocial practice.

Practice in child and adolescent mental health is difficult, complex and leads rarely to clear-cut outcomes. There is a tension between the wish for certainty — policy demands for clear outcomes and prescribed methods of intervention — and the complexities of people's lives and the difficulties they face, complexities that arise from the interaction of psychological, biological and environmental factors. These 'real' conditions faced by people in difficulty, distress and suffering test professionals and demand the capacity to bear uncertainty, face difficult feelings raised by contact with disturbing situations, and take a broad perspective with regard to how to understand the relative impact of the many and various factors that contribute to mental health difficulties in children, young people and their families. Living with uncertainty, bearing 'not knowing' and being able to think about both internal psychological and external environmental factors are qualities that social work brings to the professional task.

Thus, as is demonstrated in this excellent book, in the current contexts social work can no longer stay on the margins of child and adolescent mental health practice and it needs to actively engage in the comprehensive CAMHS agenda, at the levels of individual case assessment and intervention and service planning and delivery. In return child and adolescent mental health practice needs social work, for the contribution it can make to understanding mental health difficulties from an inclusive perspective, and with this book Steven Walker has written an account of such clarity and balance that an active reading will provide practitioners with a comprehensive basis for undertaking this work. There is now a text for social workers that comprehensively connects social work to child and adolescent mental health.

Professor Stephen Briggs
Vice Dean
Adolescent Department
Tavistock Clinic, London

Introduction

Doubt is not a pleasant condition. But certainty is absurd
Voltaire

Child and adolescent mental health (CAMH) can be a confusing, frightening and upsetting area of social work practice. It can also be immensely rewarding. Apart from the emotional impact of trying to help and support sometimes very ill children, social workers quickly find this area of practice is full of uncertainty. This book aims to allay your fears and help you cope with the many challenges of working with troubled children and young people by providing emotional and intellectual resources based on available knowledge and underpinned by core social work values and theories. However, the science, empirical evidence and variety of theories that inform child and adolescent mental health is not certain. Part of the social work task in this area of professional practice is to manage uncertainty and ambiguity and develop a capacity for doubt.

The world of the child or young person suffering mental health problems is a lonely, isolated one. Often it is a silent agony that corrodes the sense of self and produces wretched feelings, fear, dismay and hopelessness. When these troubles surface and become noticed by peers, parents or professionals their responses are too often punitive, rejecting, blaming or inconsiderate. We can think of these reactions as manifestations of defences against the overwhelming feelings of pain, suffering, fear, guilt and rage produced in adults caught up in the emotional turmoil of disturbed and disturbing children and adolescents.

Adults can thus also feel helpless, confused and frightened in the same way that the mental health problems in children are expressed. This book tries to reduce the gap between children and young people and others concerned about their mental health. It offers practitioners in this quintessential area of social work practice ways of helping, supporting and managing the internal and external resources necessary to respond appropriately. The book fully reflects the key purpose of social work which has been defined as:

A profession which promotes social change, problem solving in human relationships, and the empowerment and liberation of people to enhance well-being. Utilising theories of human behaviour and social systems, social work intervenes at the points where people interact with their environments. Principles of human rights and social justice are fundamental to social work. (International Association of Schools of Social Work and the International Federation of Social Workers 2001)

This powerful statement from a representative body of social workers from around the globe states quite clearly the twin elements that enshrine modern social work practice: the relationship between the external social world and the inner psychological experience of the individual that causes many children and young people pain and suffering. This social care text will be demanded by students, qualified practitioners, employers and training organisations keen to respond to the policy and practice imperatives prompting the new government focus on emotional well-being and child and adolescent mental health problems.

At the end of 2008 there were 22,000 children unable to access specialist CAMH services (CAMHS) due to long waiting times. The numbers of young people waiting more than 26 weeks ranged from 3.5 per cent to 18 per cent (www.rip.org.uk/files/prompts/p4/csm2.pdf). This means

TABLE INTRO. 1 VULNERABLE GROUPS IN UK WITH MENTAL HEALTH DISORDER

Vulnerable groups in UK with mental health disorder	Number	Proportion
Total child population 5–15 years	8.1 million	10%
Children in care (England)	61,000	45%
Generalised learning disability	194,000	33–50%
Victims of child abuse	80,000 annually	Not known
Homeless young people (16–21)	32,000	60%
Young offenders (15–20)	12,000	40–95%
Children with a parent who has a mental health problem	2 million	20%
Refugee children	60,000	40%
Children who have witnessed domestic violence	240,000	25%

Source: Joy, van Poortvliet and Yeowart 2008

that social work caseloads are containing increasing numbers of disturbed or troubled young people. Table Intro.1 illustrates the size of the problem and the particularly vulnerable groups of children and young people.

Seminal research nearly 15 years ago (Kurtz, Thornes and Wolkind 1995) came to similar conclusions as the latest independent review into child and adolescent mental health services (CAMHS). This starkly illustrates the lack of progress in this important area. Part of the aim of this book is to ask how this could be the case and what social work can do to improve things for a child similar to one born in 1995 when that research was published; who at age five showed disturbed behaviour at primary school, at eight years of age the early signs of depression, at 11 started self-harming and now aged 14 has been admitted to an inpatient psychiatric unit with a serious mental health problem which will have consequences for the rest of their lives. Does this serve as an indictment of government indolence or illustrate society's ambivalence about mental health and children's emotional well-being?

There is no coherent national strategy for CAMHS primarily because it falls between the Department of Health and the Department of Children, Schools and Families who each consistently fail to comply with the practice of the much-lauded government strategy of *joined up thinking*. Children's mental health needs have to compete with other demands in child protection and other children's services and especially the health care system and the Primary Care Trusts who are responsible for commissioning services but are struggling to manage their role. Multi-agency partnerships are meant to be the *modus operandi* of CAMHS but there are problems because of the different expectations from each partner agency of what CAMHS outcomes should be. Part of the problem with the organisation of CAMHS is whether to conceive it as a comprehensive or specialist service – in other words a preventive or a reactive provision. A preventive focus requires a planned training and educational programme for primary care, social work, health and education staff. Reactive provision is against universalist principles, is likely to be more costly in the long run and cannot contribute to health promotion.

The increasing trend towards including children and young people as active rather than passive recipients of health and social care means that the task of developing robust methods for obtaining children and young people's perceptions is important. Enabling them to collaborate in the design of research studies and to be consulted fully about the areas they consider important to research can only enrich these studies. The impact such research has in terms of the immediate effect on the child or young person and also on later service and practitioner development are areas requiring attention from researchers involved in this area of work. This highlights the need for continued vigilance and effort by social workers in the area of children's rights.

Children are also not a homogeneous group. The age ranges from childhood to adolescence incorporates several developmental stages which suggest attention should be paid to the design of developmentally appropriate methods of intervention. It is important in this context to continue the task of finding out what works best for which children in what circumstances, and to link this with why some children fail to develop mental health problems even in highly disadvantaged situations.

In 2008 the Secretary of State for Children, Schools and Families said that children and young people's emotional well-being was everybody's business – meaning it was not the sole responsibility of specialist Tier 3 child and family consultation services or the medical psychiatric professionals. In the same way that social workers have argued for decades that child protection is not their sole responsibility so social workers can now accept that they too have considerable responsibilities in the area of child and adolescent mental health. I hope this book provides you with the necessary resources to be able to engage more confidently in this area of work and, above all, enable you to reflect on your practice and on your own history so that by combining both experiences, you can offer the most important resource to troubled children and adolescents – yourself.

This book has been organised into three parts which could be described as the micro, meso and macro paradigms that embrace the corpus or the *Gestalt* of what I perceive to be a modern, progressive social work practice. Part I, Social work assessment and intervention, focuses on the micro level by first considering in Chapter 1 what role social work can play in CAMHS and how to develop knowledge and skills to help safeguard and promote the development of children with additional or complex needs. Then Chapter 2 reviews the importance of child development and attachment to understanding children's emotional experiences. It describes risk and resilience factors in the emotional well-being of children and young people and will help social workers consider how to synthesise child development and attachment theories in effective CAMH assessment. Chapter 3 considers the problematic definitions of mental health problems and the importance of multiple perceptions to children and young people's well-being by analysing the distinction between common and complex mental health problems. Social workers will be helped to evaluate the risk factors for complex mental health problems in young people.

Part II, Applying the skills of social work, examines the meso paradigm of CAMH by reviewing and critically analysing the most appropriate social work skills and methods relevant to practice in this area. Chapter 4 will enable social workers to develop familiarity with contemporary assessment tools, relevant methods and models of intervention and in particular to understand the key issues and skills relevant to effective risk management in working with troubled young people. Chapter 5 describes both the obstacles to and ways to achieve effective multi-disciplinary work and will help social workers review effective strategies for inclusive, integrated practice. Particular attention is given to help develop partnerships with other agencies to identify and analyse potential problems and appropriate responses to the mental health needs of children and young people. In Chapter 6 the importance of understanding the impact social policy changes have in either protecting or adversely affecting children's mental health is highlighted. Social workers need to consider how family and community resources can be harnessed to help support the emotional well-being of children and young people by developing knowledge and skills in relation to family functioning and community development. The impact of traumatic issues or events such as war, genocide and forced migration on the emotional development of refugee and asylum seeking children is given particular attention.

Part III, The context of social work with children and young people, is considered initially in Chapter 7 through the main legislative and policy framework for CAMHS and explains how this engages with and supports other children's services. In particular social workers will be helped to understand the ways in which the Human Rights Act and the UN Convention on the Rights of Children supports CAMHS. Chapter 8 describes what is meant by culturally competent practice, illustrating the importance of cultural identity to the mental health of children in a diverse society. This goes on to explain how understanding of oppression and discrimination influences contemporary social work practice to better address the mental health needs of Black and ethnic minority families. Chapter 9 examines the meaning of religion and spirituality as dimensions of children's emotional well-being and actively considers how social workers can learn to practise in CAMHS in a way that values and respects children and young people's beliefs. It illustrates how to adapt assessment and therapeutic interventions to embrace the diversity of personal and family belief systems.

Terminology

The term children and young person is used throughout this text generally to include people up to the age of 18 years. Specific reference to infants will be used to describe work with children up to five years, school age children up to 12 years and adolescents up to 18 years of age. These are, of course, arbitrary distinctions covering a wide variety of developmental and cognitive differences, but they will hopefully help the reader navigate to areas of specific interest whilst avoiding unnecessary repetition or confusion. The term parent/carers is used to highlight the important role played by non-biological adults in the upbringing of children and young people.

Family is a term used in its broadest sense to incorporate diverse forms of social groupings that do not necessarily fit the nuclear, heterosexual majority model, such as same-sex couples, step-families, single parent and communal families. Black is used in the text to include every ethnic group subjected to institutional and personal racism that results in the devaluing of ethnic minority culture. The terms psychological or mental health problems, rather than disorder or illness, are used generically to cover psychiatric terminology that is not appropriate for the intended readership and to avoid unnecessary repetition of the variety and severity of different emotional and behavioural difficulties faced by children and young people. Emotional well-being is a term increasingly appearing in the modern literature and policy guidance regarding children and young people and is used in this text synonymously with mental health.

Part I

Social Work Assessment and Intervention

Chapter 1

The Social Work Role in CAMHS

Learning objectives

» Describe and define modern social work practice in the context of constant social, economic and political change.

» Understand the challenges and dilemmas of social work practice with children at risk of developing mental health problems.

» Develop knowledge and skills to help safeguard and promote the development of children with additional or complex needs.

» Articulate the social work contribution to multi-agency work in children's services and CAMHS.

Introduction

The code of ethics for social workers (British Association of Social Workers [BASW] 2005) under the section on human dignity and worth makes explicit the expectation that professional social workers will:

• respect human dignity, individual and cultural diversity

• value every human being, their beliefs, goals, preferences and needs

• respect human rights and self determination

• seek partnership and empowerment with service users and with carers

• ensure protection for vulnerable people.

Contemporary social work practice continues to define itself in a changing legal, professional and organisational context within which social care staff are expected to safeguard the welfare and meet the increasingly complex needs of modern children and young people with fewer resources, increasing provision by the voluntary and private sectors and a retrenchment of the welfare state.

Social work is a part of the wider children's workforce and all programmes of post-qualifying education and training in social work with children and young people, their families and carers need to demonstrate they are enhancing competent and effective practice (General Social Care Council [GSCC] 2005a). Good continuous professional development and pre-qualifying training needs to be developed in relation to 'outcomes for children' as defined in the Government Green Paper *Every Child Matters* (2002) and described in more detail in the national framework for local change programmes published by the Department for Education and Skills (DfES) as *Every Child Matters: Change for Children* (DfES 2003).

Programmes must also provide evidence that they are developing practice and assessing outcomes in accordance with the National Service Framework for Children, Young People and Maternity Services (DfES and Department of Health [DoH] 2004). One of the fundamental aims of these specialist requirements is to ensure that social workers, wherever they are employed and whatever their specific roles and responsibilities, are able to promote and protect the well-being and welfare of children and young people.

This is part of the historical evolution of social work, which has included debates about the merits of generic versus specialist practice and the creation of false dichotomies between radicals citing the economic and political context as the locus for addressing social and psychological problems, and others proposing a psychosocial model seeking to address the internal psychological resources and resistance within clients. This chapter examines the developing role and nature of social work practice and articulates a modern, progressive model of practice in child and adolescent mental health (Walker 2001b).

Children and young people with mental health difficulties are increasingly coming to the attention of social workers practising in a variety of contexts such as: Adoption and Fostering, Child Protection, Care Proceedings, Mediation, Drug and Alcohol misuse services, Adult Mental Health services, Youth Justice, Family Support, and Education Welfare. National and international research demonstrates an increase in the number, range and the complexity of emotional and behavioural disturbance in children and adolescents (Audit Commission 1998; Mental Health Foundation 1999; Micklewright and Stewart 2000; Office for National Statistics 2006; Rutter and Smith 1995; Singh, Leung and Singh 2000; Walker 2001a). It is estimated that one in five children and young people under the age of 20 will experience psychological problems (World Health Organization [WHO] 2005).

The explanations offered for this contemporary phenomenon are as diverse as the methods and models of assessment and intervention employed to tackle the problem (Carr 2000). The following are all cited in the literature as risk factors (Cooper 1999 and Sutton 2000; NCH Action for Children 2007; Richardson and Joughin 2000):

- social exclusion
- parental separation and divorce
- rise in lone parent households
- racial discrimination
- child abuse
- increase in alcohol and substance misuse
- widening of the gap between rich and poor
- genetic predisposition
- retrenchment of the welfare state
- parental mental illness
- intimate partner abuse.

Equally, there is interesting research examining the circumstances, characteristics and dynamics of children and young people from high risk groups who *do not* develop mental health problems (Dulmus and Rapp-Paglicci 2000; Rutter 1999; Vostanis 2007). It is *as important* to determine the reasons for such resilience and protective factors, if social workers are to contribute fully to enhancing the mental health prospects of children and young people, and prevent problems rather than constantly reacting to difficulties (Walker 2004).

Workforce development

Recent government research illustrates the contemporary context of modern family life with one million children growing up with alcohol-addicted parents; 350,000 with at least one parent dependent on drugs; 140,000 families experiencing multiple and serious deprivations, with children more likely than others to be involved in crime, fail at school, be bullied or run away from home. One in eight children is considered to be growing up in a situation where they may be at risk (Home Office 2008). These features of family life today have endured for decades in some communities but are no less a shocking indictment of government social policies. They emphasise the critically important contribution social workers have to make.

The role and function of the social care workforce in social policy has been the subject of much discussion throughout the relatively short history of the social work profession (Adams, Dominelli and Payne 1998; Barclay 1982; Butrym 1976; Central Council for the Education and Training of Social Workers [CCETSW] 1989; Davies 1981; Giddings 1898; Kemshall 1993; O'Hagan 1996; Payne 2002; Richmond 1922; Titmuss 1958). The specific manifestation of that role and function in work with children and young people with mental health problems continues to receive little attention in the context of multi-disciplinary working, child protection, methods and models of therapeutic intervention and post-qualifying training (Adams, Dominelli and Payne 2002; Brearley 1995; Copley and Forryan 1997; Davies 1997; Higham 2009; Howe *et al.* 1999; Ruch 2009; Tovey 2007; Trevithick 2000).

Even the new Approved Mental Health Practitioner (AMHP) role replacing (and some argue subverting) the old Approved Social Worker role is focused on adult mental illness rather than child and adolescent mental health. The training requirements for the duties of an AMHP under the Mental Health Act 2007 specify that they play a key role in the care and protection of people with mental disorders and are expected to be accountable for the decisions they make. Children are hardly mentioned at all in the Specialist Standards for post-qualifying social work education and training for social work in mental health services (GSCC 2007a). The assumption is that mental health social work is about adults for adults with adults.

Under section 18 of the Mental Health Act local social services authorities are required to approve professionals as AMHPs, who may be social workers, nurses, occupational therapists or psychologists, to discharge the functions conferred on them by the Act. The Act stipulates that 'no person shall be approved by a local social services authority as having appropriate competence in dealing with persons who experience mental disorder unless he/she is approved by the local social services authority as having appropriate competence in dealing with such persons'. Under the Mental Health (Approval of Persons to be Approved Mental Health Professionals) (England) Regulations (2007) local social services authorities can only approve professionals who have successfully completed AMHP training approved by the GSCC. The problem is that former Approved

Social Workers (ASWs) are being redesignated as AMHPs, thus perpetuating the adult focus of their training and practice.

The arguments for a stronger social work role in CAMHS can be traced back to the emergence of the child guidance movement in the 1920s which led to the development of specialist clinics staffed by psychiatrists, psychologists and social workers. This inter-disciplinary model was based on assumptions about the totality of needs of children and young people referred due to concerns about their emotional and behavioural development. Nevertheless, criticism of the actual practice within these clinics could be made, because of a perceived neglect of social and environmental factors in relation to the causes of difficulties or the focus of intervention, despite the presence of social workers in the team.

Social workers in the child guidance clinics traditionally placed more emphasis on a psychoanalytical approach to their practice born from advanced training and a specific job title of psychiatric social worker (Lask and Lask 1981). The advantage of this was that it enabled practitioners to specialise and to share a common language and theoretical base with other clinic staff. The disadvantage was that assumptions and expectations of these social workers varied within and outside the child guidance clinics. Parents, teachers, health visitors and other social workers all had different expectations of the role and function of clinic social workers. They might be expected to offer individual psychotherapy, family counselling and parental guidance, or conduct risk assessments, and get involved with child abuse investigations.

All these diverse agendas put the clinic social workers in ethical and sometimes legal difficulties as they strived to balance the therapeutic requirements of their cases with procedural imperatives. Within the clinics other staff might expect social workers to support parents while intense therapeutic work was undertaken with children, or to meet with couples who required parenting advice or welfare rights information. The 1970 reorganisation of the delivery of children's services in local government within social services departments, and the advent of generic social work training, heralded an important change in the development of the role of social workers in child guidance clinics. The steady retrenchment in the welfare state, the trend towards care management and the changes in emphasis between preventive and protective social work meant the role of the specialist child mental health social worker was questioned.

The notion that social workers were behaving like therapists, or an elite branch of the profession, isolated them from fieldwork colleagues, bombarded by high levels of demand. Social work managers could argue that the clinic social workers were an expensive speciality, when resources were needed in child protection assessment. In addition, the debate around postmodernism, social constructionism and evidence-based practice combined to accelerate the culture of managerialism and the search for more cost-effectiveness in social work organisations (Leonard 1997; Parton 1994; Payne 1997; Pease and Fook 1999).

Social work practice in child and adolescent mental health work, like other clinic specialisms, is notoriously hard to quantify in outcome evaluation (Davis *et al.* 1997; Davis and Spurr 1998; McGuire, Stein and Rosenberry 1997). The increasing trends in child and adolescent mental health problems placed enormous strains on the child guidance, or renamed child and family consultation, services. Long waiting lists developed throughout the 1980s and 1990s forcing services to prioritise cases of high risk or severe disturbed behaviour, and neglecting children with emerging difficulties where preventive work could stop problems becoming entrenched and more difficult to resolve in the long term (Mental Health Foundation 1999).

The role and function of the specialist child mental health social worker began to mirror that of the fieldworker, forced to adopt short-term crisis interventions and spend disproportionate amounts of time on assessment, rather than longer-term effective work (Walker 2001a). The eclipse of specialist social work training in this area of practice, and the increasing culture of purchasing external family support or therapeutic services, has led to a reduction in the overall skills base available within social work. This places unfair pressure on voluntary and charitable family support projects, who are encouraged to try to help with complex circumstances beyond their scope. Child and family social workers in statutory local authority teams are therefore often left to handle risky, complex, multi-factorial situations in which the emotional and behavioural needs of children and young people are not being adequately met (Herington 2007).

Activity 1.1

o   Review a selection of classic social work textbooks and locate evidence related to the mental health needs of children and young people.

o   Reflect on the reasons for the inclusion or exclusion of this subject.

The evidence on adult mental health problems demonstrates conclusively that one of the biggest risk factors in developing adult mental health problems is a history of untreated or inadequately supported childhood mental health problems (DoH 1998b, 2001; Howe, G. 1999). An examination of the organisational framework in which child and adolescent mental health services are being planned and delivered currently helps illustrate the potential for a more definitive role for social work. This role embraces both a preventive and therapeutic model, grounded in psychosocial principles and consistent with community social work principles.

CAMH service development

In Britain recent government policy initiatives have prompted the reconfiguration of services for children and adolescents suffering from, or at risk of developing, mental health problems (DoH 1997a, 2000; Health Advisory Service 1995; DfES and DoH 2004). These are reflected in similar policy changes in many other countries while research into the effectiveness of different organisational forms of service delivery and the range of preventive and therapeutic support is being undertaken by the World Health Organization, the European Parliament and major university and independent research bodies. Child and adolescent mental health is a global issue.

Child and adolescent mental health services (CAMHS) have enjoyed something of a renaissance in recent years after decades of under-investment, rising demand and increasing waiting times for children and young people suffering psychological problems. At the same time social work has witnessed the continuing erosion of its original practice principles which employed a psychosocial framework to understand human difficulties resulting from a combination of external stressors and internal conflict.

Activity 1.2

o   Consider the discussion above and think about where you believe your social work practice style fits in.

o   In a team meeting or student group seminar initiate a discussion about the way your team practises or student group is being taught to practise.

The social work literature has recorded and debated the demise of the therapeutic dimension to social work practice while expressing a mixture of regret and ambivalence about its replacement with a care management or administrative model of practice (Adams *et al.* 2002; Payne 1997; Stepney and Ford 2000; Trevithick 2000).

Debates about the role of social work have peppered the modern history of the profession but in the 1980s sharply focused on the reaction to the Barclay Report and CCETSW paper 31 (CCETSW 1989). These documents provided social work educators and theorists with evidence to advance their arguments for social work to be part of the progressive movement which embraced community activism, resistance to oppressive state processes and solidarity with marginalised groups in society; or part of a residual welfare system, resisting any identification with social justice and seeking to maintain citizens within the limits of minimalist welfare provision (Corrigan and Leonard 1978; Dominelli 1988; Egan 1981; Howe, D. 1999; Jordan 1990).

However, changes in the way services for children and young people are currently being organised are opening up the possibility for social workers to practise in ways that many will find both satisfying and challenging, and that offer a contrast to the care management role currently prescribed. The opportunities to employ therapeutic skills based on a holistic model of social work practice are increasing in the statutory and voluntary sectors as well as health trusts and education departments employing social work practitioners (Walker 2003; 2004).

The policy towards multi-disciplinary working has been given added impetus following legislative changes and policy guidance that now enables easier joint budgeting between agencies and the creation of multi-disciplinary teams (Children Act 2004; Health Act 1999). The new Children's Trusts, Integrated Children's System and the Children's Plan (2007), are designed to set the framework for improvements in front-line work (see Chapter 7). This new environment is opening up possibilities for creative joint work where the sharing of skills, knowledge and expertise can enhance the quality of support offered to vulnerable children and young people where social workers are essential partners.

The welfare context

The foundation of children's welfare is based on the Every Child Matters policy launched in 2003 and since developed to improve the life chances of all children, reducing inequalities and helping them achieve what they want out of life. The resulting Common Assessment Framework and Common Core Skills and Knowledge provide a framework in which social workers seeking to deploy their full range of skills with troubled children and young people will find many opportunities (DoH and Department for Children, Schools and Families [DfCSF] 2004). Guidance based on research designed to produce a common language amongst professionals and support staff has started the long-awaited process of breaking down some of the cultural and practice barriers within the children's workforce. These barriers have regularly featured in public criticisms of agencies when a child dies or a mental health patient causes harm.

Whilst the recent focus in children's services has been on child protection or safeguarding children and the arguments around the role of extended schools in child protection, less attention has been paid to important changes in CAMHS already underway. These were heralded after research in the late 1990s provided evidence of increasing levels of significant mental health problems among children and young people worldwide (Goodman and Scott 1997; Rutter 1995; Singh *et al.* 2000; World Health Organization 2005).

Activity 1.3

o   At your next team meeting allocate some time to begin a discussion of media representations of CAMH.

o   Consider how such images affect the wider public, other professionals and young people.

Commentary

Media representations of young people tend to illuminate risk to others as with adult mental health; however, they are given extra zest by the idea of young people being 'out of control'. Young people's behavioural management is thus focused upon and finds expression in anti-social behaviour orders, school exclusion and custodial youth justice measures which have been criticised as punitive and reactionary responses. The underlying emotional and psychological causes are rarely acknowledged or addressed. Similarly, younger children who are challenging parents, carers and teachers are often wrongly diagnosed with attention deficit hyperactivity disorder (ADHD) and too readily labelled as aggressive, wilful or beyond control rather than perceived as having emerging mental health problems due to abuse, deprivation or neglect.

Social workers using their rich theoretical base and empirical evidence can assess how these reactions to children's distress can represent a misunderstood phenomenon, raise primitive feelings of blame and retribution and drive a desire for a seemingly easy quick-fix solution (Briggs 2002; Salzberger-Wittenberg 1981; Yelloly 1980).

The British government, in its *National Priorities Guidance, Modernising Health and Social Services,* stated that one of its mental health objectives was to improve provision of appropriate high quality care and treatment for children and young people by building up locally based child and adolescent mental health services (DoH 1999b). This would be achieved through improved liaison between primary care, specialist CAMHS, social services and other agencies. The problem is that CAMHS straddles the traditional ambivalence towards troubled children and young people. This raises the uncomfortable prospect of different agency staff perceiving troubled young people either as victims or villains, hindering multi-disciplinary understanding.

By 2004 the new Children Act set the seal on a series of initiatives undertaken by the Department of Health and the DfES including: Every Child Matters, The Next Steps and Change for Children with five outcomes linked to national targets and indicators which are in turn linked to a range of inspection criteria (DfES 2003). These related to improving inter-agency communication, shared databases, collaborative working, and the creation of Children's Trusts, local safeguarding children's boards and National Children's Commissioners.

These structural changes are failing to enable the more difficult practice changes in culture to take place between previously disparate services. Trying to meld the knowledge and value bases of education, social work and health will take much longer as staff get to grips with the implications of the deceptively easy rhetoric of collaborative and integrated working.

The National Service Framework for Children, Young People and Maternity Services 2004 (NSF) also set out laudable aims to enhance child health, welfare and reduce inequalities, narrow professional boundaries and focus on patient-centred care (DfES and DoH 2004). But these have not been linked to specific time-limited targets, or crucially, any extra resources. Part 9 of the NSF relates to CAMH and aspires to improve capacity, inter-agency working, early intervention and effective provision. In terms of CAMHS there are already signs that primary care health and education staff are concerned about the lack of skills and knowledge contained in their qualifying professional studies which fail to equip them to meet the expectations in the NSF.

New roles – old responsibilities

CAMHS are thus currently undergoing substantive changes in the way they are organised, staffed and delivered. The government failed in its intention to increase capacity in the CAMHS workforce by 2006 in order to create an improved comprehensive service after years of neglect. New multi-disciplinary primary mental health worker (PMHW) posts are being created to help improve capacity and fill the gap in provision between specialist Tier 3 CAMH services and primary Tier 1 services (Gale, Hassett and Sebuliba 2005). These posts are attracting many social workers due to their preventive, early intervention remit where social workers can use their full repertoire of knowledge and skills to the best advantage of troubled young people. Social workers are ideally placed to make a significant contribution to CAMHS through this role and by expanding on their existing roles in work with children and families.

Previous epidemiological studies that estimated the level of need in defined health authority areas always showed that the existing CAMHS was understaffed even though the level of demand was a fraction of the actual need for services in the community. The National CAMH Support Service set up to assist in the development of improved services produced detailed guidance and a prescriptive definition of the role of the PMHW. There are seven key components to the role:

- liaison
- consultation
- training
- supervision
- intervention
- strategic planning
- research and development. (Gale *et al.* 2005)

The liaison role anticipates the PMHW 'facilitating collaboration between all agencies…to enable the definition of the best approach to meet the mental health needs of the child' (p.41). The role of consultation replicates some of the tasks mentioned in the roles of supervision and intervention. The term consultation is open to multiple interpretations and will mean very different things to different professional staff. The potential for tension and/or confusion being generated between line managers and PMHWs seeking to offer advice and support is high, particularly where there are child protection concerns.

The training role is likely to become a focal point of pressure given the predicted shortfall in workforce numbers, but it offers an opportunity for experienced social workers to enrich their practice. The guidance from the NCSS suggests 'regular multi-agency training programmes should be offered to the range of professionals working with children…enabling them to recognise and manage child mental health problems at an early stage' (National CAMHS Support Service, p.55). The latest Post Qualifying Framework for social workers has the potential to enable social workers to gain specialist and advanced experience and training and gain employment in developing CAMH services.

The guidance states that 'the intervention role can be provided on two levels – through joint work with Tier 1 staff or direct work with children and families' (p.21). Joint work requires time and planning, the building of trusting relationships and negotiation of roles and appreciation of different working practices. In addition to the enormous waiting lists in Tier 3 together with hidden latent demand in the community it is expected that PMHWs will initially be subjected to considerable pressure to undertake large volumes of work.

The role of strategic planning is an interesting one in the context of the reconfiguration of children's services outlined in the 2004 Children Act and should appeal to many social workers. The guidance suggests the role 'includes the development and agreement of joint agency protocols for pathways of intervention, treatment or care...and contribution to the development of inter-agency structures to ensure joint planning and collaborative working relationships.' (p.63)

Finally the role of research and development envisages PMHWs 'identifying service needs and gaps across agencies with regards to children's mental health and obtaining users' views and involving users in the design and delivery of accessible CAMH provision' (p.78). The implications of this are profound. Needs assessment and analysis are notoriously difficult to implement . This hampers the production of statistically robust data with which to assist evaluation and planning. Involving children in service development is also difficult as it raises tricky ethical considerations, however, social workers' commitment to evidence-based practice and the paramountcy of children's welfare will equip them to undertake this role.

From emerging evidence on the development of CAMHS provision across the tiers, it has become increasingly clear that dedicated, quality support of universal services is required if the child's journey through CAMHS, in relation to their mental health needs, is to be seamless and comprehensive. The NSF for Children, Young People and Maternity Services (DoH 2004) emphasised the need for a balance and range of services that should be available to children and their families, in order that all levels of mental health need are met. This includes ensuring that professionals and workers at Tier 1, in daily contact with children, have sufficient knowledge of children's mental health needs in order to:

- identify those who need help
- support those with mild or minor problems
- refer to specialist services when appropriate.

To ensure that Tier 1 professionals and workers are enabled to develop their knowledge and skills base, it is important that they have access to high quality support, consultation, training and the provision of direct intervention in partnership with other agencies. Social workers aspiring to work as PMHWs have a clearly defined route available via the Post Qualifying Award in Social Work (PQSW) or other advanced training to equip them to undertake this role and bring a vital perspective to the emerging skills, value and knowledge base of this fascinating new job.

However, a system of PQSW education able to meet the needs of individuals and society rather than the challenges of globalisation must be based on a more sophisticated analysis of human autonomy, action and identity than suggested by the abstract ideologies of neo-liberalism (Lorenz 2005). Changes in the requirements of PQSW education currently suggest a reordering of the relationship between PQSW education, government and the social work profession modelled on neo-liberal ideology (Galpin 2009). The harnessing of a business-focused modernisation agenda to PQSW education undermines social work practice.

Current global discontent, along with the dissatisfaction experienced by social workers, may provide a foundation on which individual social work practitioners can draw together as a profession to find common ground with academics to find a new way forward. This would enable social work education to support the development of a motivated and stable workforce able to support economic and global concerns whilst maintaining anti-oppressive and anti-discriminatory practice that truly empowers all individuals in promoting acceptance and a broadening of our understanding of what, and who, is valued, regardless of their ability to contribute to a global economy in the form of inclusion in the labour market (Ferguson and Lavalette 2004).

It could be argued that higher education in England now represents the 'glue' that binds practitioners' professional development, competency and intellectual abilities, to their social work values and beliefs (Galpin 2009). PQSW education supports practitioners' contributions to meeting the challenges of a globalised economy while promoting practice designed to enable service users to develop individual economic power in the form of inclusion in the labour market (Lorenz 2005). However, learning also has a social and democratic purpose in terms of enabling, empowerment and freedom (Fieldhouse 1996).

The broader context of service provision

Mounting evidence has accumulated over recent years to highlight the need for policy and practice changes in the organisation and delivery of services for CAMH (Audit Commission 1999; Goodman 1997; Kurtz *et al.* 1995; Mental Health Foundation 2001; Pearce 1999). In the context of demand outstripping resources, it is acknowledged that changes in staffing arrangements and access routes to a range of appropriate and acceptable services is required. Better inter-agency co-operation, and an enhanced skills base, are key to improving effectiveness and efficiency. There is also a pressing need to offer accessible provision to socially excluded children and young people from the most disadvantaged environments who are often very difficult to engage in, and sustain, meaningful work to address their mental health needs (Arcelus, Bellerby and Vostanis 1999; Davis 1997; Vostanis 2007).

The four-tier pyramidal structure in Figure 1.1, adopted for child and adolescent mental health services (Health Advisory Service 1995), offers at first sight a rational framework for helping troubled children.

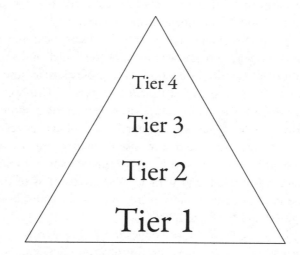

Figure 1.1 Tiers of CAMHS

From the broad Tier 1 base where many primary care staff can assess and intervene with minor problems, the structure ends at the Tier 4 apex where a few very specialist staff support the most disturbed children and young people. Social workers can work at all four tiers in many contexts, in the statutory or voluntary sector, in inter-disciplinary teams or in uni-professional roles. The four-tier structure is limited because children and young people do not fit neatly into the categories for increased intervention as the seriousness of their problems grows.

At Tier 1 the opportunity is for preventive work to tackle problems that have just emerged or are less entrenched and more able to yield positive outcomes. However, with the increasing trends in prevalence and complexity of problems at younger ages, demand outstrips resources, and social workers at Tier 1 may feel out of their depth or have to prioritise high risk work. The consequence is that children vulnerable to developing more serious mental health difficulties are neglected by the system, or are deterred from engaging with help, until they present for help and support in a more unavoidable way. The key is to make mental health services for children and young people acceptable and accessible in non-stigmatising community localities.

Previous government initiatives have tried to address this problem, and a national programme of research was commissioned to evaluate responses from local authorities and health trusts trying to meet the challenge of finding better ways of responding to this need (DoH 1997b). The key aspiration is that innovative responses should create preventive, early intervention inter-agency working, and more effective interprofessional co-operation, thereby resulting in better outcomes for troubled children within their own communities. The evidence from this research, however, was that evaluations were difficult to quantify and generalise from the specific characteristics of different forms of service delivery and research methodologies being employed (Kurtz 2001).

Linking specific interventions with agreed outcomes is also problematic due to the network of variables potentially impacting on a child or young person's development. One important issue to emerge is the way children acquire different at risk labels such as looked after, excluded or young offender, and the variety of perceptions of their needs from the care system, education system or youth justice system. Each professional system has its own language and methodology with which to describe the same child, invariably resulting in friction between agencies and misconceptions about how to work together and integrate interventions. In this climate the mental health needs of such children can also be neglected.

The increased use of voluntary agencies and unqualified family support staff is one facet of the strategy to provide more people to help parents quickly, rather than placing them on long waiting lists for specialist CAMH help, while their children's behaviour deteriorates. But without adequate training, supervision and support, these staff can be ineffective and potentially do more harm than good. Their limited knowledge base may prevent them assessing accurately and lead them to interpret a child's behaviour as wilful rather than a reaction to adverse circumstances, for example. The evidence (Davis *et al.* 1997; Dulmus and Rapp-Paglicci 2000; Durlak and Wells 1997; Oullette, Lazear and Chambers 1999) suggests that the way forward is to bring services closer to the children and families requiring them.

This means more integrated provision at the primary or Tier 1 level, with multi-disciplinary staff receiving training and support to intervene in ways that meet the needs of the local community. In addition a community work dimension is required to energise and mobilise the latent strengths of individuals and groups who can act as grassroots facilitators to help create preventive resources when and where they are needed. Such an organisational model requires a systems-level method of evaluation in order to test its effectiveness in delivering better outcomes for children and young people.

Activity 1.4

○ Investigate your local service catchment area and find out where the primary mental health workers are located, or what local provision is being offered by the voluntary and independent agencies for troubled children and young people.

○ Find out their service eligibility criteria and map that against the threshold limit of your service.

Commentary

A system of care made up of multiple agencies working together acknowledges that troubled children have multiple needs which require at different times, different combinations of a broad range of health and social care agencies. However, there is some evidence that just altering the service delivery configuration of CAMHS will not, of itself, translate into improved outcomes for troubled children (Morrissey, Johnsen and Calloway 1997). Future research needs to embrace evaluation of both the organisational and the therapeutic impact, and how these two variables interact.

A social work role for child and adolescent mental health

The GSCC (2005b) Specialist Standards and Requirements for post-qualifying training programmes for social workers supporting children and young people, their families and carers are expected to incorporate:

• the physical and mental health needs of children and young people (including a knowledge and understanding of how to use the services that exist to meet those needs)

• the risks associated with and the impact of drug and alcohol misuse on the lives of young people (including a knowledge and understanding of how to use relevant services to address these risks)

• the needs of children and young people with physical impairments and/or learning difficulties (including a knowledge and understanding of how to use the services that exist to meet those needs)

- the needs of young people involved with the youth and family justice systems (including a knowledge and understanding of how to use the services that exist to meet those needs)

- the needs of children and young people in asylum seeking families and unaccompanied asylum seeking children (including a knowledge and understanding of how to use the services that exist to meet those needs)

- the needs of children and young people accommodated, looked after and leaving care (including a knowledge and understanding of how to use the services that exist to meet those needs and the nature of the specific responsibilities of corporate parents, such as those associated with responsibilities for development and educational attainment)

- the social, psychological and legal issues associated with private fostering arrangements and their implications for child welfare.

It is clear that within the above standards and requirements the issues of mental health and emotional well-being are quite explicit. In addition the framework details a number of specific user-focused values which need to be firmly embedded in social work practice with children and young people, their families and carers. These are:

- engaging with others to develop trust

- exploring ways to share control over decision-making with young people and their families

- respect for others, including respect for difference

- honesty and openness

- an ability and a willingness to look at the needs of children and young people in a holistic way, setting problems alongside overall interests, talents and abilities and drawing on an awareness and appreciation of the diversity of lifestyles and experiences of children and young people in society.

Drawing on the traditions of social work practice in specialist CAMH settings it is possible to describe a model of contemporary practice which can complement the organisational changes currently being implemented in children's services and articulate with the GSCC specialist requirements. Such a model is based on psychosocial principles, but applied in the context of a community-oriented perspective. It is a model that can be utilised by social workers in a variety of contexts – not necessarily within specialist or non-statutory services. Social workers constrained by the limitations of the care management role, or repetitive assessment work, could find such a model both satisfying professionally and more effective (Walker 2004).

Without such a holistic tool there is a risk of colluding with neglectful parents seeking to pathologise the individual child or other agencies' narrow perspectives and failing to identify emerging mental health problems. The association of child mental health with a medical/pathological labelling process, or a genuine belief that only the parents require support to cope with their child's moods and behaviour, could disadvantage children.

A psychosocial model of social work practice offers the optimum framework to take account of all the individual child, family and environmental variables interacting to produce the identified difficulties. The model described in this book offers practitioners the opportunity to apply a flexible framework within which they can choose the appropriate method of assessment and intervention themselves, or contribute to multidisciplinary collaborative work, and evaluate the work of other professional or volunteer staff in the community.

The original characteristics of a psychosocial model of social work are typically described as understanding the person as well as the problem they are presenting. This means adopting a framework which accepts the notion of the inner and outer worlds of the service user which may be in conflict, resulting in repetitive, self-destructive behaviour (Woods and Hollis 1990). While this framework has a strong identification with psychodynamic methods of application, it is unhelpful to characterise it as narrow Freudianism or imply it is antipathetic to the needs of Black and working class clients (Dominelli 1988; Jordan 1990; Marsh 1997).

What it does is offer another resource to consider with clients whose anxiety, defence mechanisms and personal difficulties are hampering their attainment of fulfilling relationships with others and hindering effective parenting. Recognition of the feelings underlying these behaviours offers a rich source of material to work with. Social work practice based on a psychosocial model therefore:

- *concentrates* on the present rather than the past
- *attempts* to help people achieve equilibrium between their inner emotional states and the pressures they face in the outside world
- *utilises* the service user's relationship with the social worker actively. (Stepney and Ford 2000)

However, a modern psychosocial model requires refinement to take account of the need for emphasis on culturally competent, empowering and community-oriented practice. Eurocentric assumptions about normative standards of behaviour against which to assess psychological functioning have been criticised as dismissive of Black and other ethnic minority constructions of self identity and development (Robinson 1995). These criticisms can be applied to any social work model of practice which relies on stereotyped, one-dimensional assessment. The advantage of such a refined model is both the explicit inclusivity and the importance of an examination of feelings generated during the helping process.

The available evidence does suggest, however, that in the context of CAMH, it is community-oriented, proactive initiatives that are delivering measurable improvements in parenting skills and reductions in child mental health problems (Davis and Spurr 1998; Hutchings *et al.* 1998; Walker 2001a). A modern psychosocial model offers the appropriate holistic perspective for social workers to engage with other professionals in the community, to work in partnership with families and employ the personal relationship skills which the majority aspire to use.

Risk and resilience factors have been well documented in the literature (Howe *et al.* 1999; Parton 1999; Rutter 1985; Taylor and Devine 1993). These include:

- the child's response to stress being determined by the capacity to appraise and attach meaning to their situation

- age-related susceptibilities which permit older children to use their greater understanding compared to younger children

- how a child deals with adversity either actively or reactively and the ability to act positively is a function of self-esteem and feelings of self-efficacy rather than of any inherent problem-solving skills

- the quality of a child's resilience to developing mental health problems or emotional and behavioural difficulties is influenced by early life experiences but is not determinative of later outcomes.

This highlights the importance of psychosocial assessment methods that take account not just of individual characteristics within the child but equally within the family and broader environment. It is unlikely that this holistic level of assessment is available to unqualified volunteers, but the advantage of the model is that it can be employed by social workers as a tool for supervision and support of such staff. There is evidence of some fresh thinking in this area (Middleton 1997; Milner and O'Byrne 1998; Walker and Beckett 2004), where attempts to offer a more sophisticated model of assessment are being made, stressing the interactive quality of assessment variables and the need for enhanced interpretative and planning skills. The emphasis is on the need for analysing and weighing the information generated during the assessment process, ensuring this is underpinned by partnership practice and service user involvement.

Causal explanations for the increase in CAMH problems are yet to be fully developed. However, some of the recent literature indicates an area where a community-oriented psychosocial practice could make an impact. It is suggested (Bradshaw 2001; Clarke, Bradshaw and Williams 2001; Furlong and Carmel 1997; Rutter and Smith 1995) that poverty on its own is not a reliable predictor for child mental health problems. Other studies emphasise findings which demonstrate a link between social class and early childhood mental health problems (Meltzer *et al.* 2000), eating disorders (Fombonne 1995) and disproportionate numbers of young Black people diagnosed with schizophrenia (Smaje 1995; Walker 2004).

What is more certain is that contemporary society is characterised by increased family discord, parental separation and a youth culture which emphasises individualistic values, notions of self-realisation and personal fulfilment which increase the risk of mental health problems emerging. The notion of emotional illiteracy has gained currency in the context of trying to understand a generation of children and young people, from every class strata, who seem to lack the internal and external resources to help them make sense of their world. Combine these characteristics with an impoverished environment and poor life chances, and the ingredients of social exclusion can be identified as a precursor to the genesis of mental health problems. A psychosocial model could add an important dimension to the current research activity attempting to gather explanatory data to help inform policy and practice in this growing area of concern (Walker 2004).

The challenge of multi-agency work

Any model of social work practice in this area has to be able to find its place within the existing and constantly changing mosaic of professional and voluntary provision located in communities and informal networks. The challenge is to create a system of multi-disciplinary expertise and resources that is accessible and acceptable to service users, and that works together. Major barriers to effectiveness in the organisation of multi-disciplinary care are the structural inhibitors thwarting attempts to cut across professional boundaries to implement 'joined up working'. These can be exemplified by the variety of geographical boundaries covered by health, social services and education authorities (Leathard 1994; Young and Haynes 1993).

Activity 1.5

- ◦ List the unique knowledge and skills that social work brings to CAMH services.

- ◦ Explain how these are differently understood and articulated to those of other professionals working in this area.

Commentary

The range of professions potentially undertaking work with children and adolescents who have mental health problems bring different skills, training, experience and knowledge to the task. The NHS Advisory Service *Together We Stand* (1995) guidance suggests that irrespective of which tier of service is involved, there are some basic attributes which all members of a multi-disciplinary service or team should possess:

- • empathetic interviewing and counselling skills

- • a working knowledge of child development

- • up to date working knowledge of child and family problems

- • understanding of the impact of major life events on children's lives

- • awareness of how the professional's own life experiences informs their approach to others

- • familiarity with manifestations of serious mental health problems.

These are consistent with a psychosocial model of social work practice, but may not be reflected in other professional training and education. If the social work contribution to multi-disciplinary team or service developments in CAMH is to flourish, differences and similarities need highlighting. One way of achieving the clarity required for interprofessional practice is to examine the characteristics of the staff and the system they create. Ovretveit (1996) argues that it is important to be able to distinguish the type of multi-disciplinary team so that:

- • *practitioners* understand their role

- • *managers* can make changes to improve service quality

- • *planners* can decide which type is most suited to the needs of a client population

- *researchers* can contribute to knowledge about which type is most effective.

In attempting to promote multi-disciplinary working in CAMH, it needs to be recognised by service managers and planners in education, health and social work that previous experience offers grounds for scepticism. It has been observed that traditionally structured hierarchies have militated against collaboration, preserved separate role identities and inhibited interprofessional working (Fagin 1992; Rawson 1994). This has thwarted repeated attempts to achieve the much-vaunted seamless service for children and families in difficulties, as recommended in the Children Act (DoH 1989) and subsequent legislative and policy documents.

The new joint commissioning environment in health and social care enshrined in the Health Act (DoH 1999c) enables new services to be created that are designed to promote better multi-disciplinary working. This framework has begun to enable creative, innovative thinking to flourish within and between agencies. There is also evidence of attempts to foster interprofessional training among primary care staff who come into contact with children and adolescents with mental health problems (Firth, Dyer and Wilkes 1999; Sebuliba and Vostanis 2001). Health visitors, school nurses, social services support staff, family centre volunteers, general practitioners, education staff and community paediatricians usually have separate training on mental health issues without much co-ordination between each other.

These staff have a critical role in helping children and families by early identification of mental health problems and appropriate intervention (Bayley 1998). Interprofessional training can reflect the aspiration that people who work together should also train together to enable a consistency of approach to the identified difficulty (Department for Education and Employment [DFEE] 1998). Internationally, there have been studies designed to identify the interprofessional training needs of staff to enable them to function in integrated service delivery systems for children and young people (Magrab, Evans and Hurrell 1997). The conclusions are that policy frameworks focused on children's service planning in Britain (DoH and DFEE 1996) missed the opportunity to recognise multi-disciplinary training as a priority and to provide incentives to universities and other training institutions to develop interprofessional training programmes.

Where staff from different professional backgrounds work in one team, or closely co-operate in community networks and have similar training, they may face a problem with the blurring of roles and identities. At some stage the separate individual professions within each team or small network might begin to lose their former identity and metamorphose into a hybrid of all participating professions. There are contemporary examples of such hybrid posts being created in the primary mental health care field, where employers typically advertise for people from any relevant professional background, provided they have appropriate training and experience.

There is as yet no definitive primary mental health care qualification or separate professional training, but the development of CAMHS is prompting consideration of new ways of delivering support, which might include more multi-disciplinary formats. This concept is already manifest to some extent with the example of the joint practitioner in learning disability, with original qualification in, for example, nursing and social work (Davis, Rendell and Sims 1999).

Empowering children and young people

Focusing on the organisation and delivery of CAMHS, as well as managing the challenges in multi-disciplinary working and training, runs the risk of neglecting the service user dimension. The evidence of adult client/ patient/service user consultation, over changes in service provision in health and social care, is limited. For children's services in general, it is unusual. Children and young people's perspectives have rarely been explored in relation to the help they are offered towards their mental health difficulties (Gordon and Grant 1997; Walker 2001b).

There is a growing literature on children's rights and the importance of enabling children and young people to influence decisions about their own health and social welfare (Alderson 2000; Wilson 1999). However, Hennessey (1999) notes that in the contemporary enthusiasm for seeking the perceptions of children and adolescents as service users, the majority of research studies are methodologically flawed in terms of reliability and validity, while very few address issues of disability, sexuality, ethnicity and gender.

Research (Alderson 2000; Freeman et al. 1996; Hill, Laybourn and Borland 1996) describing some of the benefits of combining focus group discussions and individual interviews using multiple age-appropriate techniques, demonstrates the efforts being put in to maximise validity. They emphasise the importance of enabling children to participate in the research design as much as possible to offset the adult bias in methodology and to develop innovative methods of eliciting children's views and enabling young people to identify their own agenda as far as possible, rather than respond to an imposed one.

The literature relating to seeking the views of children is increasing and in doing so is addressing methodological and ethical challenges

(Christiansen and James 2000; Walker 2001b). Professional social work values of partnership and participatory work combined with skills in direct work with children are strongly indicated in this potentially empowering area of practice. A psychosocial model, as described above, is consistent with these values provided they are applied in the context of the local community, and focus on strengths as much as difficulties.

The behaviour and emotional affect of children and young people designated with symptoms of mental illness can be considered in different ways within a variety of professional discourses. The dominant discourse is that of medicine, and especially psychiatry, which continues to refine classifications of symptoms into universal descriptors (American Psychiatric Association 1994; WHO 1992). Yet behaviour and expressed emotions can be interpreted widely depending on the theoretical base of the professional involved and the specific cultural and historical context of their manifestation.

A child's behaviour could be assessed as genetic predisposition by a physician, a specific disease requiring treatment by a psychiatrist, cognitive distortions by a psychologist, repressed unconscious desires by a child psychotherapist, or a consequence of environmental disadvantage by a social worker. It is therefore important for social workers to acquire knowledge and understanding of these competing paradigms (Coulshed and Orme 1998; Hacking 1999; Taylor and White 2000), and locate them in a sceptical and inquisitive stance, in order to generate a range of resources to apply to the situation they are seeking to improve. Taking a community-oriented, psychosocial perspective enables social workers, uniquely, to place a child and young person's behaviour in a context which can synthesise and evaluate all the potential explanations.

As well as understanding why some children develop mental health problems, it is crucially important to learn more about those who in similar circumstances do not. Research is required to analyse the nature of these resilient children to understand whether coping strategies or skills can be transferred to other children. Positive factors such as reduced social isolation, good schooling and supportive adults outside the family appear to help. These are the very factors missing for asylum seekers, refugees and other ethnic minority families who live in deprived conditions and suffer more socio-economic disadvantages than other children.

The Department of Health refocusing children's services initiative (1995) together with the Quality Protects programme (1999a), and new assessment guidance (2000), were all evidence of a historical policy shift prompted by research into family support services and the limitations of the child protection system (DoH 1995; Statham 2000; Thoburn, Wilding and Watson 1998), designed to influence social work education, training and practice, and improve effectiveness. More policy developments (see Chapter 7 for details) have begun to reflect more clearly the CAMH issues. The future benefits for social work in the area of CAMH are likely to be substantial.

A more sophisticated modern discourse is beginning to be articulated, in which the compartmentalising of social work knowledge, theory and values is being challenged, in order to stretch the boundaries of practice possibilities (Lane 1997; Walker 2003c). It is not inconsistent to embrace the notion that social work practice in CAMH can shift to a more community-oriented, service user influenced, psychosocial model. This proposed synthesis is not especially new. Forty years ago the Seebohm Report (HMSO 1968, p.1) put forward a radical view of the role of personal social services that envisaged organisational and philosophical changes to the preceding fragmented, inadequate provision:

> We recommend a new local authority department providing a community based and family oriented service which will be available to all. This new department will, we believe reach far beyond the discovery and rescue of social casualties: it will enable the greatest possible number of individuals to act reciprocally giving and receiving service for the well-being of the whole community.

Combining a psychosocial model with community practice is not the contradiction it might superficially appear. As the organisational framework of health and social welfare is being modernised, the opportunity arises for intellectual agility on the part of social workers. Children and adolescents with mental health problems require creative and flexible solutions to their pain and suffering. The onus is on social workers to draw from their deep reservoir of knowledge and skills and apply them in contemporary circumstances to meet the needs of troubled young people in an acceptable, accessible and socially inclusive way.

Key chapter points

- The role and function of social work with children and young people with mental health problems continues to receive little attention in the context of post-qualifying training, multi-disciplinary working, child protection and methods and models of therapeutic intervention.

- The evidence demonstrates conclusively that one of the biggest risk factors in developing adult mental health problems is a history of untreated or inadequately supported childhood mental health problems.

- The opportunities to employ therapeutic skills based on a holistic model of social work practice are increasing in the statutory and voluntary sectors as well as in health trusts and education departments employing social work practitioners.

- Better inter-agency co-operation and an enhanced skills base are key to improving effectiveness and efficiency in CAMHS. There is a pressing need to offer accessible provision to socially excluded children and young people from the most disadvantaged environments who are often very difficult to engage, and sustain, in meaningful work to address their mental health needs.

- The available evidence suggests that it is community-oriented, proactive initiatives that are delivering measurable improvements in parenting skills, preventing the emergence of mental health problems and improving emotional well-being among children and adolescents.

- Staff from different professional backgrounds working in one team, or in community networks with similar training, may face a problem with the blurring of roles and identities. At some stage the separate individual professions within each team or small network might begin to lose their former identity and metamorphose into a new hybrid profession.

Chapter 2

Child Development
and Attachment

Learning objectives

» Describe the differences between mental health, mental health problem and mental disorder.

» Explain the importance of theories of human growth and development to CAMH.

» Describe risk and resilience factors in the emotional well-being of children and young people.

» Consider how to synthesise child development and attachment theories in effective CAMH assessment.

Introduction

Human growth and development are foundation elements of modern social work education and training. Within the expanded degree level curriculum and the post-qualifying framework the subject of child development and its link to mental health problems or emotional well-being requires a depth of attention if social workers are to feel confident in working with and supporting troubled children and adolescents. The spectrum of child development and mental health problems covers a wide arc from 'normal', through common and uncommon to complex and rare. This chapter will focus on the link between child development and mental health problems commonly experienced by children and adolescents. The concept of 'normal' is highly problematic yet it is a term that regularly appears in textbooks and is used by professional staff to try to measure and quantify the individual experience of troubled young people.

Defining normal is difficult due to the number of variables affecting a child or adolescent's behaviour or mood. Class, ethnicity, gender, language, culture, sexuality, religion and age are some of the factors that militate against generalising across populations. Within each factor there are sub-variables and distinctions, so for example it is problematic to make general assumptions about the age of adolescent transition and what is 'normal' behaviour at this time in a multi-cultural, ethnically rich and diverse society.

It is important to recognise that because something is statistically common does not mean it is easier to manage and that for an individual young person, their parents/carers, friends or teachers it can be part of complex and very difficult circumstances. It is not easy to distinguish between different levels of meaning and symptom severity, as we shall see later on, but the available evidence has been evaluated to help you feel better able to understand what might be happening in certain situations you are more likely to encounter and how you can use social work knowledge and skills to make a positive difference. The task is not helped by a variety of terms used by doctors, psychiatrists and psychologists in general or specialist contexts to describe the same thing. Thus we find the terms mental illness, mental health problem and mental disorder used interchangeably. Their use with children and young people and/or their parents/carers is also problematic because of the impact such language might have, and where other explanations for odd behaviour or changes in mood have previously been offered.

Social workers themselves may be very hesitant to use essentially medical language and descriptions when assessing children and young people. The word 'mental' can trigger a variety of associations and responses often conditioned by individual, family and societal attitudes. Media representations of mental illness can reinforce, or sometimes challenge, stereotypes. However, research demonstrates that there is still considerable stigma attached to the label mental illness/disorder/problem, with children themselves reflecting adult prejudice, ignorance and rank fear. Social workers are not immune to such beliefs and influences but it is important that you keep an open mind and not quickly leap to diagnose wrongly, or equally deny that a child may be developing mental health problems.

> The task of gathering information about possible causative factors (of child mental health problems) is complicated by the fact that it is adult carers, worried about children, not the children themselves that usually present asking for help. Children may not agree with parental interpretations of events and indeed may not even accept that there is a problem at all. (Fonagy *et al.* 2005, p.112)

Definitions and distinctions

The terms mental health problem, mental health disorder and mental illness are often used synonymously in both professional practice contexts and in the evidence-based literature. This can be confusing particularly for non-specialists and service users and their families. Table 2.1 offers a guide to help clarify the differences between these terms and how to measure their use in particular situations.

TABLE 2.1 MENTAL HEALTH PROBLEMS, DISORDERS AND ILLNESSES

Mental health problem	Common difficulties recognised as typically of brief duration and not requiring any formal professional intervention	Sutton (2000)
Mental health disorder	Abnormalities of emotions, behaviour, or social relationships sufficiently marked or prolonged to cause suffering or risk to optimal development in the child, or distress or disturbance in the child or community	Kurtz (1992)
Mental illness	A clinically recognisable set of symptoms or behaviour associated in most cases with considerable distress and substantial interference with personal functions	WHO 1992

A mental health problem can be distinguished from the term disorder by the degree of seriousness and the length of time the condition lasts. The assumption is that most people will recognise these symptoms and understand they do not require specialist or intensive intervention. Mental health disorder has echoes of the concept of child abuse to social workers familiar with the Children Act definition and the concept of significant harm. Note the idea of abnormality of emotions and the notion of them being sufficiently marked or prolonged. This parallel is useful in as much as it reveals how imprecise these definitions are and how open they are to interpretation. Who decides what is abnormal: the worker, parent or child? How is the notion of sufficiently marked or prolonged measured and against what standard? Mental illness takes us into the realm of medicine and clinical guidelines and diagnostic criteria usually applied to the most serious difficulties and those that are statistically rare. Whereas, at the other end of the scale, the terms emotional well-being or emotional literacy are becoming popular among the wider public and professionals even though it would be hard to find agreement about a definition of what these terms mean.

The behaviour and emotional affect of children and young people designated with symptoms of mental health difficulty can be considered in different ways within a variety of professional discourses. The dominant discourse is that of medicine and especially psychiatry, which continues to refine classifications of symptoms into universal descriptors (American Psychiatric Association 1994; WHO 1992). Yet behaviour and expressed emotions can be interpreted widely, depending on the theoretical base of the professional involved and the specific cultural and historical context of their manifestation.

Mental illness was constructed in the context of a debate among psychiatrists about the criteria for diagnosing specific mental health problems. Previously they had relied on a constellation of symptoms based on adult measures to distinguish children and adolescents whose condition was outside the normal experience. A recent study drew attention to the limitations in psychiatric diagnosis and, by implication, the medical model it embodies (Pickles *et al.* 2001). This study found that not all children with symptoms of mental disorder showed marked impairment and, conversely, some children had significant psychosocial impairment without reaching the clinical threshold for diagnosis.

If it is problematic to define mental *illness* or disorder, then it is equally difficult to define what is meant by mental *health* for children and young people. It can mean different things to families, children or professionals, and staff from different professional backgrounds might not share the same perception of what mental health is. A multi-disciplinary group agreed (Health Advisory Service [HAS] 1995) that mental health in childhood and adolescence is indicated by:

- a capacity to enter into and sustain mutually satisfying personal relationships

- a continuing progression of psychological development

- an ability to play and to learn so that attainments are appropriate for age and intellectual level

- a developing moral sense of right and wrong

- the degree of psychological distress and maladaptive behaviour being within normal limits for the child's age and context.

Defined in this way, mental health is a rather ideal state, which depends upon the potential and experience of each individual, and is maintained or hindered by external circumstances and events. According to Hadfield (1975) the child who is mentally healthy 'will obviously be both efficient and successful, for all his energies are employed to their full capacity. He will have a strong will and character, and be intelligent and moral'. This rather minimalist definition can be contrasted with a more fulsome contemporary definition of the HAS version offered by the Mental Health Foundation (1999) who suggest that children who are mentally healthy will have the ability to:

- *develop* psychologically, emotionally, creatively, intellectually and physically

- *initiate*, develop and sustain mutually satisfying personal relationships

- *use* and enjoy solitude

- *become* aware of others and empathise with them

- *play* and learn

- *develop* a sense of right and wrong

- *resolve* (face) problems and setbacks and learn from them.

Mental health is also described as: 'a relative state of mind in which a person…is able to cope with, and adjust to, the recurrent stress of everyday living' (Anderson and Anderson 1995).

This definition of mental health introduces the idea of relativity and seems to advance the notion of coping with and adjusting to everyday living. Do Black children and young people have to cope with and adjust to the everyday stress of racism? Can mental health be achieved by tolerating unemployment, poor housing or social exclusion? Social workers practising in a psychosocial context will be attuned to the social dimension affecting children's mental health. They need to consider how they define the terms mental disorder and mental health and whether their practice aims to help children and young people 'adjust to the stress of everyday living' or challenge those stresses within a personal helping relationship.

These definitions and the subtle distinctions between mental illness and mental health are important in the sense that they set the context for how social workers and others conceptualise difficulties experienced by children and young people. Examples later in this text will illustrate how education, youth justice and social work staff can all offer quite different explanations for the same behaviour with significantly different outcomes to intervention. So it is very important to be as clear as you can be about what it is you are observing and what sources of knowledge are informing those perceptions. Acquiring a label of mental illness can not only be stigmatising in the short term but can have profound longer-term consequences for a young person in terms of relationships, employment, education and personal health or life insurance.

Recognition

A nationwide survey of child mental health discovered that children under 15 years of age with obsessive-compulsive disorder were going undetected and failing to receive appropriate help despite the availability of safe and effective treatment (Heyman *et al.* 2001). Further evidence for the difference in professional perceptions of mental health problems is shown by another survey conducted among GPs. It revealed that they were only identifying 2 per cent of the 23 per cent of children attending GP surgeries who had some form of severe psychological or emotional problem (Mental Health Foundation 1993). These findings are worrying because primary care is one of the most crucial gateways for children and young people to gain access to appropriate services and resources and for signposting to accessible and acceptable support in this area.

Table 2.2 is based on the Child Health Questionnaire (CHQ) which is a popular assessment tool that can be used to begin the process of building a picture of a child or young person's life experience. The domains mirror those that appear later in child development models and the Common Assessment Framework. They are all very useful tools to use to help you and the young person and their parents/carers begin a conversation to explore how things are, what areas are of concern and to begin to construct a hypothesis or assessment about the child and why they have become a concern to others.

Activity 2.1

○ Consider the assessment tool above.

○ What are the assumptions informing its design?

○ Write down the advantages and disadvantages of using it.

The way children and young people are characterised in popular culture or in media representations as either dangerous, insatiable tearaways or passive, angelic cherubs captures the ambivalence in adult attitudes to children and young people. This translates into policies and practices to manage the social manifestations of childhood and adolescent experience. Essentially this means offering punitive, restrictive or paternalistic, patronising responses to their behaviour, experiences and needs rather than recognising and helping

TABLE 2.2 DOMAINS ASSESSED BY THE CHILD HEALTH QUESTIONNAIRE (CHQ)

Health-related quality of life

Physical activities

Low score – Greatly limited in performing all physical activities, including self-care

High score – Performs all types of physical activities without limitations

Pain and discomfort

Low score – Extremely severe, frequent and limiting bodily pain and discomfort

High score – No pain or limitation due to pain and discomfort

School/Friends – Physical limitations

Low score – Greatly limited in schoolwork or peer-group activities due to physical health

High score – No limitations in schoolwork or activities as a result of physical health

School/Friends – Emotional/Behavioural limitations

Low score – Greatly limited in schoolwork or peer-group activities due to emotional/behavioural problems

High score – No limitations in schoolwork or peer-group activities due to emotional/behavioural problems

Self-esteem

Low score – Very dissatisfied with abilities, looks, family/peer relationships and life in general

High score – Very satisfied with abilities, looks, family/peer relationships and life in general

Family functioning

Family activities

Low score – Child's problems very often limit and interrupt family activities or are a source of family tension

High score – Child's problems never limit and interrupt family activities nor are they a source of family tension

Family cohesion

Low score – The family's ability to get along is rated as poor

High score – The family's ability to get along is rated as excellent

Perceived impact of child and adolescent health on parents

Impact on time

Low score – Parent experiences marked limitations in time available for personal needs due to child's physical and/or psychosocial problems

High score – Parent doesn't experience limitations in time available for personal needs due to child's physical and/or psychosocial problems

Impact on emotions

Low score – Parent experiences a great deal of emotional worry/concern as a result of child's physical and/or psychosocial health

High score – Parent doesn't experience a great deal of emotional worry/concern as a result of child's physical and/or psychosocial health

Source: Landgraf, Abetz and Ware 1996

with mental health needs. Adult perceptions and the beliefs of those with the power to influence health and social policy and service provision are important in determining the context in which social workers have to try to support troubled and troubling young people.

It is adults who have constructed these definitions of mental health or mental health problems and designed the assessment tools such as the CHQ. There is little evidence of children or young people being consulted about how *they* define mental health or mental health problems. This is consistent with adult behaviour towards children in general, and at one level it springs from protective instincts. However, given the dominance of white, middle class males in psychiatry, it can be argued that the values they represent will be reflected in concepts of mental health problems and remain unchallenged for the most part. In so doing they will not incorporate the views, opinions and perceptions of children themselves. This therefore risks alienating children and young people and failing to communicate with them properly about a vitally important part of their lives.

It is important to try to understand the emotional world of children and young people if assessment and intervention strategies are going to meet their needs. The vocabulary, the perceptions and the culture of emotional and behavioural difficulties that children and young people employ need to be incorporated into the education, training and development of social workers and other staff engaged in this work. A psychosocial perspective offers a holistic tool with which to assemble all the important information about a child or young person that incorporates her or his internal as well as external context. Social work values and principles of empowerment are at the heart of good practice in child and adolescent mental health.

Prevalence and problems

Recent evidence indicates that 10 per cent of children up to the age of 18 years in Britain have a diagnosable mental health disorder. Higher rates exist among those living in inner city environments. One in five children and adolescents have a mental health problem which although less serious still requires professional support (Audit Commission 1998; Office for National Statistics 2004). It has been further estimated that CAMHS are only reaching a minority of the population in their catchment areas requiring help. This indicates a large number of children and young people who are not receiving the necessary support and help to relieve their suffering. The research shows for example that 1 in 17 adolescents have harmed themselves – representing 200,000 11–15-year-olds. At the other end of the age spectrum there are increasing numbers of children under seven years of age being excluded from school due to uncontrollable behavioural problems. The increased rate of suicide over the last 28 years in children and adolescents is a cause of increasing concern and a stark indicator of the mental health of young people (McClure 2001). Table 2.3 shows the prevalence and range of specific problems affecting children.

TABLE 2.3 PREVALENCE OF MENTAL DISORDERS	
Problem	**Percentage of children affected**
Emotional disorders	**3.7**
Anxiety disorders	3.3
Separation anxiety	0.4
Specific phobia	0.8
Social phobia	0.3
Panic	0.2
Agoraphobia	0.1
Post traumatic stress	0.2
Obsessive compulsive	0.2
Generalised anxiety	0.8
Other anxiety	0.9
Depression	**0.9**
Depressive episode (full ICD criteria)	0.6
Other depressive episode	0.2
Conduct disorders	**5.8**
Oppositional defiant disorder	3.0
Unsocialised conduct disorder	0.8
Socialised conduct disorder	1.3
Other conduct disorder	0.6
Hyperkinetic disorder	**1.5**
Less common disorders	**1.3**
Autistic spectrum disorder	0.9
Tic disorders	0.1
Eating disorders	0.3
Mutism	0.1
Any disorder	**9.6**

Source: Office for National Statistics 2004

Activity 2.2

o   Consult with your friends, neighbours, relatives and partner about their perceptions of the behaviour and emotional world of children and young people these days.

o   Now consider these impressions with the data on prevalence and causation and explain the differences.

Child and adolescent development

Understanding the key elements of human growth and development theoretical resources relevant to CAMHS are critical to social workers seeking to assess and intervene appropriately in the lives of troubled young people. Summaries have been assembled below. They have been simplified to aid clarity and comparison and should be seen as part of a wide spectrum of potential, rather than deterministic, interactive causative factors in the genesis of CAMH problems. Some social psychologists criticise the emphasis in child development theories on normative concepts and suggest enhancing the judging, measuring approach towards one that embodies context, culture and competencies (Woodhead 1998).

Attachment theory

Attachment theory is linked to Bowlby who considered a descriptive, explanatory framework for helping understand interpersonal relationships between children and parents/carers (Bowlby 1979). Bowlby focused on the period from six months to two years of age and suggested that the developing infant becomes attached to adults who demonstrate sensitivity and responsiveness in social interactions. Towards the age of two years the child begins to use attachment to these familiar people as a secure base to explore from and return to. Ainsworth *et al.* (1978) progressed this concept and introduced the notion of attachment patterns or styles. Attachment theory has been subject to criticism because of its early link with the concept of maternal deprivation and the implicit sexist connotations, and more recently by critics from psychoanalytic theories, ethnologists and systemic theorists. These are some of the important assumptions underpinning attachment theory:

•   *adaptiveness* – human attachment behaviours and emotions are adaptive and derived from human evolution that evolved selection for social behaviours that enabled survival

•   *critical period* – when the child is between six months and two years of age

TABLE 2.4 SUMMARY OF DEVELOPMENTAL CONCEPTS

Age range					
Theory	**1**	**2–3**	**4–5**	**5–11**	**12–18**
Eriksen's psychosocial stages of development	The infant requires consistent and stable care in order to develop feelings of security. Begins to trust the environment but can also develop suspicion and insecurity. Deprivation at this stage can lead to emotional detachment throughout life and difficulties forming relationships	The child begins to explore and seeks some independence from parents/carers. A sense of autonomy develops but improved self-esteem can combine with feelings of shame and self-doubt. Failure to integrate this stage may lead to difficulties in social integration	The child needs to explore the wider environment and plan new activities. Begins to initiate activities but fears punishment and guilt as a consequence. Successful integration results in a confident person, but problems can produce deep insecurities	The older child begins to acquire knowledge and skills to adapt to surroundings. Develops sense of achievement but marred by possible feelings of inferiority and failure if efforts are denigrated	The individual enters stage of personal and vocational identity formation. Self perception heightened, but potential for conflict, confusion, and strong emotions
Freud's psychosexual stages of development	The oral stage during which the infant obtains comfort from sucking the breast milk of the mother, and the gratification from the nutrition	The anal stage when the anus and defecation are the major sources of sensual pleasure. The child is preoccupied with body control with parental/carer encouragement. Obsessional behaviour and over-control later in childhood could indicate a problematic stage development	The phallic stage, with the penis the focus of attention is the characteristic of this psychosexual stage. In boys the Oedipus complex and in girls the Electra complex are generated in desires to have a sexual relationship with the opposite-sex parent. The root of anxieties and neuroses can be found here if transition to the next stage is impeded	The latency stage, which is characterised by calm after the storm of the powerful emotions preceding it	The genital stage whereby the individual becomes interested in opposite-sex partners as a substitute for the opposite-sex parent, and as a way of resolving the tensions inherent in oedipul and electra complexes

TABLE 2.4 SUMMARY OF DEVELOPMENTAL CONCEPTS *cont.*

Age range Theory	1	2–3	4–5	6–11	12–18
Bowlby's attachment theory	This stage is characterised by pre-attachment undiscriminating social responsiveness. The baby is interested in voices and faces and enjoys social interaction	The infant begins to develop discriminating social responses and experiments with attachments to different people. Familiar people elicit more response than strangers	Attachment to main carer is prominent with the child showing separation anxiety when carer is absent. The child actively initiates responses from the carer	The main carer's absences become longer, but the child develops a reciprocal attachment relationship	The child and developing young person begins to understand the carer's needs from a secure emotional base.
Piaget's stages of cognitive development	The sensori-motor stage characterised by infants exploring their physicality and modifying reflexes until they can experiment with objects and build a mental picture of things around them	The pre-operational stage when the child acquires language, makes pictures and participates in imaginative play. The child tends to be self-centred and fixed in their thinking believing they are responsible for external events	The concrete operations stage when a child can understand and apply more abstract tasks such as sorting or measuring	This stage is characterised by less egocentric thinking and more relational thinking–differentiation between things. The complexity of the external world is beginning to be appreciated	The stage of formal operations characterised by the use of rules and problem-solving skills. The child moves into adolescence with increasing capacity to think abstractly and reflect on tasks in a deductive, logical way

- *robustness* – attachment to familiar people is easily developed in children even under stressful conditions

- *experience* – infants have no innate preference for their parents over strangers. They will attach to anyone who is kind and friendly but they learn preferences for some adults who provide continuity over time

- *monotropy* – even with several carers the infant will develop over time a hierarchy or bias towards one caregiver

- *internal working model* – experience enables the child to construct a system of beliefs, expectations and emotions about themselves and others. This helps them handle new social situations with peers and teachers, for example

- *disruption* – although attachment is considered to be robust, significant separation from a familiar or preferred caregiver, or frequent changes of caregiver that interrupt attachment, can give rise to mental health problems.

TABLE 2.5 ATTACHMENT BEHAVIOURS AND PATTERNS IN CHILDREN AND ADOLESCENTS

	Secure-autonomous	Avoidant-dismissing	Ambivalent-preoccupied-entangled
Infant	Secure	Insecure-avoidant	Insecure-ambivalent-resistant
Child	Secure-optimal	Defended-disengaged	Dependent-deprived-coercive
Adolescent	Autonomous-free to evaluate	Dismissing	Preoccupied-entangled-enmeshed

Table 2.5 offers a useful quick reference to help you understand and assess the developmental stage and attachment trajectory of the child or young person you might be working with. What follows below is a more detailed explanation of these behaviours and patterns (Ainsworth *et al.* 1978; Crittenden 1999; George and Solomon 1996; Howe *et al.* 1999):

Secure and autonomous patterns

INFANT

Parents/carers of secure infants tend to be good at reading their children's signals. There is synchrony between them involving mutual reciprocal interactions. Clear patterns begin to be perceived by infants that help them to make sense of their own and their parent/carer's behaviour. A parent/

carer who is available emotionally, responsive and comforting can generate a soothing, comfortable environment. This helps infants to locate and support their own understanding of their own and others' emotions and behaviour. It also:

- enables the child to access, acknowledge and integrate their thoughts and the full range of their feelings
- allows the child to acknowledge the power of feelings to affect behaviour.

CHILD

Instead of using crying, following and protesting to signify emotional arousal and distress, the young child begins to learn to deal with their feelings cognitively using language and mental processes. Emotional competence develops so that secure children show good affect recognition. The child has increasing confidence in acknowledging and managing difficult and anxiety-provoking emotions. Secure children function well in family life, classroom behaviour and in peer relationships.

They are reasonably co-operative, and able to draw upon a range of strategies to cope with the demands of social relationships. They show less emotional dependence on teachers and are more likely to approach teachers in a positive manner.

- The secure child is generally popular with their friends. They show good empathy, tend to be included in group activities and show low levels of conflict in their play.
- Secure children are less likely to be victimisers or victims, have higher self-esteem and are skilled at conflict resolution.

ADOLESCENT

Secure autonomous adolescents acknowledge the value and impact of attachment relationships. The influence of such relationships on personality development is recognised. They can tolerate imperfection in themselves, their parents and those with whom they are currently in close relationship. When describing attachment experiences they are able to provide specific, concrete examples that are coherent and reflective.

- They remain constructively engaged with a problem rather than attempting to avoid it or becoming angry at its apparent intractability.
- They feel comfortable with closeness, and enjoy good self-esteem.

Avoidant-dismissing patterns

INFANT

Carers who feel agitated, distressed or hostile towards their infants are less likely to respond to the infants' own distress. They may try to control the situation by ignoring the baby or trying to convince the infant they are not 'really' upset. This undermines the child's confidence in their own perceptions. The pattern that develops is that the parent/carer becomes emotionally less available and psychologically distant. They withdraw when the child shows distress and indeed are more available the quieter the infant. In turn the infant learns to become subdued and downplay feelings of upset, need or arousal in order to remain in emotional proximity to the carer.

CHILD

Avoidant children are less likely to seek support from their carers/teachers. Their attachment style becomes more detached, cool – even socially acceptable. They have learned that their carers feel more comfortable with behaviour that is low in emotional content. Achievements are valued more highly than emotional closeness.

Avoidant personalities tend to modify their own behaviour as a way of defending against social rejection. Some children may become compulsively compliant with high anxiety levels in getting tasks 'right'. If parents or teachers display unhappiness or disapproval the child feels responsible, unsettled, ashamed or guilty.

ADOLESCENT

Avoidant-dismissing patterns can be demonstrated ranging from being socially reserved to being compulsively self-reliant. They tend to minimise the emotional effects that relationships have on them. There is, if anything, a systematic avoidance of negative experiences and memories. The adolescent has a strong need to keep focused on practical tasks. Anything or anybody who distracts them will make this adolescent feel agitated, anxious or angry. Aggressive behaviour is likely to erupt at these moments. Equally this adolescent is keen to keep to the rules and seems over-vigilant when other people appear to break rules. Thus a heightened sense of justice, right and wrong can be observed.

Ambivalent-preoccupied-entangled patterns

INFANT

Carers who are inconsistent with their babies' needs are experienced as unpredictably unresponsive. Infants feel emotionally neglected and when they begin to explore and seek independence their parents/carers feel uncomfortable. These infants have to increase attachment behaviours in order to break through the lack of carer responsiveness. The infants' behaviour is characterised by crying, clinging, making constant demands and shouting or tugging. Separation anxiety may be pronounced. The parent is in behavioural terms 'non-contingently responsive', i.e. their responses bear no relation to the behaviour of the child.

Thus the clinging, demanding behaviour increases as the infant learns that persistence will gain a reaction. However, this might be a biscuit or a physical assault. So the infant compensates by becoming hyperactive, maximising the opportunities to gain comfort and attention whenever the carer feels able to provide it. The infant begins to construct a self-image with feelings of worthlessness, not being liked or valued. This leads to feelings of doubt, despair and inadequacy.

CHILD

As the child increases in age it can raise the level of demands and persistence. A parent may threaten to leave the home or request the child to be looked after by the local authority. This only further increases the child's levels of distress, anger and despair. Alternatively where severe physical neglect occurs a child may lapse into passivity, helplessness and depression.

Family relationships can be characterised by high levels of active, demanding behaviour by parents and children. Threats and counter-threats are traded about who cares and who loves who in an impulsive, disorganised atmosphere. Relationships feel emotionally entangled and enmeshed with parents and children learning to lie, deceive and coerce to survive.

Ambivalent children show poor levels of concentration. They might suggest they are feeling unwell in an unspecified way in order to secure a socially acceptable attachment. They are characteristically lacking in self-reliance, failures are always the fault of others, and they see themselves as perpetual victims. These children quickly become known to teachers.

ADOLESCENT

In adolescence the more extreme coercive behavioural strategies become increasingly disruptive, attention-seeking and difficult to control. Life is lived at a heightened pitch of dissatisfaction and anger. Anti-social behaviour, conflict, control problems and poor concentration are observed. Feelings of guilt and personal responsibility are largely absent.

Parents and peers can be subjected to threats and intimidation to make them respond and provide. There is a struggle taking place between anger with, and seeking approval from, parents. These adolescents exhibit a need to be close but to be dependent on someone who may abandon them arouses strong feelings of anxiety. They feel a strong sense of powerlessness and describe parents/carers and practitioners as either wonderful and loving or hateful and cruel – there are no shades of grey.

It is important to recognise that these characteristics are distilled from practice and research evidence covering a wide variety of working and professional contexts. Complexity has been sacrificed to some extent to assist comprehension, therefore it is important to recognise:

- Within these generalised characteristics there is a range and overlap.
- Some children are reserved and show mildly avoidant-dismissing patterns.
- Some children are prone to reactive characteristics with mildly ambivalent-preoccupied patterns.
- Don't be fooled by first impressions.
- These classifications are based on white ethno-centric assumptions.
- Research studies tend not to distinguish between girls' and boys' differentiated socialisation.
- Poverty, unemployment and homelessness are important mitigating factors.
- The effects of sexual, physical and emotional abuse can be mistaken for attachment problems.

Integrating systemic and attachment theory

Linking child development with attachment theory can provide a sound theoretical knowledge base with which to assess a variety of situations you may encounter. An additional refinement would be to integrate systemic theory (developed in the 1970s when individual models of functioning were found to be limited by their exclusion of other familial relationships) with attachment theory to enable a synthesis of the individual with the family context. This means using the concept of family development and family attachment, in conjunction with individual development and attachment. The question of how to develop these two theories, both of which are fundamentally focused on family relationships and their impact on children's development, is engaging researchers.

In terms of their relevance to practice, government and health and social care agencies are keen to standardise assessments of children and families. The theoretical underpinnings are critical here as standardising the collection of information is relatively simple but making sense of the data requires complex theoretical frameworks if holistic practice is to be achieved. Children have different attachments to each of their parents so it is not possible to understand a family based on just one of these relationships. Similarly adult attachment security relates to specific relationships and may alter or develop over time. Recent research increasingly indicates that both child and adult categorisations are subject to change rather than remaining fixed over time (Cook 2000; Feeney 2003). The ideas from both attachment and systemic theory are needed to aid practitioners in their assessment of a family.

Activity 2.3

o Reflect on the discussion above and consider how it challenges or reinforces your preconceived ideas about attachment and child development.

o List three implications for your intervention strategies in relevant work.

Commentary

Although intervention is often informed by attachment data it may occur at the individual, dyadic, marital or family system level. Using attachment derived data does not necessarily result in an attachment intervention. Because of the connections between systems, interventions at family or marital levels can bring about change in the child's attachment relationships.

Adolescent well-being

Adolescence is acknowledged to be an under-researched area of child and adolescent mental health development. Service provision for this age range of young people is poor. It therefore warrants particular attention. A research study commissioned by the Nuffield Foundation (Hagel 2004) looked at the mental health of adolescents in the UK over the past 25 years, and found that adolescent emotional problems (such as depression and anxiety) have increased for both girls and boys since the mid 1980s. Adolescent conduct problems showed a continuous rise for both boys and girls over the whole 25-year study period. The strength of associations between these problems and poor outcomes later in adulthood have remained similar over time... and are not the result of an increasing tendency for parents to rate teenagers as problematic, but the result of real changes in problem levels.

Marked changes in family type (such as increases in the numbers of single parent families) over the period were *not* the main reason for rising trends in behaviour problems, and changes in socio-economic indicators were not the main reason either, although there is now a social class gradient in emotional difficulties that was *not* there before. The research study also observed that, while studies from, for example, the Netherlands and the US have shown either no increase, or even recent decreases in levels of psychosocial difficulties, the trend has continued upwards in the UK.

Why is it important to promote adolescent well-being?

In the short term interrupting poor mental health as soon as possible in the childhood and adolescent years will reap instant rewards for young people. Those who are supported and have more positive mental health can learn better and are more likely to fulfil their social, academic and training potential. It is likely that intervening more effectively and imaginatively could significantly reduce adolescent mortality (through reducing suicide rates) and improve life experiences. If we can accurately assess mental health problems, and we know both how to intervene and also that intervention may work, then there is an ethical imperative to do something as soon as we can.

Enhancing health and educational outcomes will benefit young people in the shorter term, but will of course benefit all of us in the longer term as well. A significant proportion of young people with mental health problems will go on to be adults with not just ongoing mental health problems, but also a range of other poor outcomes as well – difficulties with relationships, unstable employment histories, involvement in crime and social exclusion. Research has shown that by the age of 28, people with continuing high levels of anti-social behaviour have cost society up to ten times more than those with no problems – these are the costs of public services such as extra educational provision, foster and residential care, and unemployment benefits, quite apart from the personal costs to the individual (Scott *et al.* 2001).

Activity 2.4

∘ Together with a colleague, each write down three lists of your own characteristics at age 14 as you felt, as your parents saw you and as your class teacher perceived you.

∘ Note the similarities and differences; think about and discuss together what concepts informed those differences.

Social policy perspectives

In addition to the classic means of understanding child and adolescent development outlined above there are other, less prominent, but just as important resources for social workers to draw upon to help inform practice in this area. Sociology may be suffering from less emphasis in government policy and occupational standards guidance but it still offers a valuable conceptual tool to enable a rounded, holistic process of assessment and intervention. Sociological explanations for CAMH problems can be located in a *macro* understanding of the way childhood itself is considered and constructed by adults:

- Childhood is a social construction. It is neither a natural nor a universal feature of human groups but appears as a specific structural and cultural component of many societies.

- Childhood is a variable of social analysis. Comparative and cross-cultural analysis reveals a variety of childhoods rather than a single or universal phenomenon.

- Children's social relationships and cultures require study in their own right, independent of the perspective and concern of adults.

- Children are and must be seen as active in the construction and determination of their own lives, the lives of those around them and of the societies in which they live. (James and Prout 1997)

An examination of the experience of childhood around the world today shows how greatly varied it is, and how it has changed throughout history. Contemporary children in some countries are working from the ages of eight and independent from the age of 14, whereas in other countries some do not leave home or begin work until they are 21 (Alderson 2000; Bilton *et al.* 2002; Hendrick 1997). The developmental norms above show how adults construct childhood and therefore how to measure children's progress and detect mental health problems. They are however set down as solid absolutes and are based on notions of adults' fears about risk, their lack of confidence in children, and are rooted in adults' own childhood experiences. These theories have had positive effects but they have also restricted the field of vision required to engage with and understand children and adolescents fully.

Early childhood studies are beginning to challenge the orthodoxy in child development theories so that children are seen as accomplishing, living, competent persons rather than not yet quite fully formed people who are learning to become adults (Early Childhood Education Forum 1998). The idea that the stages have to be accomplished sequentially ignores the different pace that different children change at, according to external and other influences. Adults simply need to reflect on themselves to see that adults of the same developmental age can be at very different stages of emotional maturity, skill and capacity. Social workers therefore need to use concepts of development and definitions of CAMH problems cautiously and sceptically. An appreciation of how these concepts are constructs reflecting historical and cultural dominant values, and how they reinforce the power relationships between adults and children, is required.

The central processes apart from physical changes are the critical process of development of self, the search for identity and the development of relationships and the changing nature of relationships.

Social workers and other professionals in the field of CAMH need to demonstrate and incorporate in routine practice an element of intellectual modesty. This can be difficult when workloads are increasing and demands on time are enormous, or there appears to be a risky situation to deal with. It is also hard to admit to not knowing or being confused or uncertain – this is not what managers, the public and policy makers expect. Yet it may be realistic and give a more accurate picture than presenting a neat, coherent explanation for a child's behaviour in a short timescale. The competitive power dynamics in inter-agency meetings or high-pressured conferences cannot tolerate ambiguity; they demand clarity, brevity and certainty. However, hasty judgements made to protect embarrassment or personal vulnerability can have long-term consequences.

Key chapter points

- As well as understanding why some children develop mental health problems, it is crucially important to learn more about those who in similar circumstances do not. Research is required to analyse the nature of these resilient children to understand whether coping strategies or skills can be transferred to others. Positive factors such as reduced social isolation, good schooling and supportive adults outside the family appear to help.

- A mental health problem can be distinguished from the term disorder by the degree of seriousness and the length of time the condition lasts. The assumption is that most people will recognise these symptoms and understand they do not require specialist or intensive intervention.

- Research has revealed that GPs were only identifying 2 per cent of the 23 per cent of children attending surgeries who had some form of severe psychological or emotional problem. These findings are worrying because primary care is one of the most crucial gateways for troubled children and young people to gain access to appropriate services and resources and for signposting to accessible and acceptable support in this area.

- Understanding the key elements of human growth and development theoretical resources relevant to CAMHS are critical to social workers seeking to assess and intervene appropriately in the lives of troubled young people. Some social psychologists criticise the emphasis in child development theories on normative concepts and suggest enhancing the judging, measuring approach towards one that embodies context, culture and competencies.

- Linking child development with attachment theory can provide a sound theoretical knowledge base with which to assess a variety of situations you may encounter. An additional refinement would be to integrate systemic theory with attachment theory to enable a synthesis of the individual with the family context.

- Early childhood studies are beginning to challenge the orthodoxy in child development theories so that children are seen as accomplishing, living, competent persons rather than not yet quite fully formed people who are learning to become adults. The idea that the stages have to be accomplished sequentially ignores the different pace at which different children change according to external and other influences.

Chapter 3

Mental Health Problems

Learning outcomes

- - - - - - - - - - - - - - - - - - - -
» Understand the distinction between common and complex mental health problems.

» Evaluate the risk factors for complex mental health problems in young people.

» Describe and appraise assessment tools commonly used in CAMHS.

» Clarify the role of social work in this area of CAMHS.

Introduction

The distinction between common and complex mental health problems is an arbitrary one and not easy to define, but it is important to think about the differences in mental health problems in order to ensure an appropriate, timely, skilled and proportionate response. Social workers need to know whether a child's behaviour or emotional state is within the 'normal' range expected for them or whether, if it is not, it is something unusual in nature or relatively common. The idea that something is common can be reassuring but it can also be a worry. If something is common then it implies that it is recognisable and many people will experience it. The common cold is an example. Calling it common suggests that there is a good chance most people will catch it as well as receiving treatment or help that is readily available. However, when we add the notion of common to mental health problems other factors come into play as people try to understand what is happening to a child or young person and experience anxiety about something they cannot see or touch like a physical illness.

This chapter aims to focus attention on what are generally acknowledged to be common mental health problems experienced by children and adolescents in terms of how prevalent they are, rather than suggesting that common mental health problems cannot be complex (ONS 2004). They can be, especially for the families and young people struggling to cope with them and the professionals trying to help. A problem may be perceived differently by many people. For example, a young person experiencing a developmental transition from child to adolescent may feel their world is collapsing and be overwhelmed by self-destructive or depressive feelings. Their parent may shrug it all off as teenage angst – a rite of passage and within normal expectations. On the other hand a child psychiatrist might perceive the same child as suffering from the early signs of a depressive illness with a risk of psychosis and self-harm.

What follows is one way of making that distinction a little clearer. By examining the criteria used to define mental health and uncommon mental health problems we can sharpen our own understanding and think more carefully about assessing, planning and intervening when discussing individual young people's experiences. We will also look closely at other psychosocial problems that may not be generally understood as mental health problems but which raise concerns about young people's emotional well-being. A holistic approach in your work will appreciate the multiple perceptions and explanations.

Reliable evidence suggests that the nature, severity and complexity of mental health problems and related needs is more acute in vulnerable groups of children including looked after children, young offenders, abused children, homeless young people and refugees (Vostanis 2007). The cumulative impact of severe stressors and chronic adversities is a major threat to children and young people's emotional well-being. Subsequent mental health problems are likely to be more severe and entrenched, and more difficult to manage and resolve in isolation from other developmental, social and educational needs.

Children with the most complex needs are least likely to reach appropriate services. Mental health problems tend not to remit spontaneously but become more complex and resistant to treatment over time, highlighting the critical need for early effective intervention and prevention. Young people whose parents have mental health problems are at particular risk especially as they may come into contact with a range of services where their emotional well-being may be obscured. A significant number of children with relatively severe and complex mental health problems are not in contact with CAMHS (Fonagy *et al.* 2005). This means that social workers are in the front-line when it comes to recognising, supporting and signposting families with troubled children and young people to the most effective care for their complex mental health problems.

The Prince's Trust recently (2009) investigated how young people felt about the state of their lives and how confident they were about their future. The findings suggested that while the majority of young people are relatively content, there is a significant core of young people for whom life has little or no purpose – with those not in education, employment or training (NEET) most likely to feel this way. These young people are at risk of developing complex mental health problems. The report also showed how support from family is key to a young person's overall well-being, yet came across many young people who simply didn't have this support. Social workers also need to acknowledge that many troubled young people have no parent/carer support and need their knowledge and skills to help them individually.

The assessment tool in Table 3.1 has been selected to provide a useful resource to social workers in specialist or non-specialist contexts. It is a well established and common instrument familiar to CAMH specialist staff but can be adapted to or incorporated into your normal assessment working procedures and patterns. It provides you and your clients with a feel for the areas likely to be of interest, and a solid checklist to use in what may at times be confusing and fast-moving situations.

Assessment tools

A recent systematic review to assess the screening efficiency of the Child Behaviour Checklist (CBCL: Achenbach 1991) and the Strengths and Difficulties Questionnaire (SDQ: Goodman 1997) in both community and clinical populations found that both instruments were beneficial in helping screen for mental health problems in young people (Warnick, Bracken and Kasl 2008). Interestingly, this comprehensive study nevertheless admitted that there were some important limitations. First, the CBCL studies included were mostly based on research in the United States while the SDQ literature was based mainly on European and Australian research. Thus the data were inadequate in assessing these instruments across race/ethnicity or cultural dimensions. Second, the lack of an accepted standard for CAMH assessment means that, given the range of diagnostic criteria within the CBCL and SDQ, accurate comparisons across the two measures are impossible (Jensen and Weisz 2002).

This means that the science behind even these well-validated assessment tools in CAMH is still rudimentary and lacking in important variables of interest to a psychosocial approach. However, by becoming more familiar with these tools you can begin to appreciate their limitations and advantages as well as to understand how more specialist agencies begin to construct assessments. You can then more successfully determine what your role is and how to complement and contribute to an assessment of a complex mental health problem. Both of these tools use a variation of a severity scale for each domain and can be completed with parents/carers and young people as part of empowering practice.

TABLE 3.1 Mental health problems assessed by the Child Behaviour Checklist

General areas:

(i) *Internalising problems scale:* inhibited or over-controlled behaviour
(e.g. anxiety or depression)
(ii) *Externalising problems scale:* anti-social or under-controlled behaviour
(e.g. delinquency or aggression)
(iii) *Total problems scale:* all mental health problems reported by parents or adolescents

Specific areas:

(i) *Somatic complaints scale:* chronic physical complaints without known cause or medically verified basis
(ii) *Delinquent behaviour scale:* breaking rules and norms set by parents and communities
(e.g. lying, swearing, stealing or truancy)
(iii) *Attention problems scale:* difficulty concentrating and sitting still, and impaired school performance
(iv) *Aggressive behaviour scale:* bullying, teasing, temper tantrums and fighting
(v) *Social problems scale:* impaired peer relationships
(vi) *Withdrawn scale:* shyness and social isolation
(vii) *Anxious/Depressed scale:* feelings of loneliness, sadness, being unloved, worthlessness, anxiety and general fears
(viii) *Thought problems scale:* strange behaviour or ideas, obsessions

---

Source: Achenbach 1991

Activity 3.1

o   Review the CBCL and SDQ and consider how you might adapt them or integrate them with an assessment using the Child Assessment Framework.

o   Discuss with a colleague from a specialist CAMH team noting areas of similarity, duplication or gaps.

Specific mental health problems

Depression

Depression is one of the most common CAMH problems. In order to understand the nature of the low mood a child or adolescent may be experiencing the following guidance can help in measuring in some way the intensity of the depression and help you organise an appropriate response (National Institute for Health and Clinical Excellence [NICE] 2005). An initial assessment should ascertain whether at least one of the following symptoms is present on most days, most of the time, for at least two weeks: persistent sadness or low (irritable) mood, loss of interests and/or pleasure and fatigue or low energy. If any of these are present, you should find out about associated symptoms that may also be experienced such as those listed below:

- poor or increased sleep
- poor concentration or indecisiveness
- low self-confidence
- poor or increased appetite
- suicidal thoughts or acts
- agitation or slowing of movements
- guilt or self-blame.

Then ask about any past history of depression, family history, associated disability and availability of social support.

If the young person has four or fewer of the above symptoms, no past or family history and some social support available then it may not be serious. If these symptoms are intermittent, or of less than two weeks' duration, the young person is not actively suicidal and has little associated disability then your intervention can rely on providing general advice and 'watchful waiting'.

If the young person has five or more of the above symptoms together with a past history or family history of depression and low level of social support then the depression is more serious. Combined with suicidal thoughts and associated social disability means more active help is required in primary care and the GP should be contacted to arrange an appointment. Together with the GP you may decide after the first appointment that a referral to a mental health professional at Tier 2 CAMHS is necessary if the young person is not coping, neglecting themselves, the relatives are more concerned or there is a recurrent episode of depression within one year of the first. If the following factors are present then an urgent referral to a child psychiatrist is needed:

- active suicidal ideas or plans
- psychotic symptoms
- severe agitation accompanying severe (seven or more) symptoms
- severe self-neglect.

Suicide

Suicide warrants particular attention for obvious reasons. It is worth considering the definition commonly accepted as well as other related terms, such as parasuicide and deliberate self-harm, to appreciate the differences between these terms and how they can get confused. Suicide refers to death that directly or indirectly results from an act that the dead person believed would result in this end. The definition of deliberate self-harm includes non-fatal or attempted suicide, but also life-threatening behaviours such as self-poisoning in which the young person does not intend to take their life as well as habitual cutting, piercing and head banging. Parasuicide is defined as serious but unsuccessful attempts to kill oneself such as any deliberate act with non-fatal outcome that appears to cause or actually causes self-harm or without intervention from others would have done so (Aggleton, Hurry and Warwick).

Trends in suicide are influenced by a variety of factors. One of the more significant is change in the lethality and ease of availability of commonly used methods of suicide. Broadly speaking the pattern suggests that in the 1970s overdose was more common, in the 1980s carbon monoxide from car exhaust fumes, and in the 1990s death by hanging. Restrictions on the availability of painkillers and the fitting of catalytic converters in vehicles have affected this pattern. Actual suicide rates may be at much higher levels due to the classification by coroners who may consider there is insufficient evidence that the injury was self-inflicted and the individual intended to die. There is also anecdotal evidence that some coroners classify some suicides as undetermined or accidental in order to spare the anguish of parents and carers.

Factors associated with suicide in young people include depression, severe mental illness and personality disorder. Substance misuse, particularly alcohol, predates suicidal behaviour in many cases. The sharp increase in suicides among 15- to 19-year-old men recently mirrors the period which has shown a large increase in the use of alcohol and drugs among young people generally (Appleby, Cooper and Amos 1999). Disrupted relationships caused by family breakdown and social exclusion in terms of unemployment are factors strongly associated with young male suicide. There is an assumption that the gender disparity in rates of suicide in young people (three males to one female) reflects the changing roles of men and women in contemporary society. This suggests that young women have higher levels of self-esteem and better coping strategies, than young men with a problematic masculine identity and an inability to acknowledge and communicate emotional difficulties (Gunnell, Wehernew and Frankel

1999). The evidence is not conclusive and it is wise not to generalise on the basis of redundant stereotypes. On the other hand there is evidence that changes to gender roles is having an effect on young women's capacity for externalising mental health problems with anti-social behaviour, rather than the traditional internalising of mental health problems.

Between 2001 and 2002 there was a 40 per cent increase in the number of young women sentenced to secure custody (Youth Justice Board 2002). The concept of the emotionally illiterate male is nothing new but as with all simplistic stereotypes, it obscures more than it illuminates. The startling increase in young male suicide rates cannot be explained by a generalised notion of the consequences of bottled up feelings or the empowerment of women. Nor can the dramatic increase in eating disorders among young females be consistent with the emotionally sophisticated stereotyped image that is projected. A more subtle and complex explanation is required.

Recent evidence confirms for example that suicide is of particular concern in marginalised and victimised adolescent groups including gay, lesbian and bisexual youth. Research suggests that despite the rhetoric of anti-discriminatory policies and professional statements of equality, heterosexist and homophobic attitudes continue to be displayed by some psychologists and social workers (Morrison and L'Heureux 2001). This can further reinforce feelings of rejection, confusion and despair in troubled young people. Other evidence warns against a narrow definition of sexual-minority adolescents that pathologises their behaviour or wrongly assumes a higher risk of self-harming behaviour (Savin-Williams 2001).

Adolescents at risk of suicide can feel that they can resolve their internal states of despair and angst by splitting away from their body. Thus by killing their physical body they believe they can liberate their psychic self from the emotional pain and suffering. Adolescents at risk of psychosis are often suicidal, but suicide is not the outcome in many cases. Working with adolescents who are suicidal means being exposed to intense and extreme emotions such as anxiety, guilt, responsibility and fear. It is highly problematic work because it is immune to predictability and because there are multiple aspects to suicidality (Briggs 2002).

Anxiety

Fears and anxieties are normal developmental challenges facing the maturing young person. The relative intensity, frequency and duration of the behaviour associated with anxiety needs to be evaluated, and their role in the course of normal development considered against the frequency of the same behaviours among non-troubled children from the same class, culture and ethnic background. There are three main anxiety problems experienced by children and adolescents (Kendall 2000):

GENERALISED ANXIETY DISORDER

This is usually characterised by unrealistic and excessive anxiety and worry that do not seem to be linked to a specific situation or external stress. Children like this tend to worry about future events such as family activities, health issues and exams or just what is going to happen in the next hour or day. A young person observed as being in a chronic state of constantly feeling on edge, can be understood as suffering with anxious apprehension.

OBSESSIVE-COMPULSIVE DISORDER

This involves recurrent obsessions or compulsions that are time-consuming, cause distress and lead to problems in everyday functioning. Intrusive thoughts or images are also characteristic and perceived as senseless and inappropriate. Common themes are contamination, dirt, violence, harm or religious concepts. Washing rituals are particularly common.

SEPARATION ANXIETY DISORDER

This is related usually to children and focuses on distress caused by and about being separated from those to whom the child is attached. It usually features children refusing to sleep away from home, staying excessively close to a parent at home; particularly problems around the time of starting school. Children are often fearful of some unspecific harm befalling their important attachment figures. School phobia is a variation of this problem and occurs when an anxious child can be comfortable in any setting other than school.

Autism

Autism has probably been around for a lot longer than the first recorded diagnosis and definition in the early 1940s. Like many problems before and since it can be evidenced in children and young people in hindsight but until the 1940s there were different explanations for those showing the characteristics we nowadays associate with autism. The cause of the problem is still the subject of constant research and much controversy but there are associations with physical disorders (i.e. rubella, 'measles, mumps and rubella' [MMR]) suggesting organic pathology as one important factor. A brief definition of autism is: 'abnormal development of language and social relationships with ritualistic and obsessional behaviours' (Kanner 1943). Key characteristics of a child or young person with autism are:

- failure to comprehend others' feelings, lack of interest in imitative or social play, and inability to seek friendships or comfort from others

- impairments in verbal and non-verbal communication and avoidance of eye contact

- resistance to change and limited interests.

Assessing autism accurately is notoriously difficult especially in pre-school age children when normal lack of socialisation and ranges in verbal communication vary widely. It is only when children attend school that those with autism tend to be identified because of the different way they behave and relate to others. It is also difficult to be certain about the prevalence of autism in the population. This is due to the complex classification systems used by health and psychiatric professionals and the way contemporary research has identified a variety of different conditions along the autistic spectrum of behaviour. What is certain is that as diagnosis and assessment skills improve in health and social care staff, more children and young people are being identified and diagnosed with autism. Current estimates suggest a prevalence rate in the general population of between 7 and 17 per 10,000 children (Ghaziuddin 2005).

Autism begins at birth but tends to be unrecognised until the child is two to three years old. There is usually a delay between parent concerns and diagnosis. This could be explained by the general lack of knowledge of child development, especially among primary health care staff who are untrained or cautious about offering an opinion. By the age of three, however, both parents and health care staff usually concur that autism could be the cause of the language delay and lack of peer relationships. In addition other people such as friends, neighbours or nursery staff are reporting a pronounced lack of sociability, inability to empathise or capacity to reflect on social situations. This quickly leads to social isolation in playgroups or nurseries, reinforcing the characteristic preference for an autistic child for solitary repetitive play.

Autism is found three to four times more often in boys than girls and half of all autistic individuals never speak. Those who can show unusual use of language in their intonation, stress placed on various words and often speak in a monotone. A significant proportion of autistic children have behavioural and emotional problems expressed in hyperactivity, short attention span, aggression, self-harm and anxiety/depression. Autistic features are often present where there is a generalised learning disability (Morton-Cooper 1988; Spender *et al.* 2001; Waterhouse 2000).

Autism is on a spectrum of severity and is highly disabling. It is one of the least prevalent conditions seen in child mental health services but because of the impact on family and social relationships it demands considerable resources. The outcome of autism is poor. There is deterioration in 50 per cent of adolescents, some of which is attributable to onset of epileptic seizures. In 30 per cent there is some improvement in behaviour and functioning, usually when onset is later, where IQ is over 60 and speech developed by five years of age. This suggests early intervention is crucial. Howlin and Rutter (1987) describe positive results from a home-based intervention consisting of behaviour modification, encouraging language and skill development, and psychological family support.

Repetitive behaviour is a major symptom of autism but there are a variety of motivations that contribute to the behaviour's occurrence – anxiety, self-soothing, self-stimulation and some more desultory states where the child may be deeply bored but not know it or may not know how to seek out and shift to another more interesting activity (Alvarez 2005). Where the activity has built up to a frenzy, the child may need to be distracted with a fairly exciting alternative. Rutter (1985) emphasises the importance of enlisting parents as co-therapists in behavioural treatments. Helping them learn problem-solving skills is important in their ongoing management of current and future behavioural problems.

Asperger syndrome

A precise diagnosis and definition is hard to obtain because there is still confusion between autism and Asperger syndrome (AS) in medical and health literature. A child with AS is likely to have better cognitive and communication skills but still experiences poor social interaction and stereotyped interests. It is estimated that the prevalence rates for AS are higher than for autism but there is little robust evidence in this area. This is partly explained because of the relatively high levels of intelligence found in such children which can serve to mask other difficulties, especially during adolescence. Asperger syndrome is more prevalent in boys and can be characterised by a notable physical clumsiness with a very characteristic monotonous speech pattern and inflection. Anxiety, depression and low self-esteem are particularly found in adolescence. As yet there is no definitive treatment or support but the social work role would include:

- assessment needs to highlight strengths of child
- parent education and support to help them understand and cope

- early identification required to intervene with social and language skills.

CASE ILLUSTRATION

Freddy is 14 with mild learning disabilities and has been diagnosed with autism. He lives with his father and younger brother, who is 12 years old. Freddy's father has declined an offer of respite care to give him a break from the stress of caring for the family. A friend helps out sometimes by taking Freddy and his brother to the local gym, but Freddy is becoming more and more withdrawn particularly since his mother left the family home. Freddy was assessed for a place at a special school for children with autism but his parents could not agree on the matter and he is now in a local school where they try hard to include Freddy but are finding him a handful. He has extra support in class and his teacher has received advice from educational psychologists and the National Autistic Society. Freddy finds it difficult to cope, however. He has been involved in fights with other boys and when he is not allowed to continue with his favourite activity of painting he has become aggressive towards teaching staff. He has no friends at school and his reading and writing is five years behind his peers. Freddy has been referred to your social work team. Your task is to assess the situation and come up with a plan of action.

Commentary

Assessment

Freddy needs to be understood in the context of his family and social environment. His behaviour needs to be seen as a means of communicating his distress which he cannot express in other ways. You need to be aware that his reported behaviours can be due to emotional problems rather than assume they are an integral feature of autism. Remember that Freddy is at a developmental transition into adolescence and his behaviours may be associated with this life stage, similar to his peers. However, Freddy will be aware that his peers have abilities he does not. The school environment may not be fully understanding or supportive of his needs. At home his father could be finding Freddy difficult to cope with now he is physically larger and stronger, but his pride causes him to resist offers of help. He is unsure about how to advise Freddy about his sexuality and curiosity about intimate relationships.

Intervention

Close observation of Freddy in school and at home together with other professional assessments will provide rich information for you to evaluate. The core aim of your intervention is to facilitate his communication and help improve the physical environments in order to provide Freddy with a degree of predictability. It is important that he can exit situations where he is over-stimulated and can retire to a safe, calm space to unwind. Individual behavioural interventions can be helpful for use in the school or home setting so that he can gain positive feedback when keeping on task. Freddy might also require counselling/therapeutic input to address anxiety problems underlying some of his troubling behaviours.

Overall educational provision may need to be reviewed to assess whether existing plans require updating or changing to reflect his emerging needs. His father will probably benefit from some individual support from you to discuss his feelings about Freddy and the break-up of the marriage. Provision of good quality information about autism could help his father gain further insight and empathy with Freddy's behaviour and future care needs. As his social worker you could assume the role of keyworker in co-ordinating planning and arranging multi-agency meetings with the family to foster collaborative and empowering relationships.

Activity 3.2

○ Imagine you have just been told that your child is autistic or has AS.

○ Discuss briefly with a colleague: how you feel, what impact this will have on your partner, siblings and extended family relationships.

○ What help would you want?

Drug, alcohol and substance misuse

Young people in the UK are more likely to drink alcohol excessively and get involved in drug use than their counterparts in mainland Europe. Social workers should consider whether the drug and alcohol misuse is a cause of mental health problems or a consequence. Alcohol and drug abuse are factors associated with anti-social behaviour, criminal activity and poor educational attainment. The interim period between adolescence and adulthood is the highest risk period for problematic drug use. This is especially so for those individuals who are described as externalised (the under-parented) and internalised (the over-parented) (Harris 2007). These young people grow up in family units of two extremes. The externalised family tend to be permissive and exert little control over the development of the young person, model poor behaviour around high consumption and exert little influence on the peer groups that their children subscribe to. The internalised group tend to be abstinent, fretful parents who over-protect their offspring from risk and responsibility, censure peer contact and thus disconnect their children from the socialisation process.

It is these attachment relationships that allow some young people to develop substance misuse problems. Economic hardships have meant that the predicted life route for many in these groups is no longer there. Semi-skilled labour markets have collapsed leaving many individuals and entire communities without job prospects. Drugs can provide the only form of purposeful activity and the only source of satisfaction to those socially excluded and economically stranded. These swift changes in the labour market have primarily influenced conventional male roles as breadwinners.

In the under-parented child, drug use tends to occur sooner, as they become increasingly detached from the cultural institutions in deference to the all important peer group. Here male behaviours and consumption is determined by the group, whilst for women it is determined by their partners. Research highlights that initially these young people's problems stem from lack of support structures in their lives, such as school and family. This social exclusion widens their separation from the mainstream. Initially drug use is a central reference point for the peer group. It serves as a group totem – not so much the reason that people come together but the excuse to come together. This commodity gives the group identity, only later to become a coping strategy in light of increased pressure from cultural separation. Eventually drugs become both the coping strategy and source of increasing turbulence (Harris 2007).

Self-harm

Self-harm among young people is a major public health issue in the UK. It affects at least 1 in 15 young people and some evidence suggests that rates of self-harm in the UK are higher than anywhere else in Europe. Self-harm blights the lives of young people and seriously affects their relationships with families and friends. It presents a major challenge to all those in services and organisations that work with young people, from schools through to hospital accident and emergency departments (MHF 2006). Levels of self-harm are one indicator of the mental health and mental well-being of young people in our society in general. Recently there has been a shift in government strategies, across the UK, towards recognising and promoting better mental health and emotional well-being for all children and young people. These initiatives may eventually do a great deal to reduce self-harm among young people but there is not yet an adequate evidence base specific to self-harm. Key questions you are likely to have or to be asked by parents/carers are:

- What is self-harm?
- How common is it among young people?

- Can it be prevented?
- How can we respond better to young people who self-harm?

Self-harm describes a wide range of things that young people do to themselves in a deliberate and usually hidden way. In the vast majority of cases self-harm remains a secretive behaviour that can go on for a long time without being discovered. Self-harm can involve:

- cutting
- burning
- scalding
- banging or scratching one's own body
- breaking bones
- hair pulling
- ingesting toxic substances or objects.

Young people who self-harm mainly do so because they have no other way of coping with problems and emotional distress in their lives. This can be to do with factors ranging from bullying to family breakdown. But self-harm provides only temporary relief and does not deal with the underlying issues. Although some very young children are known to self-harm, and some adults too, the rates of self-harm are much higher among young people, and the average age of onset is 12.

There is relatively little research or other data on the prevalence of self-harm among young people in the UK or on the reasons why young people self-harm. It is clear that self-harm is a symptom rather than the core problem. It masks underlying emotional and psychological trauma, and successful social work for responding to self-harm must be based on this fundamental understanding. The evidence on reasons why young people self-harm shows that there are a wide range of factors that might contribute.

Young people report that there are often multiple triggers for their self-harm, often daily stresses rather than significant changes or events (MHF 2006). These include things like feeling isolated, academic pressures, suicide or self-harm by someone close to them, and low self-esteem or poor body image which can make them feel unstable and even hate themselves. Many described how self-harm gets out 'all the hurt, anger and pain' but that relief is so short-lived they do it many times. Crucially, young people talked about having no alternatives: 'I don't know how to release my feelings in any other way.' Many also explained that their self-harm is about feeling dead inside and that self-harm 'brought them back to life' and made them feel 'something – alive and real'. Because young people often find release or even positives from self-harm it can be difficult to envisage coping with life without it: 'I have found the decision to stop harming myself infinitely more difficult than the decision to start.'

Self-harm is a difficult issue for many people to understand and deal with – whether they are the person who has self-harmed or the person discovering it. It is very important that social workers who come into contact with children and young people have a basic understanding of what self-harm is, why young people do it, and how to respond appropriately. It is clearly important to avoid being judgemental towards young people who disclose self-harm. Young people want to be treated with care and respect and with an acknowledgement of the emotional distress they are experiencing.

Evidence from professional staff reinforces the point that it is very important not to focus exclusively on the self-harm itself but on the reasons why the young person has self-harmed. It is very important that you understand that a young person disclosing self-harm needs to know that the fact they have been able to disclose shows strength and courage. It is equally important that when hearing a disclosure you allow the young person to take the discussion at their own pace, foster trust and respect the right of the young person to act on their own judgement as to what and how much to say. The majority of young people say that they were more likely to speak to close friends about their self-harm than to family or any professional or organisation (Fortune, Sinclair and Hawton 2005). This highlights the need for greater awareness, and better information to be distributed not just among young people who self-harm but also among those friends and family to whom they might disclose.

RISK ASSESSMENT

Some young people may self-harm just once or twice. For others it can become a habitual response to any overwhelming situation. They might self-harm several times per day during difficult periods in their life. Therefore, it is important that the issue is addressed immediately and assessment is the gateway to understanding and future management. It is rare for self-harming behaviour to exist in isolation. Self-harm often follows on from earlier problem behaviours and illustrates that an addictive quality exists across a range of behaviour. The literature supports the view that for young women there are well-established links both with eating disorders and overdosing. Any risk assessment should be able to answer the following:

- What makes the person harm themselves?
- Do they want to die when they commit the act of self-harm?
- Have they felt this way before?
- Have they had any previous help with self-injurious behaviour?
- Do they still feel like harming themselves?
- Do they want help?

Your risk assessment needs to be directed to four main issues: assessment and management of the current episode; identification and management of associated problems; identification and promotion of the child and family's resources, and prevention of repetition.

INITIAL STEPS

All young people who have self-harmed should receive prompt medical attention. Intent should be assessed. Workers need to obtain sequential details about the events that occurred in the 48 hours preceding the act of self-injury and explore circumstances surrounding the act or planned act: the reasons, the method, the degree of planning, the location of the act, the presence of a suicide note, the expected extent of injury, any actions after the attempt, whether drugs were consumed (prescribed or illicit), the likelihood of being stopped in time or revived, the extent of the desire to die, feelings about living. It is essential that workers establish any previous acts of self-injury as well as trying to establish the young person's behaviour before, during and after the incident, and any major life events they may recently have experienced.

IDENTIFYING OTHER PROBLEMS

Work with the young person to devise a list of the most important current problems. Self-harm in young people is associated with depression, drug or alcohol abuse, behavioural problems and physical illness. There is often an association with family difficulties, including parental discord and violence, parental depression or substance abuse, role models of self-harming behaviour in the family, abuse of all kinds and bereavement. Other associated problems include bullying at school, peer role models of self-harm, models of self-harm in the media and educational difficulties. Some young people who self-harm have associated mental health problems and so it is important to look for evidence of major depression, anxiety, psychotic or paranoid symptoms, misuse of alcohol or illicit drugs or withdrawal (especially withdrawal from amphetamines or cocaine).

PROMOTING THE CHILD AND FAMILY'S RESOURCES

Factors in the child that protect them from self-harm, or from repetition of self-harm include:

- being particularly good at something (e.g. a sport)
- positive peer relationships
- good school attendance and academic achievement
- positive plans for the future.

Family factors that reduce the risk of self-harm include:

- a close relationship with at least one positive role model
- parenting styles that encourage rather than punish
- clear methods for communication within the family.

Coping resources, e.g. family, friends, also need to be examined. Access to appropriate coping resources reduces the risk of self-injury and of suicide. Your role may focus on increasing the number of appropriate coping resources and consider who else should be involved, such as friends, relatives and external organisations.

PREVENTING REPETITION

This should begin with an assessment of the risk factors for frequent repetition since motivations for self-harming behaviour change over time and context. Assessment of mental state and continuing intent to self-harm will usually require that the young person be interviewed without the parent. There is no evidence that encouraging children and young people to talk with professionals about their feelings and plans precipitates self-harm (Calder 2007). Factors suggesting there is continuing intent include:

- a clear statement that the young person intends to harm themselves again (such a statement should always be taken seriously)
- depression
- unresolved personal or family problems (particularly if these appeared to precipitate previous self-harm)
- hopelessness
- clear plans to self-harm
- easy access to dangerous methods
- frequent previous attempts.

Marfe (2003) identified four very useful risk categories to help social workers analyse the information they have collected:

THE YOUNG PERSON AT EXTREMELY HIGH RISK:

Has made previous attempts at serious self-harm; clear intentions of a wish to die and has made a deliberate premeditated suicide attempt. The young person will have obtained the agent (tablets, etc.) prior to the day of attempt and believes the agent or themselves will cause significant harm, and has specifically arranged a time when he or she reckoned to be alone. They will usually have left a note, regrets they were unsuccessful on the first attempt and appears to be extremely depressed or despondent.

THE YOUNG PERSON AT HIGH RISK:

Has tried to self-harm seriously or made a suicide attempt that was planned and gives clear reasons for their actions which still pose a risk. They will have deliberately bought the agent that day, or previously, and be aware that the agent is harmful. They will usually leave a note, be alone when the attempt was made and still be experiencing suicidal feelings. They will be regretful or uncertain about the failed attempt at serious self-harm and appear extremely depressed.

THE YOUNG PERSON AT MODERATE RISK:

Will have a history of deliberate self-harm, risk taking or impulsive behaviour, a history of poor stress coping mechanisms but has no clear intention or a wish to seriously self-harm. They can give clear reasons for their actions – but they no longer pose an obvious risk. They may have made an attempt to self-harm deliberately, but with no actual suicide intent. The young person will have obtained the agent impulsively that day but not be fully aware of the effects of the overdose. Any attempt at self-harm would have been made while others were in the vicinity and they may have informed others of their actions. The young person is glad they did not die but may still be considering other forms of self-harm.

THE YOUNG PERSON AT LOW RISK:

Has no history of previous deliberate self-harm or risk-taking behaviour, no history of poor stress coping mechanisms and has no intentions to, or wish to, self-harm seriously. They can give clear reasons for their actions which were never intended to pose a risk and have made the self-harm actions known to others appropriately. Any accomplished self-harm occurs when others are in the vicinity or they are not planning self-harm of any kind.

One of the things that self-harm offers young people is a way to feel in control of something in their lives. Even those young people who speak directly to an adult feel that once they had done this, all decision-making and control were taken from them. They were not being consulted about the services that might be contacted, or about the exact sort of help and information that would support and help them deal with their self-harm. Many were unsure – and felt unable to ask about – who else would be told or involved after they had disclosed private and sensitive information. Young people say (MHF 2006) that lack of control exacerbates the self-harm. It is also apparent that many young people who self-harm are afraid that the only coping strategy that has been keeping them functioning might be taken away from them.

> My friend went on to tell my head of year who in turn said it was necessary to inform my mother. I felt as though I had no say in what was happening and I felt out of control. Thus the self-harm increased. My mother was shocked and forced me to go to the doctor's the next day. My doctor looked at me differently once I told her why I was there. It was as if I were being annoying and wasting her time. She saw my arm and told me that it was only superficial and that she would make enquiries as to what should be done with me.

> The one time I trusted them enough to tell them I had cut myself again, they rang my mother then and there. It made me hate being there even more, and I lied and lied and told them I didn't even consider it whenever I got angry anymore when truthfully it was so much in my mind, and the fact I had been so restricted in cutting myself I was actually now obsessed with it. (MHF 2006, pp. 14–16)

Fear of losing control and not being consulted with fully and appropriately about decisions in their lives are not the only barriers to disclosure. Evidence shows that most young people do not have anyone they feel they can talk to about this private and sensitive issue, apart from their immediate friends, and they certainly do not know how they might be able to contact more formal support services. In addition, they may be worried that if they do disclose their self-harm, their choices for the future may be compromised. Anecdotal evidence from young people shows that they worry that they will not be able to work in professions such as teaching, nursing or childcare because of the public perception that people who self-harm are 'dangerous' and should not be allowed to work with children.

MOVING FORWARD

Young people who engage in self-harm can find it hard to talk about the subject and are often afraid of the reaction they may receive. Almost all of them feel guilty and ashamed. The reaction a young person receives when they disclose their self-harm can have a critical influence on whether they go on to access supportive services. Young people who have self-harmed want responses that are non-judgemental and which are caring and respectful. Social workers need to recognise that dealing with disclosure requires them to exercise their existing core professional skills, *not* to have a completely new set of skills.

Research indicates the difficulty faced by services and individuals in delivering services that young people who self-harm will engage with (Fortune *et al.* 2005). The vast majority of the adolescents surveyed felt that they could cope on their own, and therefore did not need to engage in services, or that services would not understand and respond appropriately. Other findings highlight the fact that if young people do seek help and/ or advice, they predominantly talk to their friends, although they also sought out a wide range of individuals and organisations for advice and/ or support. On the whole the respondents felt that the contact had been helpful: relatives were the least helpful and voluntary organisations the most. The type of support they found most helpful was face-to-face contact.

A number of different approaches have been taken in an attempt to intervene and/or 'treat' individuals who self-harm. Systematic reviews evaluating the effectiveness of various interventions after incidents of self-harm have been published, but are inconclusive and focus on a narrow methodological base. Further research is needed to fill these gaps. Out of those few interventions which have been evaluated to date, three appear to be promising:

- crisis cards (or green cards)
- problem-solving therapy
- dialectical behaviour therapy.

Activity 3.3

o Arrange to attend a multi-agency meeting to discuss liaison, joint working and collaborative practice and how to respond to the increasing levels of self-harm.

o Before the meeting reflect on the above and think about what your particular contribution could be.

Commentary

Social workers need to affirm their commitment to putting the voices of young people who self-harm at the centre of policy. Service delivery responses to young people who self-harm are still patchy, and many services and projects do not have the support and the resources that they should. The research demonstrates how far reaching the issue of self-harm is for young people. The guilt and secrecy associated with self-harm impacts on their daily lives in:

- relationships
- the clothes they wear
- interactions with their friends
- sense of self-worth.

There are considerable barriers that prevent young people who self-harm from seeking support. The most fundamental one is the fact that many young people do not feel that the professionals they deal with, and/or the services on offer, are meeting their needs (or indeed even recognising what they need, if they are focusing solely on the self-harm). Services and individual practitioners need to become a lot more appropriate, accessible and effective, and young people also need to be equipped with the skills to maintain their own good mental health and to tackle self-harm as early as possible. The voices of young people who self-harm are not being heard, leaving many young people still at a point where they feel that the only way they can negotiate crises and difficulties is through self-harm. At the same time, almost all those young people very much want to be able to move on and stop their self-harm.

Crime, youth justice and anti-social behaviour

The predominance of 'punishment' as a cultural response to anti-social and youth crime in the UK has often meant that the public framing of provision for responding to vulnerable young people persistently involved in criminal activity has been dominated by punitive language. Mental health and emotional well-being are rarely considered in these contexts. There is an absence of any measured consideration of how best to respond effectively to the personal characteristics and social circumstances of these troubled young people (Whyte 2007). The final decade of the twentieth century saw a greater emphasis on personal and individual accountability and responsibility and a move away from a model of shared responsibility resulting in more young people appearing in criminal processes. This has been associated with more and new mechanisms for dealing with youths through formal, legal and criminal processes, whether in youth or adult courts, rather than through diversionary and better integrated social educational, health and welfare mechanisms emphasised by the UN Convention on the Rights of the Child.

THE COST OF ANTI-SOCIAL BEHAVIOUR

Evidence suggests that conduct disorder in children and young people costs £1.5bn up to the age of 25, and much more if projected forward into their futures (Joy *et al.* 2008). These costs include involvement in the criminal justice system, education, health and foster care costs, and lost earnings. Yet conduct disorder is treatable. A study into the efficacy of parenting programmes showed that, on average, two-thirds of children under ten years whose parents took part showed improvement, with effects detectable for up to four years. But at the same time, research in 2006 suggested that three-quarters of children with a diagnosable problem of any kind were not receiving sustained, appropriate treatment over three years. The same source indicated that less than half of children with a diagnosable problem were getting support from any professional.

Evidence supports the view that multiple difficulties relating to social adversity, socialisation and social control, particularly parental supervision, are common to many young people who offend persistently. They often have an inter-related set of problems differentiating them from those who get into trouble once or twice, are often well known to social services departments for non-offence reasons, and many have a history of local authority care (Hagell and Newman 1994). According to Rutter (2005) the following are causal factors in the development of anti-social behaviour that have increased in recent years:

- family disruption
- increase in educational expectations
- major decision-making around drugs and sex
- prolongation of financial dependence on parents.

Contributory factors are the effects of cultural conflict, media portrayal of male and female role models, and the increasing levels of toxins and pollutants in the environment, food and drink. The relative increase in affluence and widening of the gap between rich and poor has also invariably highlighted differences between social class groups and the sense of exclusion and alienation felt by increasing numbers of disaffected young people. The de-classification of certain recreational drugs and the relaxation of licensing laws and availability of high strength alcohol has contributed to disinhibited social behaviour. In addition the cumulative effects of all the above have contributed towards a reduction in community cohesion and civic responsibility. The following conclusions can be drawn from research considering the patterns of violence in different age groups:

- There is a continuity in problem behaviour from childhood to adolescence, especially physical aggression.

- Chronic physical aggression during elementary school increases the risk of violence persisting.

- Physical aggression peaks around the second year of life but then will show different developmental trajectories.

- Violence is unlearned, not learned. Early violence is common and most children become gradually less violent from the time they start school, although indirect aggression increases.

- Social influences seem to compromise the processes that help to contain violent behaviour. It suggests the quality of early relationship experiences is important. (Broidy *et al.* 2003)

Practitioners from different disciplines require a shared understanding of how different practice approaches can complement each other within a framework directed by effectiveness principles. Concern about pathologising or medicalising social conditions can only be overcome with a shared understanding of the importance of promoting positive mental health as a crucial element in any effective response to serious and persistent youth crime. This needs to be located within the provision routinely available for the most risky and vulnerable young people. Although research on the relative success of different approaches remains limited, a collaborative approach that involves health and social systems in planning, inter-disciplinary training and the delivery of services can build on the strengths of each system and help to establish connections that seem critical to structured intervention, aftercare and maintenance, and community reintegration (Whyte 2007).

Eating disorders

Assessment of young people with eating disorders should be comprehensive and include physical, psychological and social needs, and a comprehensive assessment of risk to self. The level of risk to the young person's mental and physical health should be monitored as treatment progresses because it may increase, for example, following weight change or at times of transition between services in cases of anorexia nervosa (NICE 2004). For people with eating disorders presenting in primary care, GPs should take responsibility for the initial assessment and the initial co-ordination of care. This includes the determination of the need for emergency medical or mental health assessment.

Young people and, where appropriate, carers should be provided with education and information on the nature, course and treatment of eating disorders. In addition to the provision of information, family and carers may be informed of self-help groups and support groups, and offered the opportunity to participate in such groups where they exist. Social workers should acknowledge that many people with eating disorders are ambivalent about treatment and recognise the consequent demands and challenges this presents. Young people with eating disorders should be assessed and receive treatment at the earliest opportunity. Early treatment is particularly important for those with or at risk of severe emaciation and they should be prioritised for treatment.

ANOREXIA NERVOSA

Most people with anorexia nervosa should be managed in the community with psychological treatment provided by a service that is competent in giving that treatment and assessing the physical risk of people with eating disorders. Young people with anorexia nervosa requiring inpatient treatment should be admitted to a setting that can provide the skilled implementation of re-feeding with careful physical monitoring (particularly in the first few days of re-feeding) in combination with psychosocial interventions. Family interventions that directly address the eating disorder should be offered to children and adolescents with anorexia nervosa.

FEEDING AGAINST THE WILL OF THE PATIENT

This should be an intervention of last resort in the care and management of anorexia nervosa. Feeding against the will of the patient is a highly specialised procedure requiring expertise in the care and management of those with severe eating disorders and the physical complications associated with it. This should only be done in the context of the Mental Health Act 1983 or Children Act 1989. When making the decision to feed against the will of the patient, the legal basis for any such action must be clear.

BULIMIA NERVOSA

As a possible first step, young people with bulimia nervosa should be encouraged to follow an evidence-based self-help programme. The course of treatment should be for 16 to 20 sessions over four to five months. Adolescents with bulimia nervosa may be treated with cognitive behavioural therapy (CBT-BN), adapted as needed to suit their age, circumstances and level of development, and including the family as appropriate.

FOR ALL EATING DISORDERS

Family members, including siblings, should normally be included in the treatment of children and adolescents with eating disorders. Interventions may include sharing of information, advice on behavioural management and facilitating communication. In children and adolescents with eating disorders, growth and development should be closely monitored. Where development is delayed or growth is stunted despite adequate nutrition, paediatric advice should be sought. Social work professionals assessing children and adolescents with eating disorders should be alert to indicators of abuse (emotional, physical and sexual) and should remain so throughout treatment.

The right to confidentiality of children and adolescents with eating disorders should be respected. When working with children and adolescents with eating disorders social workers should familiarise themselves with national guidelines and their employers' policies in the area of confidentiality. In the absence of evidence to guide the management of atypical eating disorders (eating disorders not otherwise specified) other than binge eating disorder, it is recommended to follow the guidance on the treatment of the eating problem that most closely resembles the individual patient's eating disorder.

Schizophrenia

This is best understood as a collection of several disorders rather than one single mental health problem. It is nothing to do with 'split personality'. It is uncommon in early adolescence but prevalence increases with age and in males. The signs to watch out for are:

- psychotic state with delusions, hallucinations or thought disorders
- significant reduction in social contacts
- deterioration in general and academic functioning
- reduction in personal care and hygiene

- in addition some young people might show a lack of emotional affect
- lack of energy or spontaneity
- lack of enjoyment.

Risk factors include:

- family history
- biochemical and brain disorder
- substance misuse which triggers psychosis.

The treatment and management of schizophrenia has been divided into three phases: initiation of treatment at the first episode; acute phase, and promoting recovery. As a social worker you might be involved at any or all of these phases.

The national guidelines make good practice points and recommendations for psychological, pharmacological and service-level interventions in the three phases of care in both primary care and secondary mental health services (NICE 2002).

THE PROCESS OF CARE

The effects of schizophrenia on a young person's life experience and opportunities are considerable. Service users and carers need help and support to deal with their future and to cope with the changes the illness brings (NICE 2002). Social workers should work in partnership with service users and carers, offering help, treatment and care in an atmosphere of hope and optimism. For most young people experiencing a schizophrenic breakdown, the level of distress, anxiety and subjective confusion, especially during first episodes, leads to difficulty in accessing services. Service users and their relatives seeking help should be assessed and receive treatment at the earliest possible opportunity.

ASSESSMENT

The focus of your intervention and joint work is to help improve the experience and outcomes of care for people with schizophrenia. These outcomes include:

- the degree of symptomatic recovery
- quality of life
- degree of personal autonomy
- ability and access to work

- stability and quality of living accommodation
- degree and quality of social integration
- degree of financial independence
- the experience and impact of side effects.

The assessment of needs for health and social care for young people with schizophrenia should therefore be comprehensive, and address medical, social, psychological, educational, economic, physical and cultural issues.

PARTNERSHIP WITH SERVICE USERS AND CARERS

Social work staff involved in the treatment and management of schizophrenia should take time to build a supportive and empathic relationship with service users and carers. This should be regarded as an essential element of the care offered. The families of people with schizophrenia often play an essential part in the treatment and care of their relative, and with the right support and help can positively contribute to promoting recovery. Parents of young people with schizophrenia often feel to blame, either because they believe they have passed on the genes causing schizophrenia, or because they are 'bad parents'. Clear and intelligible information should be made available to service users and their families about schizophrenia and its possible causes, and about the possible role families can have in promoting recovery and reducing relapse.

Whatever treatments are offered, it is essential to engage the service user in a collaborative, trusting and caring working relationship at the earliest opportunity. Professionals should take into full account the particular nature of schizophrenia, which may affect a young person's ability to make judgments, to recognise that they are ill, to comprehend clearly what professionals might say to them and to make informed decisions about their treatment and care. Every effort needs to be made to ensure that a service user can give meaningful and properly informed consent before treatment is initiated, giving adequate time for discussion and the provision of written information.

CASE ILLUSTRATION

Douglas is a 17-year-old embarking upon A level studies at his local sixth form college. He transferred there from his secondary school following poor exam grades at GCSE and a spate of bullying. His parents have noticed him becoming more withdrawn, staying in his bedroom a lot and declining to socialise with his dwindling friendship group. Douglas provokes arguments with his younger sister and frequently flies into an uncontrollable rage, while at other times he seems far away and in a world of his own. His personal hygiene has worsened and he occasionally talks to himself. The college rang last week and said that he had been missing a lot of classes and they were very concerned.

Activity 3.4

○ Review the material in the above section of the chapter together with the content of the case illustration.

○ Imagine your office has been contacted by Douglas's parents and your task is to meet with them to discuss the way forward.

Commentary

Social work professionals should provide accessible information about schizophrenia and its treatment to service users and carers. This should be considered an essential part of working in this area. In addition to the provision of good quality information, families and carers should be offered the opportunity to participate in family or carer support programmes, where these exist. Because many young people with actual or possible schizophrenia have difficulty in getting help, treatment and care at an early stage, early intervention services should provide the correct mix of specialist pharmacological, psychological, social, occupational and educational interventions at the earliest opportunity. Where the needs of the service user and/or carer exceed the capacity of early intervention services, referral to crisis resolution and home treatment teams, acute day hospitals or inpatient services should be considered.

The choice of antipsychotic drug should be made jointly by the individual and the clinician responsible for treatment based on an informed discussion of the relative benefits of the drugs and their side effects. The individual's advocate or carer should be consulted where appropriate. Cognitive behavioural therapy (CBT) should be available as a treatment option for people with schizophrenia. Family interventions should be available to the families of people with schizophrenia who are living with or who are in close contact with the service user. Counselling and supportive psychotherapy are not recommended as discrete interventions in the routine care of people with schizophrenia where other psychological interventions of proven efficacy are indicated and available. However, service user preferences should be taken into account, especially if other treatments are not locally available.

Attention deficit hyperactivity disorder (ADHD)

ADHD is for some social workers and health professionals a controversial subject. It is believed by some that there is over-diagnosis and over-use of stimulant medication to control children's natural boisterous behaviour, and by some that the problem of ADHD is more widespread and under-diagnosed (Timimi and Maitra 2005). Diagnosis of ADHD has multiplied in recent years as have concerns about the short- and long-term side effects of drug treatment. Others accept that it is a real problem and a behavioural syndrome characterised by the core symptoms of hyperactivity, impulsivity and inattention. While these symptoms tend to cluster together, some children are predominantly hyperactive and impulsive, while others are principally inattentive. Not every young person with ADHD has all of the symptoms of hyperactivity, impulsivity and inattention. However, for a person to be diagnosed with ADHD, their symptoms should be associated with at least a moderate degree of psychological, social and/or educational impairment (NICE 2008).

Moderate ADHD in children and young people is present when the symptoms of hyperactivity/impulsivity and/or inattention, or all three, occur together, and are associated with at least moderate impairment, which should be present in multiple settings (for example, home and school or a healthcare setting) and in multiple domains such as: achievement in schoolwork or homework, dealing with physical risks and avoiding common hazards, and forming positive relationships with family and peers), where the level appropriate to the child's chronological and mental age has not been reached. Determining the severity of the disorder should be a matter for clinical judgement, taking into account the severity of impairment, pervasiveness, individual factors and familial and social context (Spender et al. 2001).

ASSESSMENT

Usually there need to be problems both at home and school serious enough to affect family functioning or academic achievement. The symptoms must have started before the age of seven and cannot be accounted for by depression or anxiety. Specific features to consider when assessing for a full diagnosis of ADHD are six or more of the following:

- failure to pay close attention to detail, makes frequent mistakes
- difficulty in concentrating on tasks or play activities
- failure to listen when spoken to directly

- failure to follow through on instructions or finish tasks
- lack of organisation
- reluctance to start tasks that require concentration
- loses items necessary to complete tasks
- distracted by irrelevant activity
- forgetful in daily activities.

Three or more of the following:

- fidgets
- cannot remain seated
- inappropriate running or climbing
- noisy
- being constantly active.

One or more of the following:

- blurts out answers before a question is completed
- failure to wait in turn
- interrupts or intrudes on others' conversations or games
- talks constantly.

CARE AND TREATMENT

Social work professionals should offer parents or carers of pre-school children with ADHD a referral to a parent-training/education programme as the first-line treatment if the parents or carers have not already attended such a programme or the programme has had a limited effect. Teachers who have received training about ADHD and its management could provide behavioural interventions in the classroom to help children and young people with ADHD.

If the child or young person with ADHD has moderate levels of impairment, the parents or carers should be offered referral to a group parent-training/education programme, either on its own or together with a group treatment programme (CBT and/or social skills training) for the child or young person. In school-age children and young people with severe ADHD, drug treatment should be offered as the first-line treatment. Parents should also be offered a group-based parent-training/education programme. Drug treatment for children and young people with ADHD should always form part of a comprehensive treatment plan that includes psychological, behavioural and educational advice and interventions.

Children and young people with behavioural problems suggestive of ADHD can be referred by their school or primary care practitioner for parent-training/education programmes without a formal diagnosis of ADHD. The diagnosis of ADHD in children, young people and adults should take place in CAMHS. When a child or young person presents in primary care with behavioural and/or attention problems suggestive of ADHD, primary care practitioners should determine the severity of the problems, how these affect the child or young person and the parents/carers and the extent to which they pervade different domains and settings.

If the child or young person's behavioural and/or attention problems suggestive of ADHD are having an adverse impact on their development or family life, social workers should consider a period of watchful waiting of up to ten weeks and offer parents/carers a referral to a parent-training/education programme. If the behavioural and/or attention problems persist with at least moderate impairment, the child or young person should be referred to a child psychiatrist, paediatrician or specialist ADHD CAMHS for assessment.

Group-based parent-training/education programmes are usually the first-line treatment for parents and carers of children and young people of school age with ADHD and moderate impairment. This may also include group psychological treatment CBT and/or social skills training for the younger child. For older age groups, individual psychological treatment may be more acceptable if group behavioural or psychological approaches have not been effective, or have been refused.

Table 3.2 briefly summarises a number of common assessment tools for specific problem identification or to begin the process of information gathering to understand further why, or indeed whether a child or young person may be troubled:

TABLE 3.2 COMMON ASSESSMENT TOOLS

Title	Author	Year	Acronym	Brief description
Common Assessment Framework	Department of Health and Department for Children, Schools and Families	2005	CAF	This should be the main and sometimes only assessment instrument to be used by all staff at the first sign of emerging vulnerability, and to act as a marker for referral to another agency or specialist service
Child Behaviour Checklist	Achenbach	1991	CBCL	The CBCL is a checklist of 12 items relating to common behaviour in young children, and has well-established validity and test–retest reliability
Child Global Assessment Scale	Schaffer *et al.*	1983	C-GAS	The C-GAS is a 100-point rating scale measuring psychological, social and school functioning
Children's Depression Inventory	Kovacs	1992	CDI	This is designed to parallel the Beck Depression Inventory but adapted to suit the developmental and reading-level needs of children. The test comprises 27 self-rating items for school-age children and adolescents.
Conners' Rating Scale Revised	Conners	1997	CRS-R	Uses observer ratings and self-report ratings to help assess ADHD and evaluate problem behaviour in children and adolescents. There are three versions – parent, teacher and adolescent self-report
Eating Attitudes Test – 26	Garner *et al.*	1979	EAT-26	The Eating Attitudes test is a 26-item self-report measure, which looks at the eating attitudes of the young person. The EAT-26 alone does not provide a specific diagnosis of an eating disorder
Framework for the Assessment of Children in Need	Department of Health	2000	FACN	A framework which provides a systematic way of analysing, understanding and recording what is happening to children and young people within their families and the wider context of the community in which they live
Health of the Nation Outcome Scales for Children and Adolescents	Gowers *et al.*	1998	HoNOSCA	These scales rate 13 clinical features on 5-point severity. There are two additional questions which assess parental understanding of the difficulties and information about services

Name	Author	Year	Acronym	Description
Harter's Self-Perception Profile for Adolescents	Harter	1988	SPPA	A 45-item self-report scale with a 4-point structured-alternative format intended to offset desirable responding. It focuses on eight specific domains. For ages 14–18
Harter's Self-Perception Profile for Children	Harter	1985	SPPC	Designed to measure multiple dimensions of self-concept. Contains 36 items and focuses on five domains of self-concept. For ages 8–13
Moods and Feelings Questionnaire	Angold and Costello	1993	MFQ	The MFQ consists of a series of descriptive phrases regarding how the child has been feeling or acting recently. Child self-report and parent/carer self-report versions are available
Relationship Problems Questionnaire	Minnis, Rabe-Hesketh and Workind	2002	RPQ	This is an 18-item questionnaire for measuring attachment disorder
Strengths and Difficulties Questionnaire	Goodman	1997	SDQ	The Strengths and Difficulties Questionnaire (SDQ) is a brief behavioural screening questionnaire that provides balanced coverage of the behaviour, emotions and relationships of children and young people. Three versions exist: the self-report for ages 11–17; the parent or teacher form for ages 4–10 and the parent or teacher form for ages 11–17
Spence Children's Anxiety Scale	Spence	1994	SCAS	This provides an overall measure of anxiety consisting of 38 anxiety items and written in child-friendly language.
Trauma Symptom Checklist for Children	Briere et al.	1995	TSCC/TSCC-A	Self-report measure of post-traumatic distress and related psychological problems in male and female children aged 8–16 years
Wally Feelings Game	Webster-Stratton	1996		Children are shown eight coloured pictures of problem situations and then asked how they would feel if this happened to them and what they would do or say to solve the problem
Wally Social Skills and Problem Solving Game	Webster-Stratton	1999		This assesses both the qualitative and quantitative dimensions of a child's social problem solving. The game uses a game-fantasy approach and 13 brightly coloured pictures of hypothetical problem situations related to object acquisition and friendship skills

Key chapter points

- The nature, severity and complexity of mental health problems and related needs is more acute in vulnerable groups of children including looked after children, young offenders, abused children, homeless young people and refugees.

- The science behind assessment tools in child and adolescent mental health is still rudimentary and lacking in important variables of interest to a psychosocial approach. However, you can appreciate their limitations and advantages as well as understand how more specialist agencies begin to construct assessments.

- Assessing autism accurately is notoriously difficult especially in preschool age children when normal socialisation and ranges in verbal communication vary widely. It is only when children attend school that those with autism tend to be identified because of the different way they behave and relate to others. It is also difficult to be certain about the prevalence of autism in the population.

- There is relatively little research or other data on the prevalence of self-harm among young people in the UK or on the reasons why young people self-harm. It is clear that self-harm is a symptom rather than the core problem. It masks underlying emotional and psychological trauma and successful social work for responding to self-harm must be based on this fundamental understanding.

- Assessment of young people with eating disorders should be comprehensive and include physical, psychological and social needs, and a comprehensive assessment of risk to self. The level of risk to the young person's mental and physical health should be monitored as treatment progresses.

- Schizophrenia is best understood as a collection of several disorders rather than one single mental health problem. It is nothing to do with 'split personality'. It is uncommon in early adolescence but prevalence increases with age and in males.

- ADHD is for some social workers and health professionals a controversial subject. Some feel there is over-diagnosis and over-use of stimulant medication to control children's natural boisterous behaviour. Others accept that it is a real problem and a behavioural syndrome characterised by the core symptoms of hyperactivity, impulsivity and inattention.

Part II

Applying the Skills of Social Work

Chapter 4

Social Work Skills and Methods

Learning objectives

» Develop familiarity with contemporary assessment tools for CAMH work with children and families.

» Utilise social work theories and models for assessing children and young people's emotional welfare.

» Recognise assessment as part of the continuum of care and therapeutic support necessary for promoting children and young people's mental health.

» Understand the key issues and skills relevant to effective risk management in working with troubled young people.

Introduction

Social work students regularly complain that there is not enough skills training on their qualifying courses – even some of the newest graduates from the three-year social work degree which was meant to expand practice learning opportunities and skills development. There are many textbooks exclusively devoted to social work skills and methods; others, like this one, are focused on particular areas of practice or client groups. It has been estimated that there are nearly 60 distinct social work skills (Trevithick 2000). The need for clarity and focus means we can usefully collate them into relevant domains for examination and exposition. This chapter will do that in the context of CAMH in general and in relation to the rest of the learning resources within the whole book.

One of the key social work tasks is that of assessment; it is a skill that has to be learned and a method of working alongside other skills and methods that we shall examine in this chapter to see how usefully they can be employed to help support children and young people suffering mental health problems. There are numerous assessment and planning systems for individual children and young people across children's services. This is complicated and can lead to the impression that more effort is being expended on assessment and ticking the boxes than on helping the child or young person to address their needs. Systems include the Common Assessment Framework, the Care Programme Approach, the Framework for the Assessment of Children in Need and their Families, the Special Educational Needs Code of Practice and the ASSET assessment used by Youth Offending Teams.

The Social Care Institute for Excellence (SCIE) 2005 knowledge review of the teaching and learning of assessment skills in social work education discovered that throughout social work education there was no single theory or understanding as to the purpose of assessment. The review acknowledged that assessment is practised differently according to the practice context and/or the function of the task. This means that when assessment is taught it is usually embedded in the social work curriculum with other learning objectives, leaving student social workers feeling they have learnt little about assessment in general let alone for CAMH. The following points are recommended in the development of good assessment practice (Lynch 2004):

- *critical thinking* – involves tapping into your natural curiosity; analysing underlying assumptions; considering multiple perspectives; reflecting; inquiring, and a certain amount of scepticism

- *knowledge* – a wide knowledge about the spectrum of problems that bring the public into contact with social services, e.g. in sexual abuse cases an understanding of child development, family systems, sex offenders, community resources, risk assessment, cultural dynamics and case management

- *principles of assessment* – recognise that using the principles of assessment alone may not provide assessment skills which are transferable to other settings and client groups

- *working in partnership* – crucial in CAMH where social care, health and other professionals are mutually dependent on each other in the care assessment process.

Assessment has been defined as a tool to aid in the planning of future work and the beginning of helping another person to identify areas for growth and change. Its purpose is the identification of needs – it is never an end in itself (Taylor and Devine 1993). Assessment is the foundation of the therapeutic process with clients. It can set the tone for further contact, it is your first opportunity to engage with new or existing clients, and it can be perceived by children and young people as a judgement on their character or behaviour. A good experience of assessment can make them feel positive about receiving help and their attitude to you and your agency. A bad experience of assessment can make matters worse, offend, and make problems harder to resolve in the long term. You can regard it as little more than a paper chasing exercise, involving form filling and participating in a process that restricts eligibility. Or you can see it as an opportunity to engage with children and adolescents in a problem-solving partnership where both of you can learn more about yourselves.

Effective assessment with Black and ethnic minority communities was highlighted throughout the UK National Service Framework for Mental Health (DoH 1999c). Standard one notes that some Black and minority ethnic communities have higher diagnosed rates of mental health problems than the general population and calls for specific programmes of service development for these communities. Standards two to six discuss the need for performance assessment to include the experience of service users and carers, including those from Black and ethnic minority communities. These reflect the anxiety among politicians and professionals regarding the disproportionate numbers of Black and ethnic minority people admitted compulsorily into psychiatric care. They suggest that in addition to the needs of Black and ethnic minority children and young people being neglected, they also represent the institutionalisation of *fear of the other*.

In seeking to understand this you need to be able to review the social context of mental health, cultural variations in emotional expression, and the wider effects of racism in producing higher levels of stress and disadvantage among Black and ethnic minority children and young people. This is then compounded by practice in psychiatric services that are perceived to be institutionally racist and insensitive to individual needs. The development of psychiatry and theories of human growth and development constructed in the eighteenth and nineteenth centuries were based on white ethnocentric beliefs and assumptions about normality. The western model of illness regards the mind as distinct from the body and defines mental illness or mental health according to negative, deficit characteristics. In non-western cultures such as Chinese, Indian and African, mental health is often perceived as a harmonious balance between a person's internal and external influences. Thus a person is intrinsically linked to their environment and vice versa.

Activity 4.1

o   What do you consider to be your strongest social work skill?

o   What do you consider to be your weakest?

o   Now make an action plan to improve your weakest skill and discuss this with your manager to investigate what education or training resources can help you.

The Common Assessment Framework

Government guidance indicates that the Common Assessment Framework (CAF) should be the main and sometimes only assessment instrument to be used at the first sign of emerging vulnerability in a child or young person, and act as a marker for referral to another agency or specialist service. Assessments have hitherto been used to make decisions about whether or not a child meets the threshold criteria to trigger delivery of a service. The concept is that the CAF should lead to a common approach to needs assessment, as an initial assessment for use by statutory or voluntary sector staff in education, early years, health, police, youth justice or social work. It is intended that this will reduce the number of assessments experienced by children and foster improved information sharing and thus help dissolve professional boundaries.

The framework is expected to contribute to the wider culture change across the children and young people's workforce by offering:

- general guidance on its use

- a common procedure for assessment

- a methodology based on the Framework for the Assessment of Children in Need and their Families

- a focus on child development and communication skills with children, carers and parents

- gaining consent

- how to record findings and identify an appropriate response

- how to share information when a child moves between local authority areas

- an explanation of the roles and responsibilities of different agencies and practitioners. (DfES 2005)

The process of the common assessment

- *Preparation* – you talk to the child/young person and their parent. Discuss the issues and what you can do to help. You talk to anyone else you need to who is already involved. If you decide a common assessment would be useful you seek the agreement of the child/young person and their parent as appropriate.

- *Discussion* – you talk to the child/young person, family and complete the assessment with them. Make use of additional information from other sources to avoid repeated questions. Add to or update any existing common assessments. At the end of the discussion seek to understand better the child and family's strengths, needs and what can be done to help. Agree actions that your service and the family can deliver. You agree with the family any actions that require others to deliver and record this on the form.

- *Service delivery* – you deliver on your actions. Make referrals or broker access to other services using the common assessment to demonstrate evidence of need. Keep an eye on progress. Where the child or family needs services from a range of agencies a lead professional must be identified to co-ordinate.

Elements of the common assessment framework
Development of baby, child or young person

- *General health* – includes health conditions or impairments which significantly affect everyday life functioning.

- *Physical development* – includes means of mobility, and level of physical or sexual maturity or delayed development.

- *Speech, language and communications development* – includes the ability to communicate effectively, confidently and appropriately with others.

- *Emotional and social development* – includes the emotional and social response the baby, child or young person gives to parents, carers and others outside the family.

- *Behavioural development* – includes lifestyle and capacity for self-control.

- *Identity* – includes the growing sense of self as a separate and valued person, self-esteem, self-image and social presentation.

- *Family and social relationships* – includes the ability to empathise and build stable and affectionate relationships with others, including family, peers and the wider community.

- *Self-care skills and independence* – includes the acquisition of practical, emotional and communication competencies to increase independence.

- *Understanding, reasoning and problem-solving* – includes the ability to understand and organise information, reason and solve problems.

- *Participation in learning, education and employment* – includes the degree to which the child or young person has access to and is engaged in education and/or work based training and, if s/he is not participating, the reasons for this.

- *Progress and achievement in learning* – includes the child or young person's educational achievements and progress, including in relation to their peers.

- *Aspirations* – includes the ambitions of the child or young person, whether their aspirations are realistic and they are able to plan how to meet them. Note there may be barriers to their achievement because of other responsibilities at home.

Parents and carers

- *Basic care, ensuring safety and protection* – includes the extent to which the baby, child or young person's physical needs are not met and to which they are protected from harm, danger and self-harm.

- *Emotional warmth and stability* – includes the provision of emotional warmth in a stable family environment, giving the baby, child or young person a sense of being valued.

- *Guidance, boundaries and stimulation* – includes enabling the child or young person to regulate their own emotions and behaviour while promoting the child or young person's learning and intellectual development through encouragement, stimulation and promoting social opportunities.

Family and environmental factors

- *Family history, functioning and well-being* – includes the impact of family situations and experiences.

- *Wider family* – includes the family's relationships with relatives and non-relatives.

- *Housing, employment and financial considerations* – includes living arrangements, amenities, facilities, who is working or not and the income available over a sustained period of time.

Social and community resources

- *Neighbourhood* – includes the wider context of the neighbourhood and its impact on the baby, child or young person, availability of facilities and services.

- *Accessibility* – includes schools, day-care, primary health care, places of worship, transport, shops, leisure activities and family support services.

- *Characteristics* – includes levels of crime, disadvantage, employment, levels of substance misuse/trading.

- *Social integration* – includes the degree of the young person's social integration or isolation, peer influences, friendships and social networks.

Activity 4.2

○ Review the above material and make a note of those elements that are less familiar to you.

○ Make sure you make time soon to discuss these in supervision or with your manager to help you understand them and integrate them into your practice.

Framework for the assessment of children in need

The Framework for Assessing Children in Need (DoH 2000) was the most comprehensive guidance to emerge following implementation of the Children Act 1989. You are expected to use this in conjunction with the CAF. Since 2001 all referrals to social service departments concerning children in need have been assessed under these guidelines in three ways. An initial assessment where the needs are considered to be relatively straightforward, such as a request for family support, a comprehensive assessment and a core assessment.

- *Initial assessment* – this provides a good basis for short-term planning and can be used as part of eligibility criteria to determine the level of need and priority. In childcare situations it is used to effect immediate child protection with a general requirement of a two-week time limit.

- *Comprehensive assessment* – this takes over from where an initial assessment finishes and where more complex needs such as mental health have been identified. Or it is initiated following changes in a service user's situation where basic, but limited information already exists.

- *Core assessment* – this is used in childcare cases and is a specific requirement under Children Act 1989 guidance for a time-limited assessment in order to help inform the decision-making process in legal proceedings where the needs are perceived to be more complex involving a number of concerns about emotional development or child abuse. The key aim is to enable all stakeholders to contribute as much information as possible, consistent with effective outcomes.

A recent research project found evidence that workers find the Assessment Framework cumbersome, over-reliant on prescribed formats and expected to be undertaken in unrealistic timescales (Corby, Millar and Pope 2002). The researchers found evidence that parents involved in these assessments felt their views were not being taken sufficiently into account. Key to parental satisfaction with the process was:

- feeling that their perceptions about their child/ren were taken into account
- reaching agreement about the nature of the problem
- maintaining optimism and a degree of sensitivity
- using the framework flexibly and creatively to maximise parental empowerment.

Recent research demonstrates that child protection assessments can become dominated by the agenda of social services departments thereby undermining the concept of inter-agency co-operation (Howarth 2002). Also in the drive to complete recording forms within specified timescales anti-oppressive practice is given a lack of attention, while the pace of the assessment is inconsistent with the capacity of the family to cope. This means already stressful situations can become unbearable and increase risks to a child or young person's emotional well-being.

Activity 4.3

- ○ Write down the ways in which you think the guidance will help in your assessment of a child and family you might be working with, and the ways in which this guidance will hinder the assessment.

Commentary

Such a comprehensive guidance framework can seem daunting to staff working under pressure on their available resources. Time is crucial in many situations and it is often difficult to obtain full information in risky circumstances. Interventions undertaken in one set of circumstances can impact on the quality of subsequent assessment – and vice versa. It is important to consider the purpose of assessment and the relationship between assessment and intervention, which can make it hard to separate their functions. The danger is that you might well feel impelled to conduct lengthy detailed assessments following the framework rigidly rather than using it as a guide to practice across a multitude of different circumstances. The skill will be in focusing on the most important aspects of the framework relevant to particular situations.

CASE ILLUSTRATION

This case study gives an example where partnership appears fraught with difficulties and may appear unachievable. You have just been told to review this case and transfer it to another area because the family are moving. Think about how you would try to work in partnership with the family while conveying your concerns to other professionals.

Father (Tommy) age 45, unemployed, disabled wheelchair user.

Mother (Shirley) age 32, left family six months ago, whereabouts unknown.

Daughter (Anne) age 11, at special school for children with learning difficulties.

Son (Adam) age six, attends primary school.

Twins (Luke and Linda) age 38 months, Steve is brain damaged and Linda has a hole in her heart. Both have developmental delays.

The family are travellers and about to move to another area. The father, Tommy, has been unco-operative with many agencies concerned about his children. He has been rude, hostile and racially abusive to Black staff. Hospital appointments for the twins have been missed and your concerns have been increasing over time. Adam and Anne bed wet and both have missed a lot of schooling. Father has a history of moving around the country – often at short notice. Tommy feels there is nothing much wrong with the children and focuses his attention mostly on the twins. He feels that professionals are exaggerating; he is a proud man and he is determined to care for his family on his own.

Commentary

Reflecting on your feelings may produce elements of fear, disapproval and frustration. Or perhaps you might be aware of a certain admiration for Tommy's tenacity and self-sufficiency. You may feel protective towards the children and angry that Tommy is not putting their needs first. As a Black worker you may want to discuss whether another worker should be allocated this case given his racist language; on the other hand you may feel it is a useful challenge to work with him. You also need to reflect on racist stereotypes of members of the Traveller community and consider activating supportive family networks at his intended destination.

Your main anxieties may stem from Tommy's lack of co-operation and from concerns about the children's developmental needs being neglected. The short-term impact on their emotional well-being and the long-term consequences of this on their personal, educational and social development are a concern. The effects on Tommy's physical and mental health of soldiering on heighten your concerns. Tommy's anger could be explored to tease out the cause and help him manage it more usefully.

- Is his attitude due to his wife's exit?

- Does he feel he is being perceived as an inadequate parent?

- Is he suspicious of professional interference?

- Can he express his feelings of helplessness?

- Does he acknowledge that his own needs are being eclipsed?

Suggesting a multi-agency case conference between the current and future professional network is useful for planning and using resources and offers a chance to share concerns and measure your level of anxiety against other perspectives. Research shows the absence of case conferences is likely to be detrimental but their occurrence is not always beneficial (Hallett and Birchall 1992). It will be useful to explore the family's wider network including grandparents, uncles, etc. as a possible source of support. Thought also needs to be given to the significance for the children of Shirley and her absence. Is their behaviour part of delayed shock, anxiety and bereavement at their loss and/or a reaction to Tommy's distress? You might think about the use of a contract with Tommy. This could set out the purposes of future involvement and what is possible or not in terms of support, help and resources consistent with the child protection plan. It could give Tommy space to outline his concerns, needs and goals.

CASE ILLUSTRATION

A review of the existing plan shows that it is only partly working. These elements are successful:

- Adam and Anne's school attendance has improved slightly.

- The house is cleaner than it used to be.

- Tommy has reduced his alcohol use.

- Tommy has allowed the health visitor to visit more often.

These elements of the plan have been less successful:

- The twins' appointments have not been kept.
- Tommy has refused larger accommodation to enable Anne and Adam to have separate bedrooms.
- Tommy often leaves the children with friends when he goes out to the pub in the evening.
- He continues to threaten social workers trying to visit.
- Tommy has undermined individual work with Anne and Adam.

As part of the review work it is crucial to assess whether the developmental needs of each child in the family are being better met. Concerns should be recorded and areas of agreement and disagreement between yourself and Tommy and any other professional noted. The review needs to consider whether Tommy's moving away is part of a pattern to avoid scrutiny or part of his cultural characteristics or indeed both. It is important to evaluate the strengths in this family as well. Tommy is determined to keep the family together. He has some understanding of their needs for schooling and health care. He has acknowledged his alcohol problem. The review may in balancing all the information still decide that Tommy cannot be worked with and that legal intervention is the only way to secure the children's welfare.

If this is the case, it is important that such a judgement is soundly based on evidence from other professionals and research, and only comes after all possibilities for engagement have been explored. If Tommy moves away quickly before further action can take place agencies at his destination need to be informed fully. Exchange of information and fluent communication is essential. Each separate agency should ensure that their specific part in the protection plan is crystal clear and formally acknowledged at transfer. Responsibility and accountability are now more sharply located with managers. These are the times when vulnerable children may be at most risk because of a combination of disruption in the care network and bureaucratic inertia.

Skills in direct work

Table 4.1 details the recommended treatments and support strategies for children and adolescents suffering mental health problems. They have been collated on the basis of considerable research into effectiveness but from an evidence base that is not yet methodologically robust. Studies examining their efficacy tend to be done by doctors in clinical settings under controlled conditions. They do not therefore match with the practice reality for social workers in non-specialist contexts undertaking several different roles. However, they serve a very useful purpose in providing knowledge and information about how mental health problems can be tackled. Many treatments and the theoretical base informing them are the same as social work methods and models of practice. Research also confirms that core interpersonal skills transcend disparate treatments, methods and models.

TABLE 4.1 RECOMMENDED TREATMENTS FOR CHILDREN AND YOUNG PEOPLE'S MENTAL HEALTH DISORDERS

Depression

For mild depression: 'watchful waiting' for up to four weeks. Non-directive therapy, group cognitive behavioural therapy (CBT) or guided self-help may be beneficial
Moderate to severe depression: psychological therapy as a first-line treatment (e.g. individual CBT, interpersonal therapy or shorter-term family therapy) for at least three months
Anti-depressant medication (selective serotonin reuptake inhibitors [SSRIs]) may be considered, particularly for adolescents, but only in combination with psychological therapy and if there is no response to psychological therapy after four to six sessions
Family therapy or individual child psychotherapy if the child or young person is still not responsive may be considered. Advice on exercise, sleep and nutrition may also help

Anxiety and phobias including obsessive-compulsive disorder (OCD) and body dysmorphic disorder (BDD)

Behavioural therapies and CBT, sometimes involving family or carers (particularly if the child is under 11 or there is high parental anxiety), or Exposure and Response Prevention (for young people with OCD or BDD who have not responded to guided self-help). However, CBT only appears to be effective in 50 per cent of cases treated in randomised controlled trials
Anti-depressant medication (SSRIs), usually in combination with a psychological therapy, may be used for social anxieties, OCD or BDD that have not responded to CBT. The provision of information, advice and support at school may also be helpful

Post-traumatic stress disorder (PTSD)

Trauma-focused CBT, adapted to suit the child or young person's age, circumstances and level of development
Eye Movement Desensitisation and Reprocessing (EMDR) is used but there has been limited research into this to date. EMDR involves focusing on a particular physical action while thinking about the traumatic experiences in order to change the individual's thoughts and feelings about those experiences

Conduct disorders including oppositional defiant disorder (ODD)

Group parent-training programmes led by a therapist, particularly for less severe conduct problems. On average two-thirds of children under ten whose parents take part show improvement, with effects detectable for up to four years
Parent training for conduct disorders in adolescents seems to have limited effectiveness
Problem-solving and social skills training may be helpful if used in combination with parent training for 8–12-year-olds, or where problems are more severe. However, the benefits may be short term
Family therapy for adolescents and young people with moderate conduct problems, combined with CBT where appropriate

Multisystemic therapy (MST) is an intensive programme that involves a therapist working with a family in their home to help them change their behaviour patterns, resolve conflicts, introduce rules that will improve the conduct of their child and reduce opportunities for delinquent behaviour. It is probably the most effective treatment for adolescents with severe and enduring problems

Therapeutic foster care with trained and experienced foster parents can help children and young people with severe and enduring problems

Medication may help in particular cases, after other forms of treatment have been tried and where conduct disorders are associated with hyperactivity

Attention deficit hyperactivity disorder (ADHD)

Parent-training programmes (developed for the management of children with conduct disorders) as the first-line treatment for pre-school children. It should also be offered to the parents of school-age children and young people with moderate ADHD. Parent training/ education can improve a child or young person's compliance, boost parental self-esteem and reduce parental stress, although it is not effective in all cases. It may also be used in combination with a group or individual treatment programme (such as CBT or social skills training) for the child or young person

Stimulant medication is the first-line treatment for school-age children and young people with severe ADHD. Research shows it can reduce hyperactivity and improve concentration in 75 per cent of treated children. However, it may lead to mild growth suppression, particularly when used for continuous treatment, so breaks are advisable. It should always form part of a comprehensive treatment plan that includes psychological, behavioural and educational advice and therapy

Group-based parent-training programme

Changes to diet and nutrition (for example, avoiding foods that contain high levels of sugar and artificial colourings, and carbonated drinks) may help some children and young people. ADHD has been linked to deficiencies in essential fatty acids, and there is evidence that taking omega-3 and omega-6 fatty acids has a positive effect on reading and spelling and ADHD-related behaviours

Exposure and Response Prevention (ERP) works on the principle that if you stay in a stressful situation long enough, you become used to it and your anxiety decreases, i.e. you gradually face the situation you fear (exposure) but stop yourself from doing your usual compulsive rituals (response prevention) and wait for your anxiety to pass

Schizophrenia

Medication (e.g. anti-psychotic medicines called 'atypical neuroleptics') is the primary form of treatment

Specialist care (e.g. support from crisis-resolution and home-treatment teams)

Psychological therapies, particularly CBT and family therapy (these have been found to benefit adults with psychosis but less is known about how much they help younger people)

Bipolar disorder

Medication (e.g. lithium, neuroleptics or mood stabilisers) is the primary form of treatment

Psychological therapies may also be used as part of treatment, e.g. to manage depressive symptoms

Eating disorders

Anorexia nervosa:
Psychological therapies (such as CBT, cognitive analytic therapy [CAT], interpersonal psychotherapy, psychodynamic psychotherapy)

Table 4.1 Recommended treatments for children and young people's mental health disorders *cont.*

Eating disorders

Family therapy focused specifically on eating disorders
Inpatient care as necessary, including psychological or behaviour therapy that focuses on eating behaviour, attitudes to weight and shape, and wider issues

Bulimia nervosa:
Self-help in the first instance
Anti-depressant drugs may also be offered as an alternative or additional first step
Family therapy
CBT for bulimia (CBT-BN), adapted to suit the patient's age, circumstances and level of development, and involving their family as appropriate
Interpersonal psychotherapy or other psychological treatments may be considered as an alternative, but further research is needed into their effectiveness
Behaviour therapy may also be used with children and young people who are being treated in hospital to help them put on weight. Treatment must involve the management of physical aspects of the condition as the risk of morbidity is high

Deliberate self-harm

Specific advice on self-management of superficial injuries, harm-minimisation techniques and alternative coping strategies for people who repeatedly self-injure. Helping young people to distract themselves from self-harm by using a red water-soluble felt tip pen to mark their skin, rather than cutting themselves
Developmental group psychotherapy with other young people who have repeatedly self-harmed may be effective in reducing repetition
Family therapy may help in addressing the issues that cause self-harm

Substance abuse

Family therapy and MST may be effective in reducing substance abuse and tackling related problems
Motivational interviewing is a form of counselling in which the counsellor discusses with the child or young person the advantages and disadvantages of changing his or her behaviour. This may be effective, as may preventative programmes in schools that build personal, social and resistance skills

Source: Joy *et al.* 2008

Methods and models of practice

The following methods and models of practice are not unique to social work nor are they an exclusive list. Within each are specific skills sets informed by sound theory and research. They have been chosen from the range of modern methods and models available to aid clarity in selection of the most appropriate components of an effective social work intervention in CAMH work (Coulshed and Orme 1998; Doel and Marsh 1992; Milner and O'Byrne 1998; Payne 1997; Walker 2005a; Walker and Beckett 2003). Discussion of the merits of defining methods and models of social work, and examination of the distinctions between terms such as practice approach, orientation and perspective, has been avoided for the sake of brevity and in order to avoid adding to the confusion already highlighted in the literature (Trevithick 2000).

Crisis intervention

Crisis intervention has become a practice with a theoretical base and can be identified by certain characteristics. Drawing on psychodynamic principles it is aimed at strengthening the child's internal psychological resources through a personal relationship within which you can positively reinforce their coping strategies. Crisis theory is described as a time when a person finds themselves much more dependent on external sources of support than at other times in their life. It has been described as having three distinct phases (Caplan 1961):

- *impact* – recognising a threat
- *recoil* – attempting to restore equilibrium but failing, leaving the person feeling stressed and defeated
- *adjustment/adaptation or breakdown* – when the person begins to move to a different level of functioning.

It is usually a set of inter-related factors and triggers that produce a state of crisis, some of which can be anticipated while others cannot. Rather than see crises as individual failures it is better to think of them as opportunities for interventions when the young person is more likely to respond. Characteristics include:

- helps the young person gain insight into their functioning and better ways of coping
- used in conjunction with risk assessment and risk management techniques
- is usually short term in nature
- relates a young person's internal crises to external changes
- can help in case of loss, bereavement, reactive depression and trauma
- based on the idea that people can return to a previous level of functioning.

DISADVANTAGES

This may be used as the default setting for social work practice as government and employers redefine modern social work to a reactive service administering problems, gatekeeping resources and referring clients on to other services. Done well it offers opportunities for advanced reflective psychosocial practice and high levels of interpersonal skill. But if it is used to ration, exclude and constrain then it is more a mechanism of social control.

Community work practice

Helping people within their own communities is endorsed by valid research as better than removing them to unfamiliar surroundings. The theoretical base of such practice is political and socialist in origins. In its narrowest definition it might exclude statutory work and identify with voluntary non-statutory sector staff engaged in pressure group action or outreach activity. A broader definition would include it as part of the repertoire of skills required in progressive psychosocial practice. It is characterised by partnership, anti-discriminatory, empowering practice aimed at reducing social exclusion and fostering self-help. It comprises these specific skills:

- galvanising
- focusing
- clarifying
- summarising
- gatekeeping
- mediating
- informing. (Henderson and Thomas 1987)

DISADVANTAGES

Young people who are homeless or in crisis are not often linked to their neighbourhoods, kinship networks or informal support, therefore it is difficult to galvanise them or enable them to accept the help offered. The community itself may be hostile to them and their behaviours as well as reflecting racist beliefs and discriminatory practices. Institutional organisation of social work practice is part of the structure of society and welfare which has let many young people down.

Systemic practice

Employing a systemic or systems model in CAMH practice will be characterised by the key notion that individual children and young people have a social context which will be influencing, to a greater or lesser extent, their behaviour and their perception of their problem. An important social context is that of the family and this has led to the practice of family therapy as a method of practice. It offers a broad framework for intervention enabling the mapping of all of the important elements affecting families as well as a method of working with those elements to effect beneficial change. Key features include:

- convening family meetings to give voice to everyone connected to an individual's problem (e.g. family group conference)

- constructing a geneogram (family tree) with a family to help identify the quality of relationships

- harnessing the strengths of families to support individuals in trouble

- using a problem-oriented style to energise the family to find their own solutions

- assisting in the development of insight into patterns of behaviour and communication within the family system

- adopting a neutral position as far as possible in order to avoid accusations of bias/collusion.

Many professionals use this model as an overarching framework to help guide their practice. It is particularly useful to use to clarify situations where there is multi-agency and multi-professional involvement in clients' lives. It can help the drawing of boundaries and sort out who does what in often complex, fast-moving and confusing situations. It also helps avoid the assumption that the individual child or young person is necessarily the main focus for intervention.

DISADVANTAGES

It can be difficult for some families to appreciate the interconnectedness of the problems of individual children with wider influences. It is a way of viewing the position, role and behaviour of various individuals within the context of the whole system, but in so doing can appear abstract, culturally insensitive and disempowering. Used uncritically it can negate the importance of individual work, as well as avoiding location of responsibility in child abuse situations.

Psychodynamic practice

The model offers a concept of the mind, its mechanisms and a method of understanding why some children behave in seemingly repetitive, destructive ways. It is the essential one-to-one helping relationship involving advanced listening and communication skills. It provides a framework to address profound disturbances and inner conflicts within children and adolescents around issues of loss, attachment, anxiety and personal development. Key ideas such as defence mechanisms, and the transference in the relationship between worker and client, can be extremely helpful in reviewing the work being undertaken, and in the process of supervision. The model helps evaluate the strong feelings aroused in particular work situations, where for example a client transfers feelings and attitudes onto the worker that derive from an earlier significant relationship. Counter-transference occurs when you try to live up to that expectation and behave for example, like the client's parent. Key features include:

- It is a useful way of attempting to understand seemingly irrational behaviour.

- The notion of defence mechanisms is a helpful way of assessing male adolescents who have difficulty expressing their emotions.

- It acknowledges the influence of past events/attachments and can create a healthy suspicion about surface behaviour.

- The development of insight can be a particularly empowering experience to enable children and young people to understand themselves and take more control over their own lives.

- The model has influenced a listening, accepting approach that avoids over-directiveness.

- It can be used to assess which developmental stage is reflected in the child or young person's behaviour and to gauge the level of anxiety/depression.

DISADVANTAGES

The conventional criticisms of this model are its genesis in a medical model of human behaviour that relies on expert opinion without too much account of the person in their socio-economic context. In its original, uncritical form it pathologises homosexuality and negates gender power relationships. It is not considered an appropriate way of working with some ethnic minority groups and on its own cannot adequately explain the effects of racism.

Cognitive behavioural practice

Practice with this model is based on the key concept that all behaviour is learned and therefore available to be unlearned or changed. It offers a framework for assessing the pattern of behaviour in children and adolescents and a method for altering their thinking, feeling and behaviour.

The intervention can be used with individuals and groups of young people. It aims to help them become aware of themselves, to link thoughts and emotions, and to enable them to acquire new life skills. Using this approach you would decide on the goals/new behaviours to be achieved with the client, those that are clear but also capable of measurement. The four major behavioural techniques are desensitisation, aversion therapy, operant conditioning and modelling. Key features include:

- using the ABC formula – what are the Antecedents, the Behaviour and the Consequences of the problem
- focusing on what behaviours are desired and reinforcing them
- modelling and rehearsing desired behavioural patterns
- combining behavioural and cognitive approaches to produce better results
- gradually desensitising a child or young person to a threat or phobia.

Behavioural approaches have appeal for staff undertaking intervention because they offer a systematic, scientific approach from which to structure their practice. The approaches go some way towards encouraging participatory practice, discouraging labelling, and maintain the client's story as central. The idea of learned helplessness has the potential to bridge the gap between psychological and sociological explanations of behaviour, maintaining the focus on both social and individual factors.

DISADVANTAGES

Usually it is only the immediate environment of the child that is examined. It is not as value-free as it claims. The scientific nature of behavioural assessment rests on modernist assumptions about certainty. There is often in practice a tendency to rush a solution after a limited assessment where the theory is skewed so that the individual client changes to accommodate their circumstances rather than the other way round. The potential to use the theory to employ anti-oppressive practice is limited because much of the theory is based on white, male, western norms of behaviour.

Task-centred practice

Task-centred work is often cited as the most popular base for contemporary assessment and intervention practice, but it may be that it is used as a set of activities rather than as a theoretically based approach from which a set of activities flows. Key features include:

- It is based on client agreement or service user acceptance of a legal justification for action.

- It aims to move from problem to goal, from what is wrong to what is needed.

- It is based around tasks which are central to the process of change and which aim to build on individual service user strengths as far as possible.

- The approach is time-limited, preserving client self-esteem and independence as far as possible.

- It is a highly structured model of practice using a building block approach so that each task can be agreed and success (or not) measured by moving from problem to goal.

Task-centred practice can serve as a basic approach for the majority of children and young people. In this approach the problem is always the problem as defined by the client. It therefore respects their values, beliefs and perceptions. This approach encourages children and young people to select the problem they want to work on and engages them in task selection and review. It lends itself to a collaborative and empowering approach by enabling you to carry out your share of tasks and review them alongside the client. Time limits and task reviews aid motivation and promote optimism.

DISADVANTAGES

Although this approach has the capacity for empowerment, it can sometimes prohibit active measures by practitioners to ensure it does empower. Although ostensibly value-free and intrinsically non-oppressive, you should continually reflect on your practice to make this explicit. The coaching role could be open to abuse, or permit you to become overly directive. The emphasis on simple, measurable tasks may focus attention on concrete solutions that obscure the potential advocacy role of practice. The approach requires a degree of cognitive ability and motivation in the child or young person that in some cases will be lacking.

Narrative therapeutic practice

Narrative therapeutic ideas have developed in recent years among social workers captivated by the notion of storytelling as a means to engage children and young people. Perhaps this development is a reaction against the increasingly technocratic age we live in and where children are surrounded and constantly stimulated by largely visual and auditory media or communication. Storytelling is advocated by educationalists attempting to reach children in schools, theatres and libraries as a way of preserving some interest in the written word. Ethnic minority communities endeavour to use storytelling in large industrialised countries as a means of recovering their cultural history and maintaining rituals obscured by the homogenised consumer-oriented culture offered by profiteering corporations.

Narrative therapeutic ideas recognise the ability children and young people have to ascribe meaning to events that serve to explain but also to influence choices about the possible courses of action. This capacity to generate and evolve new narratives and stories to make sense of experiences involves the use of culturally shared myths, legends and fairy stories. Thus therapy is seen as not just offering new perceptions and insights but lies in the very nature of the conversation taking place. Narrative therapists such as White and Epston (1990) suggest that problems are derived and maintained from the *internalisation* of oppressive ways of perceiving the self. These notions can be reinforced by parents who constantly criticise a child or who only respond negatively to behaviours. Key characteristics include:

- The technique of *externalising* the problem whereby the social worker encourages the child to objectify or personify the problem outside of themselves.

- The child can separate themselves from the problem instead of being seen and related to by others as *the problem.*

- Engages the child or young person in a process of exploring and resisting the problem as an unwanted impediment rather than as an integral part of their psychic constitution.

- Enables a troubled young person to begin the process of challenging self-defeating and overwhelming self-concepts.

Children and young people who are suffering from psychological distress requiring therapeutic help may be either too young or too old to engage in cognitive and verbal communication about their feelings and experiences. Younger ones may be more at ease with activities and play materials to aid expression while older teenagers will often be difficult to engage and open up having learned the basic defence of silence. But they will all know something of fairy tales, myths and legends. Every culture has them and they are usually told during early childhood in a verbal parental or carer ritual as old as time. Earliest school literature incorporates these stories in education curriculum precisely because they are familiar and accessible.

As part of the healing process literature is an often underrated asset. Yet it carries information about families, emotions, morality, relationships and so much else in a way that can enable very damaged children to use devices such as fairy stories to help understand themselves at a deeper level. Fairy stories have the capacity to capture the child's imagination because they usually involve fantastical creatures, transformational experiences or complex predicaments in which the child can immerse themselves and relate to their inner world.

DISADVANTAGES

A child's repressed feelings and worst fears cause inner conflicts that can manifest in acting out behaviour or anxiety states leading to mental health problems. These defences may be a necessary phase through which the child needs to pass before being able to change. Impatience on your part may be unhelpful. Fairy stories operate at the *overt* level where concepts of right and wrong and other moral dilemmas may seem obvious to you. But the story also operates at a *covert* level carrying important messages to the conscious, preconscious and unconscious mind that will affect the child's sense of culture.

Risk assessment and risk management

Assessment of risk and its management has become a dominant theme in social work in the past decade. It is a crucial skill, especially in work with particularly vulnerable young people. As with other aspects of the profession – such as the move to competence-based training and the increased emphasis on evidence-based practice – the concern with risk assessment has been a reaction to a wider demand for the greater public accountability of professionals in all spheres. In social work several highly publicised failures to protect clients and the public from dangerous people have ensured that the spotlight of concern has been kept on practice skills and standards. Despite the fact that the highly publicised failures – mainly in childcare and mental health work – represent a minority of social work cases, their impact on practice has been considerable. This has led to policy and practice in relation to risk and its management becoming focused on dangerousness, particularly so in work with offenders and mental health and significant harm in relation to children and elders. This puts undue pressure on work that is already highly sensitive in many cases and paradoxically may provoke the very behaviour that it seeks to prevent.

Activity 4.4

○   Think about a recent piece of work in which you were considering the risks in the situation.

○   On reflection, do you now feel you underestimated or overestimated the risks, or got them about right?

○   What do you now think were the factors leading you to that perception?

Partnership practice

Partnership practice, whilst apparently being at odds with some of the control requirements of social work, is in fact one of the methods through which a balance between the care and control aspects of the job can be sought – if not always attained. Activity 4.5 is intended to clarify this.

Activity 4.5

o   Write a paragraph describing how you think working in partnership with service users can help to integrate the requirements of both care and control.

o   In doing this you might find it helpful to re-read briefly the section above on the social construction of risk.

Commentary

In the section on social construction we discussed the social and cultural factors involved in the definition and perception of dangerousness. Working in partnership involves a genuine commitment to the attempt to understand the world from the client's perspective and communicating this effectively without necessarily condoning any particular behavioural expression of their perception of the world. Partnership however also involves mutuality – there is an expectation that the client will be willing to make a similar attempt to understand the perceptions and behaviours of others. Obviously the worker has the professional responsibility to enable clients to work on problems in this way when initially the nature of their problems may inhibit the flexibility which this entails. This will involve entering the social and cultural context of the client, rather than attempting to promote change by imposing an alien cultural context.

For example, in the case of verbal behaviour which is causing problems for the 'rap' fan due to the perception of it as abusive, the worker may begin by encouraging the teenager to share their tastes in music. Whilst not directly confronting the issue, this approach may eventually enable the teenager to understand the origins of the problem and work on it in ways which are rooted in their social and cultural context, rather than demanding they conform immediately to cultural standards which are alien to them.

In such ways partnership practice can work with the social and cultural relativity which, as we have seen, is a characteristic of assessment practice. What may be seen as the problem of ambiguity and uncertainty which in some circumstances leads to draconian attempts to control, can in this way be turned into a positive strength in the attempt to care and enable. The above example demonstrates the integration of knowledge, skills and values which we discuss further later on. In this case, knowledge of cultural diversity, the skills of interpretation and negotiation in building partnership, and the values of individualisation and respect for uniqueness and diversity are the foundation of such partnership practice. It is important to acknowledge that the commitment to partnership should not be misinterpreted as an invitation to relinquish boundaries in professional relationships. Loss of boundaries can place social workers at risk.

Risk to social workers

An interesting aspect of the moral panic about risk and dangerousness is that the risk to social workers from dangerous people and the adverse attention of politicians and the media has not been of such concern. The risk of abuse and physical threat or attack for social workers is considerable and social workers – particularly in residential settings – are among those who share the highest risk of assault at work. The recognition of this risk should be an important consideration for all social workers, their managers and the organisations within which they work.

As we shall see later, too narrow a focus on assessing risk to others can lead to a neglect of risk to self. Neglecting the wider context in which clients exist – psychologically and socially – can result not only in inadequate assessment of their needs but also of the dangers to workers which may be inherent in this context. Service users may experience the bureaucratic requirements that form part of assessment processes as a further burden or imposition from a system perceived as hostile and inaccessible. Already frustrated by the problems of their immediate context, the service user may find a ready scapegoat in the worker who can come to represent and embody the problem. Unacceptably, though unsurprisingly, this can result in misplaced aggression directed at the worker. Two factors that can contribute to this potential for misplaced aggression are neglect of the client's context and failure to maintain boundaries.

Neglect of the client's context

In attempting to fulfil the requirement to protect allegedly vulnerable others, the worker may unwittingly reinforce the client's perception that they are being labelled remorselessly as the problem. Systems theory points to the way in which family and social systems manage problems by identifying problems as caused by individuals which are in fact a result of dysfunctional systems, not any particular individual within them. In focusing too narrowly on assessment of the alleged problem person this theoretical insight and the practice which should lead from it are forgotten.

The result of this is that the scapegoating which may have been contributing to the client being identified as the problem in the first place is reflected for the client in the assessment process. The client may then respond – as they perhaps have in their social context – with aggression. Thus, by neglecting the client's systemic context, the worker becomes part of the dysfunctional system and any therapeutic potential of the professional encounter is reduced dramatically – sometimes to the extent of verbal or physical violence occurring.

Failure to maintain boundaries

Unfortunately partnership practice can easily be misinterpreted as standing in the client's shoes. The attempt to empathise with the client is often described in these terms but empathy, or understanding, is not standing in their shoes. This, in any case, is impossible and can also be misperceived by clients as the creation of a mutual acceptance of their position and their response to it. This can be a flawed position in the sense that inevitably such misperception – if shared by worker and client – will result in the worker eventually belatedly having to affirm the difference of their position. This, in turn, can lead to feelings of rejection and betrayal in the client and the resultant danger of aggressive reactions.

We will now move on to explore the difference between danger and risk and the importance of regaining an understanding of the social work process in assessment. As we shall discover, it is simply not possible to provide unambiguous checklists to identify dangerous people, or rules to eliminate risk to self or others reliably. What is possible to acquire is the knowledge, skills and values of the social work profession and integrate them in a social work process in order to minimise danger and manage risk as effectively as possible.

One of the consequences of pressures to reduce risk and eliminate danger from social work has been an obsession with the production of checklists such as eligibility criteria, assessment schedules and risk assessment scales. As recent Department of Health reports have acknowledged this has been at the expense of attention to the process aspects of social work intervention. The tendency has been for practice to become narrowly focused on aspects of the individual such as dependency or dangerousness, rather than on the whole person-in-context. This is counter to – and in extreme cases can threaten – the established values and effective practice of social work which emphasise individualisation, respect for the person and a holistic approach which takes full account of the social and cultural context.

Activity 4.6

○ Make some brief notes describing several disadvantages of viewing risk solely as danger and intervention as about risk control.

Commentary

Ironically the danger of such practice is that in pursuing the ultimately unattainable goal of entirely risk-free practice, workers may overlook the risks attached to intervention. Removing a child allegedly in danger from its family opens the child up to other dangers which can be equally damaging. The rights of young people could be neglected in order to control the risks they pose to themselves or others. It is possible to lose sight of the individual-in-context, their strengths and the creative potential for development and growth this brings. Social work values include recognising the uniqueness, diversity and strengths of individuals. Focusing too narrowly on one aspect of the individual (e.g. dangerousness) may limit opportunities for interventions that can enable children and young people to build on their strengths to become less dangerous. You may also overlook the risks to yourself. An over-eagerness to control risks posed to others can expose workers to unacceptable levels of risk to themselves. This can result not only in serious harm to the worker, but add to the guilt and other problems experienced by the client involved in violence against the worker.

Defining risk

You can do this by thinking about two approaches to risk in social work. As social work develops its understanding and practice in relation to risk, two contrasting approaches have emerged: the safety first approach which can be paraphrased as CYB (cover your back) and the risk-taking approach which subscribes to the view that risks are an inherent part of social life. If individuals are to be fully engaged in social life some risk is inevitable. Both terms are problematic:

• Competent social work should not be entirely 'defensive' and preoccupied with covering your back.

• Risk taking has connotations of an advocacy of taking risks which is counter-intuitive to many and easily misconstrued as irresponsible in view of the vulnerability of many service users.

Characteristics of the risk control perspective

• *Definition:* risk is negative – danger, threat.

- *Priority principles:* professional responsibility and accountability.
- *Practice priorities:* identification (assessment scales) and elimination (procedural, legalistic).

Characteristics of the risk management perspective

- *Definition:* positive – risk is part of life, balancing risks and benefits is part of individual's development, being self-determining and personally responsible.
- *Priority principles:* self determination, anti-oppression.
- *Practice priorities:* solution-focused, partnership practice, empowerment.

The benefits of the risk management perspective are that they are in keeping with the values and practice of modern social work. It emphasises the process of maximising benefits as well as minimising risks, rather than the procedure of identifying and eliminating risk, and builds on strengths. The drawbacks are that it relies heavily on highly developed professional competence and judgement and requires the commitment of the client to partnership. It also requires intellectual/cognitive competence in the client. It involves ambiguity and uncertainty, is poorly understood by the public and requires supportive management practice and organisational policy. Risks to social workers are virtually ignored. As understanding and practice in relation to risk develops it becomes clear that there needs to be an integration of the best of both approaches. Eliminating or totally controlling risk in social work is impossible. It is undesirable to think of risk and the social work task in relation to it in this way because:

- evidence and intuition suggests it is impossible and thus resources are wasted
- risk is part of social life
- practice which is effective in terms of promoting individual responsibility and social competence can not be reductionist – it must recognise the person-in-context and build on strengths
- social work agencies have responsibilities in law in relation to certain client groups. Individual social workers must neither neglect these responsibilities nor accept unlimited liability – whether or not there are legal requirements
- the social and individual costs of control can outweigh the social and individual benefits

- social work routinely brings its practitioners into contact with dangerous people and entails professional judgements which are potentially castigated by management, organisations and the media.

Activity 4.7

○ What do you feel are the shortcomings in your practice guidance and legislative context for the effective management of risk in your agency service?

○ Review the material above and list three priority factors you consider could improve your current risk assessment and risk management practice.

Commentary

A generic framework for risk assessment practice which can take into account the two perspectives on risk and the tensions between the various practice requirements has been influential since first described by Brearley (1982). His framework is based on the clear definition of danger, risk, predisposing and situational hazards, and strengths.

Listing the hazards and strengths provides a way of quantifying the balance between them. You then need to identify what other information can be obtained to help analyse the whole situation, before reaching a conclusion and making a judgement about the decisions to be made. Decision-making needs to be more explicit. Plans should flow logically from the assessment. There is a need for a guiding framework. If decisions are not clearly linked to the findings of assessment, accountability for actions is difficult to support. In the event of unsuccessful outcomes there is no way of analysing which aspect of the situation could account for this and how future interventions could be amended in the light of it. Following local custom and practice rather than agency procedures leads to inconsistency in practice, is therefore open to complaint from service users on the grounds of inequity of treatment, and is in any case insupportable in terms of professional accountability.

Failing to convey decisions affecting families' welfare undermines the potential for partnership practice currently and/or in the future. It also (as with the above) means that there is not a clear audit trail linking referral, assessment, intervention and outcome. Managers failing to indicate their endorsement of the social worker's action means there is no record of the agreed intervention which is mutually binding and this may lead to disagreement later about what was in fact agreed. This can be potentially hazardous to the social worker in situations where harm occurs to clients or others. Having explored this particular aspect of risk work we will conclude our discussion of risk work in relation to childcare with a summary of some general implications for practice drawn from the discussion so far.

Competent practice in risk work should:

- adopt a systemic, holistic perspective on need (as well as identifying risk)

- appropriately employ well-validated criteria of risk within a coherent framework of assessment and consequent, clearly related, intervention

- explicitly involve parents and children, recording their perceptions and opinions

- avoid gender bias in assessment, recommendation and intervention (attention often focuses unreasonably on mothers in abusive situations)

- utilise multi-disciplinary processes of assessment and decision-making

- be explicitly shared in supervision, recorded and endorsed at every stage by managers.

The impact of adversity on an individual's development depends on when it happens and how long it lasts. Young people's life chances and experiences are also closely linked with the overall socio-historical context. An important study found increasing polarisation in education, work, health, family formation and civic participation (Schoon et al. 2002). The pathways to successful adult adaptation are influenced by young people's early experiences and are shaped by the resources and support available to each individual throughout childhood and adolescence. Educational qualifications play a particularly important role in predicting adult outcomes.

Yet it is important to recognise that young people's achievements are not preordained, and it is the whole life course that influences individual development, not just the early years. Therefore it is never too early or too late to increase access to the material, emotional or cultural resources that can enable an individual to realise her or his potential fully.

Key chapter points

- The Social Care Institute for Excellence 2005 knowledge review of the teaching and learning of assessment skills in social work education discovered that there was no single theory or understanding as to the purpose of assessment. The review acknowledged that assessment is practised differently according to the practice context and/or the function of the task.

- Social workers need to recognise that children's views can be obscured or implicitly silenced by a combination of vulnerability due to their ascribed role as 'the problem', a fear of professionals with the power to punish, or a therapeutic stance that tries to equalise all members of the family.

- Whatever method or model of intervention is used, any potential for change can be liberating or constraining, it can generate enlightenment or promote feelings of anger, loss and bereavement. Maintaining a degree of professional optimism with realism and managing uncertainty with a modest and respectful approach offers skilful social workers the potential for being a useful resource to children and adolescents.

- The evidence base for individual work with children and young people is relatively sparse. Many of the changes that take place may just not be outwardly measurable in terms of behaviour or symptomatology. There are pragmatic difficulties in making individual subjective measures of internal change that are not readily comparable especially when considering the cultural diversity between and within ethnic minority communities.

- Assessment of risk and its management has become a dominant theme in social work in the past decade. It is a crucial skill especially in work with particularly vulnerable young people. As with other aspects of the profession – such as the move to competence-based training and the increased emphasis on evidence-based practice – the concern with risk assessment has been a reaction to a wider demand for the greater public accountability of professionals in all spheres.

Chapter 5

Multi-disciplinary and Interprofessional Working

Learning objectives

» Reflection on the core skills required for working collaboratively across organisations including during interprofessional CAMH meetings.

» Describe the obstacles to and ways to achieve effective multi-disciplinary work.

» Review effective strategies for inclusive, integrated practice.

» Work in partnership with other agencies to identify and analyse potential problems and appropriate responses to the mental health needs of children and young people.

Introduction

The fragmentation of service provision for children and young people and adults means that where a child may be at risk of harm from a parent/carer with a mental health problem, their needs may be eclipsed by the focus on containing and supporting the adult. This chapter will examine the barriers to working together and the ways of reducing or removing those barriers in children's services to offer resources to social workers concerned to achieve greater collaboration and co-operation. Networking and working successfully in a group are core skills for all staff and fundamental learning requirements for social workers, who strive to safeguard the well-being of children, young people and their families.

Collaborative or partnership working are terms used frequently in the practice guidance and professional literature without a great deal of reflection about what the terms mean or how to realise them in practice. The Oxford Concise English Dictionary (11th edition, 2004) defines a professional as 'a person having impressive competence in a particular ability'; this could relate to all individuals involved in the child's care from all specialities whether statutory, voluntary or independent. It could also be argued that it relates to parents and informal carers who may have extensive experience and knowledge about an individual child and their situation. Indeed it could be argued that children and young people are themselves the experts.

The dictionary continues by defining multi-disciplinary (inter-agency or interprofessional is not defined) as 'involving several academic disciplines or professional specialisations', and continues that collaboration is 'working jointly on an activity or a project'; however, co-operation appears to be the most relevant word to use, defined as 'work together towards the same end' along with 'help someone or comply with their requests'.

Traditionally, health services have tended to focus their attention on a particular problem. For example psychiatric services focus on mental health, drug and alcohol services on drug and alcohol abuse, and paediatric services on physical health. CAMHS guidelines often concentrate on the management of a single mental disorder instead of taking a holistic and co-ordinated approach to care and treatment of the whole person. Too often young people complain that specialist CAMH services focus on their symptoms or diagnostic label and ignore their social needs.

This narrow approach, however, does not reflect the complexity of health problems experienced by children and adolescents, as young people with mental health problems in one area often experience difficulties in other areas of their lives. Physical problems may be a consequence of mental health problems while emotional well-being can be adversely affected by a physical illness. Individual professions and services must pay more attention to the high levels of multiple problems in young people, and they need to develop strong collaborative relationships with each other if they are to provide adolescents with effective help for their problems. For example a young person with depression may very well also have drug and alcohol problems and ADHD. This is where social workers can make a big contribution to a troubled young person's emotional well-being by taking a whole-person holistic view of their experiences and circumstances.

In Australia, where similar challenges are faced, financial incentives are used to encourage mental health services to broaden their treatment programmes and improve co-ordination with other services (Sawyer et al. 2000). Better research is needed to provide more understanding of the mechanisms that give rise to the broadly based problems experienced by adolescents so that young people do not get referred to different specialists. A social worker can be a valuable asset to a young person trying to navigate around a confusing, disjointed health system by taking on the role of advocate and keyworker.

Activity 5.1

o Make a list of all the individuals you work with. Remember to note not just the practitioners you work with on a daily or weekly basis, but those professionals who you may contact infrequently.

o Within your practice area reflect upon the barriers that you can see in working effectively with all your colleagues both within your agency and across agencies.

Commentary

Some barriers can be geographical, related to distance between childcare practitioners. This is especially a problem in rural areas where distances may be considerable. Other barriers could relate to traditional thinking and the inability to see beyond the aims and objectives of the organisation. It is more important to focus on the child or young person rather than the needs of the organisation; however, sometimes the systems put in place make it difficult for individual practitioners to move away from this. All professions have unique philosophies which are derived from their educational experiences, working practices and surrounding environment. This can lead to clashes across agencies when differing priorities arise.

Health, social care and education may not have a common understanding of emotional well-being, significant harm or care management. This means careful negotiation is required to ensure a balance of power is maintained to support the child and their family. An example of this may be the way that issues of confidentiality are dealt with both within a particular agency and also across agencies. While it is clear to all childcare practitioners that confidentiality cannot be guaranteed, endeavouring to gain consent to share information with appropriate parties is tricky.

The organisational context

The traditional model of service delivery in community CAMHS in Britain began formally over 50 years ago, when the first child guidance clinic opened in East London in 1948 after earlier efforts to help children with emotional and behavioural difficulties. One of the difficulties highlighted in a seminal piece of research was the gap which had been steadily growing for decades between the primary care sector and the specialist child guidance service (Kurtz *et al.* 1994).

A four-tier structure was designed in 1995 to streamline the referral process for children who could be helped with minor emotional and behavioural problems at Tier 1 by GPs, teachers, social workers and health visitors (see Chapter 7 for more detail). This progressed through the tiers to Tier 4 where very disturbed young people who were at risk of harming themselves or others could be supported by highly specialist staff in forensic work or eating disorders for example (HAS 1995).

The aim of primary care professionals in schools, community nursing, health visiting and social work was to intervene with children and families at Tier 1 who were causing concern but where problems had not become entrenched or severe. Any assessed requirement for specialist help could be referred through to the specialist Tier 3 or Tier 4 child and family consultation service or units dealing with severe and life-threatening problems. Delays in receiving help put pressure on primary care staff who were responsible for maintaining contact and support to the referred child and family, whilst simultaneously trying to manage ever-expanding caseloads of other children who were beginning to cause concern.

Figure 5.1 illustrates how you could plot the level of co-operation, collaboration and co-ordination in your particular work context using a sliding scale to see where the depth of co-operation is shallow or deep, the degree of collaboration, and how this affects co-ordination between agencies.

In theory the existing CAMHS should already have facilitated interprofessional working, but in practice every part of the four-tier structure from primary care through to regional specialist units was overstretched. In planning the nature of new interprofessional teams, service managers need to consider what kind of team would be desirable in order to meet the government policy objective and be effective in relieving the suffering of children adolescents and their families.

When new teams integrate too quickly, in order to maximise their effectiveness under the scrutiny of evaluation, they can neglect to attend to uncomfortable and potentially conflictual issues which can be quite normal in interprofessional team formation (DeBell and Walker 2002). One way of achieving integration is the development of a core training programme for all staff. This could cover a range of relevant subjects designed to promote emotional well-being in young people, including:

- CAMH
- attachment theory
- emotional impact of divorce and separation
- child protection
- domestic violence

- bereavement and loss
- parenting programme
- anti-discriminatory practice
- Human Rights Act.

Apart from increasing the knowledge and skills base of individual practitioners who came with different levels of prior training and staff development, the delivery mode of the training itself should not be profession-specific, unlike much conventional training. It should be delivered not just to whole teams but to the whole CAMHS service. The added benefit would be closer integration within teams and across the whole CAMHS service.

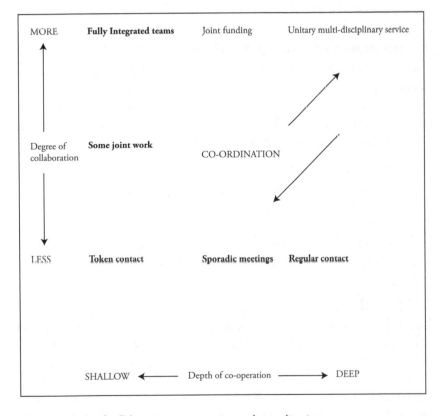

Figure 5.1 Scale of collaboration, co-operation and co-ordination

Management

Team management is a controversial subject where the challenge in interprofessional teams is to establish a structure which allows appropriate autonomy for practitioners from different professions but permits the team co-ordinator to control the use of their time to where need was most pressing (Onyet, Heppleston and Bushnell 1994). Establishing clear lines of accountability is crucial where staff are still employed by separate agencies. The accessibility of a named person within the CAMHS structure provides a focus and a voice at strategic forums. This enables a new service to have a clear identity, streamlined communications and a distinctive profile within a multi-dimensional organisation. The multi-agency nature of the service requires highly tuned negotiating skills to enable effective liaison with each of the partner agencies.

Development of a new practitioner

One of the issues to emerge from developing new interprofessional CAMHS services is whether at some stage the separate individual professions within each team will begin to lose their former identity and metamorphose into a new kind of practitioner taking on characteristics of their colleagues from different professional backgrounds.

Activity 5.2

- ○ Imagine you are applying for a new job in a new interprofessional team tasked with supporting children's mental health and emotional well-being.

- ○ List your fears and anxieties about how you feel you might get on with staff from a different professional background.

Commentary

There are contemporary examples of such hybrid posts being created in the primary mental health care field, where employers typically advertise for people from any relevant professional background, with appropriate training and experience. There is as yet no definitive primary mental health care qualification or professional training but in 2005 a set of competencies was articulated (Gale *et al.* 2005) which provided an excellent framework (see Chapter 1 for details); this is an obvious development in the medium term. The concept of the joint practitioner with qualification in, for example, nursing and social work, is not new (Davis *et al.* 1999).

In CAMH the education, health and social work structural hierarchies have militated against collaboration, preserved separate role identities and inhibited interprofessional working (Dimigen *et al.* 1999; Fagin 1992; Rawson 1994). This has thwarted repeated attempts to achieve the much-vaunted seamless service for children and families in difficulties as recommended as far back as the Children Act (DoH 1989). The new joint commissioning environment in health and social care enshrined in the Health Act enables new services to be created specifically, and this has generally enabled creative, innovative thinking to flourish within and between agencies (DoH 1999c; Kurtz 2001).

There is evidence of attempts to foster interprofessional training among primary care staff who come into contact with children and adolescents with mental health problems (Firth *et al.* 1999; Mun *et al.* 2001; Sebuliba and Vostanis 2001). Staff such as health visitors, school nurses, social services support staff, family centre volunteers, general practitioners, education staff and community paediatricians usually have separate training on mental health issues without much co-ordination. These staff have a critical role in helping children and families, by early identification of problems and appropriate intervention (Bayley 1998).

Interprofessional training can reflect the aspiration that people who work together should also train together to enable a consistency of approach to the identified difficulty (DfEE 1998). Internationally, there have been studies designed to identify the interprofessional training needs of staff to enable them to function in integrated service delivery systems for children and young people (Magrab *et al.* 1997). The conclusions are that policy frameworks focused on children's service planning missed the opportunity to recognise interprofessional training as a priority and to provide incentives to universities and other training institutions to develop interprofessional training programmes (DoH/DfEE 1996).

Staff who train and work together from different agencies are likely to feel less inhibited about offering much welcome consultation, advice, training and support to other staff. This can help bridge some of the gaps left by policy limitations and resource shortages unable to deliver the desired interprofessional environment.

Networking or tangling?

Establishing new teams in an existing professional network of statutory and voluntary providers within established agencies and a dynamic context of changing resources and multiple initiatives is not easy. There are opportunities for collaboration between these providers and new teams but there are also challenges in fitting in without duplicating or undermining existing good work. Changes in the network in areas such as school health provision, the Quality Protects/Every Child Matters programme in social services, together with Health Action Zones, Youth Offending Teams, Sure Start, On Track, Education Action Zones, Connexions, Children's Trusts and fluctuations in the voluntary sector, emphasise the importance of collaborative meetings to enhance opportunities for maintaining and improving working together principles and integrated provision rather than causing confusion.

There is some potential for confusion about specific services, however, because of the variety of voluntary and statutory agencies working in the broad area of family support especially in disadvantaged locations (Hetherington and Baistow 2001). Church, voluntary and charitable groups have existed in these locations for many years and created their own distinctive role within the diverse range of formal and informal provision of welfare services. There is in these circumstances the prospect of duplication of effort, or at worst, mixed messages to families from different agencies. The interprofessional nature of new teams carries the potential for enabling a better understanding of how the overall picture of support services fits together and a sharing of ideas about how to tackle mental health problems in young people. As we shall see later, no one professional or voluntary service provider can claim omnipotent certainty in this very complex practice area.

In order for the policy imperative to work there needs to be a vertical information cascade within the CAMHS tiered structure and outside in the broader children and families services framework as well as horizontal lines of communication. This is essential for more fluid communication between agencies to ensure as far as possible that the right service is supporting the right families at the right time (Remschmidt 2001; Richardson and Joughin 2000; Walker 2001b). Within the government's focused CAMH strategy, teams are liaising with specialist services providers in efforts to achieve the following:

- streamline the referral processes between each service
- exchange referrals and share in consultation
- avoid families or referrers feeling passed around the system.

The interprofessional nature of new staff groups, with their emphasis on offering short-term intensive input, advice, information, parental guidance and direct work with children, are indicative of a non-stigmatising acceptable service, to enable young people to feel comfortable about accessing help (Read and Barker 1996). These services can also contribute to principles aimed at working together in line with government policy on collaboration between agencies by delivering care and support in children's own homes or in preferred contexts such as schools.

The issue of roles and boundaries between different professionals has long been debated in the literature on health and social care (Munley, Powers and Williamson 1982; NISW/DoH 1982). The contemporary emphasis on joined up working and interprofessional care has promoted joint training and qualification in working with people with learning disabilities and people with mental health problems. Recent initiatives to expand the role of nurses and social workers contribute to a blurring of roles often approved by clients (Pearce 1999; Snelgrove and Hughes 2000; Williams *et al.* 1999). The stigma of CAMH problems deters many young people from gaining access to the right help at the right time. Combined with the profound feelings of guilt experienced by parents, which prevents them seeking support, this means there is enormous unmet need in the community (Repper *et al.* 1997; Walker 2002).

The initiative to encourage innovative service delivery in CAMHS offers the opportunity to team members of the positive benefits of skill mix and sharing knowledge leading to a blurring of former professional identities to the benefit of service users. There is other evidence that paradoxically, the encouragement of interprofessional working actually reinforces boundaries within the network between professions (Brown, Crawford and Darongkamas 2000).

It is possible that as new teams continue to train together and develop generic working there may be some resistance to relinquishing former roles, and even strengthening of the boundaries between professions. The challenge for service managers will be to preserve the distinctive individual professional expertise base but not at the expense of service coherence. When attempting to engage children and families already suffering under the pressure of racism and discrimination it is important that children, families and carers have the maximum choice when engaging with services aiming to meet their needs (Bhui and Olajide 1999). In addition new teams would benefit from formal service user involvement, especially children and young people separately from parents or carers, at the clinical audit, monitoring, review and strategic planning levels of the service (Alderson 2000; Barnes and Warren 1999; Treseder 1997). Conventional uni-professional services have tended to miss this opportunity for empowering service users.

Dissolving the boundaries between professionals carries with it the opportunity for narrowing the gap between service user and practitioner. Much of the contemporary literature on CAMHS development debates the ethical, professional and practical issues raised in considering how genuinely to engage service users as partners in the process (Christiansen and James 2000; Kent and Read 1998; Nixon and Northrup 1997; Walker 2001c).

There is as yet no substantial evidence base for effectiveness in support services for children and adolescents with mental health problems. One of the few contemporary attempts to collate the available methodologically robust research emphasises the importance of specifying what intervention works for which families with what problems (Carr 2000). Much of the available data is corralled into separate professional boundaries. It is significant therefore that in any new interprofessional CAMHS provision new methodologies for research reflect the new service configuration by moulding together qualitative and clinical quantitative data.

Useful evaluation tools

Two popular instruments are currently available to help social workers, parents/carers and young people to evaluate the services they receive for help with emotional well-being and mental health problems. These instruments are designed to facilitate the collection of young people's perspectives. Their use is important in the audit, research and outcome evaluation process to help improve the individual and collective service user experience as well as to contribute towards interprofessional service planning and development.

Health of the Nation Outcome Scales for Children and Adolescents (HoNOSCA)

This was developed as a measure of clinical outcome for use within CAMHS. The Health of the Nation Strategy (DoH 1992) was to improve significantly the health and social functioning of mentally ill people. Subsequently the Royal College of Psychiatrists Research Unit developed the Health of the Nation Outcome Scales (HoNOS), a brief pen and paper instrument that was designed to assess the health and social functioning of people with mental health disorders. HoNOS could thus be used in conjunction with other information-gathering processes to measure treatment outcome effectiveness.

Specifically HoNOSCA provides a global assessment of the behaviour, impairments, symptoms and social functioning of children and adolescents with mental health problems. The tool takes the form of a numerical record of routine clinical assessment, a set of 13 scales plus a further two optional scales, completed by the keyworker/CPA team or equivalent. Each scale measures a type of problem commonly presented by children in mental health services. A completed HoNOSCA score sheet is a measure of present state and provides a profile of 13 severity ratings which can be added together to make a total score. HoNOSCA does not replace case notes or standardised measures. It is intended that it is used as an integral part of a minimum data set (Gowers *et al.* 2000). The key characteristics of this evaluation tool are:

- short, simple, acceptable and useful
- adequate coverage of clinical and social problems
- sensitive to improvement, deterioration or lack of change in child over time
- known reliability and relationship to other established instruments
- simple indicators for comparative local and national use.

A wide range of health and social domains are considered in these scales – psychiatric symptoms, physical health, functioning, and social relationships are included in the tool (see Table 5.1).

TABLE 5.1 HEALTH OF THE NATION (HoNOSCA) SCALES

Scale item	Section
Disruptive/aggressive behaviour	Behaviour
Overactivity and attentional difficulty	
Non-accidental self-injury	
Alcohol, substance/solvent misuse	
Scholastic or language skills	Impairment
Physical illness/disability problems	
Hallucinations and delusions	
Non-organic and somatic symptoms	
Emotional and related symptoms	
Peer relationships	Social
Self-care and relationships	
Family life and relationships	
Poor school attendance	
Lack of knowledge – nature of difficulties	Information
Lack of information – services/management	
Each scale item scored in range 0–4	

Source: Gowers *et al.* 2000

Severity is measured in the following 5 point scale where: 0 = no problem, 1 = minor problem requiring no action, 2 = mild problem but definitely present, 3 = moderately severe problem, 4 = severe to very severe problem

It is important to recognise the limitations of this evaluation tool. For example it does not predict risk; it is a measure of the preceding work period. It does not produce a medical diagnostic label and although it is not designed for use in primary care it could be employed particularly in the context of a review or case ending process with a young person. On their own HoNOSCA ratings say little about whether an outcome is related to the care provided. Outcomes assessment should also include the intervention used, and the context of the situation, for instance, the diagnosis, or other events which might have a bearing on change. (See HoNOSCA 2010 for further details.)

Quantitative measures that examine changes in symptoms that caused the initial concern are commonly used to evaluate outcome in CAMH services. Inpatient and day patient units are the intervention prescribed for some of the most disturbed young people, those whose development is being hampered significantly by family circumstances, or who have life-threatening problems. There are very few reliable studies that have examined the outcome of these interventions because they are all different in size and type of client population. Social workers will probably be more interested in combining these with qualitative measures that address questions to do with:

- how a child or young person is functioning in their social environment
- gaining their accounts of what they define as success
- whether they can get on better with mates
- whether they feel more able to cope with stress.

The Experience of Service Questionnaire (ESQ) was introduced by the Commission for Health Improvement (CHI) in 2002 as a way of ascertaining the views of children and young people in contact with CAMHS. The main format is reproduced in Figure 5.2 to give you an idea of its design and purpose. (For more detail about the use of the ESQ and the functions of the Healthcare Commission, which has since taken over the work of the CHI, please see CHI 2010.) For each item in the questionnaire young people and/or parents tick the circle that best describes what they think or feel.

At a broader level innovative services exemplify the practical results of efforts to encourage interprofessional working aimed to improve the quality, delivery and co-ordination of all services for children and young people (DoH 1998; Rodney 2000; Tucker et al. 1999). In the history of CAMHS, there has always been a recognition that interprofessional effort needs to be brought to bear on the difficulties of troubled children. That model has now been updated with new initiatives functioning to fulfil an interprofessional role within a service struggling to cope with increased demand.

	Certainly true	Partly true	Not true	Don't know
I feel that the people who saw me listened to me	☐	☐	☐	☐
It was easy to talk to the people who saw me	☐	☐	☐	☐
I was treated well by the people who saw me	☐	☐	☐	☐
My views and worries were taken seriously	☐	☐	☐	☐
I feel the people here know how to help me	☐	☐	☐	☐
I have been given enough explanation about the help available here	☐	☐	☐	☐
I feel that the people who have seen me are working together to help me	☐	☐	☐	☐
The facilities here are comfortable (e.g. waiting area)	☐	☐	☐	☐
My appointments are usually at a convenient time (e.g. don't interfere with school, clubs, college, work)	☐	☐	☐	☐
It is quite easy to get to the place where I have my appointments	☐	☐	☐	☐
If a friend needed this sort of help, I would suggest to them to come here	☐	☐	☐	☐
Overall, the help I have received here is good	☐	☐	☐	☐
What was really good about your care?	☐	☐	☐	☐
Was there anything you didn't like or anything that needs improving?	☐	☐	☐	☐
Is there anything else you want to tell us about the service you received?	☐	☐	☐	☐

Figure 5.2 Experience of Service Questionnaire (ESQ)

This model could be the genesis for a new primary mental health care professional, within a preventive configuration, with implications for training, qualifications, accreditation and employment which demonstrably reflect an interprofessional perspective. The concept of early intervention is critical in CAMH because there are few opportunities to make an impact in the developmental windows that present in young people before problems become entrenched. Failure to intervene successfully at this age inevitably produces a vulnerability to later mental health problems in adulthood, with all the social, interpersonal and economic consequences for those individuals, their families and society.

The evidence supports the notion that it is possible to establish, with relatively little difficulty, interprofessional teams which are able to integrate with all care staff, within the social environments of children and families (Falloon and Fadden 1995). As the evidence base for effectiveness builds in this area of work, further research will be required to examine the long-term consequences of new CAMHS initiatives to contribute to the refinement of studies into interprofessional working in this and in other children's services.

Working together

Leathard (1994) believes that in present practice most practitioners working within teams, which would include childcare professionals who are safeguarding children and young people, feel that working collaboratively is a good approach and that this is a more frequent occurrence than in the past (Wilson and James 2002). The value of this approach is especially true when resources are shared and the needs of the child and family dominate the discussion. Morris (2000) agrees in her report for the Joseph Rowntree Foundation and National Children's Bureau on barriers to change in the public care of children. She adds that social services, education and health services have been endeavouring to work jointly at local, strategic and national level.

In actuality practitioners who are often arranged in specialist groups tend to retreat behind professional lines every time important developments to interprofessional working are made. Morris also comments that there are often gaps between intention and practice. When concerns or issues arise that bring professionals into conflict rather than working the issues out as an interprofessional team, individual professional groups often withdraw behind their professional identities and roles and are unable or unwilling to offer inter-agency support (Corby 2000; Leathard 1994). This frequently occurs when a crisis or issue arises, instead of individuals supporting each other across agencies and sharing experiences for caring for the child and family. Professionals tend to seek support from colleagues from the same professional background believing there would be greater understanding of the stress involved (Morris 2000; Wilson and James 2002). It is crucial therefore to explore and learn to overcome the barriers which prevent practitioners working together to safeguard the emotional well-being of children and young people.

Activity 5.3

o   Are the barriers to inter-agency co-operation inevitable and insurmountable?

o   How might you tackle those barriers and try to overcome them?

Commentary

Kearney, Levin and Rosen (2000) suggest that although the interfaces between organisations will change all the time (usually through structural change) the difficulties of working across the interface remain. These blocks to communication and action are not totally removable – they exist as an inevitable by-product of the boundaries between different agencies and practitioner groups. Their presence is therefore inevitable. However, the power of these blocks to affect practice is variable and if recognised and attempts made to overcome them by the practitioner as well as the agency, their power is significantly reduced. Rather than deal with each block individually, there are a number of steps that we can take collectively to reduce their power (Walker and Thurston 2006).

Willingness to ask the 'naive' question

If the combating of ignorance about other agencies is the way to reduce blocks to inter-agency working, one of the most useful techniques the practitioner can utilise is the insistence on asking the naive question. This technique makes a virtue out of asking for an explanation when you don't understand, you half-understand, or when you do understand but know that others do not.

Understanding and valuing the other perspective

It is important to accumulate the minimum amount of relevant knowledge that enables us to see the world from others' point of view. Once the knowledge about the other practitioner's role and perspective has been gained, good inter-agency work demands that this be put into practice. This means that the differences that individual practitioners bring must be included in the inter-agency process rather than ignored, bulldozed over or pushed into a corner. Some strong element of compromise is suggested here rather than seeking a 'right' or 'superior' answer.

The dissemination of knowledge

The practitioner needs to be able to communicate, in an intelligible fashion, the essential characteristics of her own agency, role and language to the other practitioners in the system. This closely reflects the ability to communicate. It implies the ability to share the information that you possess in such a way that colleagues appreciate what you are saying, what it means in terms of your agency and its pertinence with regard to the particular case.

The ability to practise in an inclusive, inter-agency fashion

This is the key to overcoming structural blocks to inter-agency work. Although poor practice can seldom be laid at the door of the individual practitioner, positive inter-agency practice can be stimulated by individuals taking control over the inter-agency element of their own practice. The ability to practise in an inter-agency, inclusive way involves a change of thinking and the development of the 'inter-agency mind-set' (Reder and Duncan 2004). This change moves from the position of 'I' and 'you' or 'they' to 'we' and 'us'. 'How can my agency sort out this child and adolescent mental health problem?' changes to 'How can we help the inter-agency team begin to address this problem?' It involves beginning to think about the work in a multi-agency fashion, to develop a cognitive map that is truly inter-agency in its focus.

Dealing with conflict

When the structural blocks to communication have been overcome and the human issues around working together have been dealt with, the potential for conflict with families and between practitioners or agencies is still present. But it is likely that this conflict is concerned with professional differences of opinion or judgement, or a reflection of differences of interest within the family. It is important, according to Furniss (1991), that these differences are not minimised or ignored, but recognised, confronted and addressed, so that the issues in question can be resolved.

> Activity 5.4
> o   Make a list of several factors that you believe are responsible for poor communication between agencies working in CAMHS.
> o   Now compare them with those below.

Factors responsible for poor communication between agencies

- power struggles between key professionals involved in the child's care
- traditional thinking with regard to services offered by specific agencies
- lack of motivation in individuals to invest time in working together
- different values and beliefs surrounding professional practice
- different and competing priorities for outcomes for the child and family
- geographical location of offices or services
- differences in terminology used across agencies
- lack of priority given to joint service planning
- concerns about client confidentiality across agencies
- lack of knowledge and stereotyping of practitioners from other agencies
- inaccessibility of staff across agencies due to different work practices
- budget restraints on local services for children and young people
- different threshold criteria across agencies for making decisions, especially around significant harm.

Confidentiality

It is important to ensure sensitively that the child or young person is aware that some information cannot be kept a secret, but will be dealt with in the appropriate manner and will not be a matter for public knowledge. However, this is more complex around issues concerning health, especially sexual health and any interventions required, where the equilibrium between patient confidentiality has to be balanced with the health needs of the individual or others (DfES 2003; Moules and Ramsay 1998). If the child or young person is seen as Fraser competent (Gillick, Wisbech and W. Norfolk AHA 1986), this will also impinge on the outcome of sharing undisclosed information given in confidence (Wilson and James 2002).

The process becomes more difficult and complex when sharing information across organisations due to concerns about breaches of confidentiality. The Data Protection Act (DPA) (1998) clearly highlights the rights of individuals to confidentiality and privacy; however, it also clearly states that this does not restrict information for individuals, children, young people or adults who are seen as vulnerable. The DfES (2003) guidance on giving information and advice when dealing with potential child abuse situations supports this view: 'sharing information amongst practitioners working with children and families is essential. In many cases it is only when information from a range of sources is put together that a child can be seen to be in need or at risk of harm' (p.14).

Hendrick (2005) highlights the current government view, which provides for the removal of all legal barriers that prevent professionals and agencies from sharing information about children, without prior consent of the child's parents or the child her/himself. This is where the confusion often lies, in that it would be difficult to maintain a transparent and trusting relationship with the child and their family if this route alone was taken. However, in some situations when the child may be at risk there could be some justification. But Hendrick (2005) suggests this should be carefully employed, especially when dealing with young offenders, as this has ramifications for fairness and justice to be seen to have been carried out. Ideal practice would be to share information, with all interested parties including the child, young person and their families after gaining consent, thus ensuring co-operation from all members of the family including the parents.

Inter-agency collaborative practice

While barriers exist it is important to acknowledge it is not a choice to decide whether or not to work across agencies; rather, it is important to reduce the barriers in a way that supports the child, young person and all the professionals involved. This is now a statutory requirement whereby a framework has to be developed for co-operation across all agencies to support the well-being of children in your local area (Children Act 2004). This approach acknowledges the role of individuals from voluntary organisations, informal carers, private and statutory organisations and the need to combine and integrate services where appropriate. The family role within this must not be underestimated. Carers often have to relay information between agencies and can still feel taken for granted by the caring professionals (Leathard 1994; Lindon 2003).

Activity 5.5

o Together with a colleague from another discipline, discuss the team you work in paying attention to the values you share, qualifications, knowledge and experience.

o Now highlight all the differences you may have and the similarities.

o Compare and contrast how these similarities and differences bring strengths and weaknesses to the group.

Commentary

The practice of multi-professional working can lead to efficient sharing of information and enhanced communication across agencies and help to ensure greater cohesiveness and effectiveness within and across organisations to safeguard the emotional well-being of the child or young person and their family. The Children Act Guidance for the NHS (1989) suggested that a plan for each child or young person was the best way forward, which may encourage multi-agency working as the

> plan devised jointly by the agencies concerned in a child's welfare which co-ordinates the services they provide. Its aim is to ensure that the support offered meets all the child's needs, so far as practicable, and that duplication and rivalry are avoided. The plan should specify goals to be achieved, resources and services to be provided, the allocation of responsibilities, and arrangements for monitoring and review. (DoH 1989, p.112)

Individual strategies for improving communication

It is important to collect evidence from all colleagues who work with the child/ren and the family. Do follow up your intuition with a non-judgemental investigation of the facts. Prepare your report in plenty of time and be familiar with the contents and be honest and as open as possible with the parents before the conference. Ensure information is kept in chronological order and is as complete as possible.

Actively listen to other members of the conference or review group and keep an open mind. Be assertive and clear when presenting your information and be prepared to challenge other members constructively. Equally you must be ready and prepared to receive constructive criticism. Remember to use professional judgement rather than emotive statements. If asked try to give a sensitive but honest opinion of the child's situation and do not let the potential for intimidation hold back your professional opinion.

Show respect and value everyone's view regardless of whether they match your own but do not be afraid to bring conflict to the group – it could actually be very helpful and open up closed communications. Remember the child/ren should be the main focus and you must maintain an anti-discriminatory attitude. Professional judgement should override any personal dislike. Afterwards ensure you receive regular supervision to discuss issues raised at conference.

Activity 5.6

○ Think about a recent case conference or interprofessional meeting you attended concerning a young person with CAMH problems.

○ Using the material above reflect on your involvement. What did you do well and what were you unhappy about?

○ Write down some points specifically designed to change your practice at future meetings.

Commentary

While it is important to reflect upon personal behaviour during a case conference, review or interprofessional meeting, this alone cannot offer the support the child/ren may require both in the short or longer term. Rather it is the behaviour of all members of the group and their ability to reflect critically on the evidence presented to them that will determine the outcome for the child. This is clearly led by the chairperson and, while an indecisive or judgemental chairperson may impair the process, Munro (2002) makes the point that a good leader will encourage group discussion, valuing all participants regardless of their role or status, and refrain from commenting on their personal opinion until later in the meeting. A further element to add could be a member prepared to play devil's advocate, who would have the role and sanction of the group to challenge any assumptions or complacency that may appear. However, the whole group has to take responsibility for the outcome of the meeting. The following points outline some group strategies for improving communication:

• Children who wish to attend need to be prepared.

• Parents who wish to attend need to be prepared.

• Remember that the child/ren remain the focus of discussion.

• Everyone needs to introduce themselves fully, along with the reason for their presence.

- Professional stereotypes must not override professional judgement.

- Members should be encouraged to share all information including confidential information.

- The group should avoid unrealistic optimism.

- Members should endeavour to remain objective rather than emotive.

- Balance must be given to ensure that valuing cultural diversity does not lead to tolerance of abuse.

- Reports from practitioners not present should receive equal weight to those presented in person.

- If the child is not present to offer their wishes and feelings this needs to be acknowledged when decisions about their future are made.

Professional skills can also be improved when practitioners share experiences, thus reducing the risk of isolation. Alongside this, efficient sharing of education and resources which focus not on the agencies' needs, but rather on the learning and supervision needs of the childcare practitioner, is helpful. This can be further supported with professional truthfulness, combining materials both about particular children and their families and also information about up to date knowledge, research and evidence-based practice leading to enhanced communication. This may facilitate collaboration both within organisations which have a variety of professionals working with children, and across organisations with professionals having a common theme of focusing on the child. Care needs to be taken to ensure that professionals who have fixed workloads are given enough time to rearrange their workload to attend case conferences and other meetings.

To work closely and satisfactorily with families requires good communication skills. To work as an advocate for the child means an ability to negotiate with other members of a team and across agencies which again requires fluent communication. Finally, to empower a child and their family means having the awareness to give information freely to ensure informed consent. In short, good communication is the oil which lubricates and enables the interprofessional team to function smoothly and successfully for the child. Good practice regarding children who are still living at home, the method of referring, use of case conferences and action plans emphasise the need to incorporate the child's needs and rights as well as parental involvement. The terms partnership and collaboration are often used interchangeably to describe both the form of organisation and method of working. Harrison *et al.* (2003) remind us that partnership working is pointless unless it can be demonstrated to have influenced policy and practice. White and Grove (2000) suggest that four elements must exist within a partnership in order for it to function:

- *Respect* – without respect between partners there can be no prospect of achieving partnership.

- *Reciprocity* – requires that partners contribute what they can on an equal basis without power resting in one agency.

- *Realism* – requires a realistic appraisal of the challenges, tasks and resources.

- *Risk-taking* – requires that agencies court failure even if this goes against instinctive practice.

For a child to voice or demonstrate their mental health problems takes great courage, and while most professionals appear to take into account the problems the child has, welfare decisions are often made *for* the child rather than *with* the child. Professionals need as a team to put the child's rights first when making decisions, and it is only when this occurs that childcare professionals can believe policies do protect the child and their rights. Great strides have been made, but with knowledge of gaps in CAMHS leaving children at risk, progressive social workers need to monitor procedures and their policy of inter-agency working continuously to ensure that decisions are made in the child's best interest.

Key chapter points

- Collaborative or partnership working are terms used frequently in the practice guidance and professional literature without a great deal of reflection about what the terms mean or how to realise them in practice.

- Communication is important not only to support and develop relationships with families, but also to be able to work well with other professionals. Clients have concerns about the standard of communication they receive and it is the professional's responsibility to ensure it improves and to acknowledge that the families personally need information throughout your contact with them.

- Research continues to reveal the gap which has been steadily growing for decades between the primary care sector and the specialist CAMH services.

- A disadvantage of the accelerated interprofessional cohesion could be that important differences and disagreements are denied or overlooked in order to present a united front under the glare of evaluation and scrutiny in a climate of scarce resources and funding rivalries between services.

- As interprofessional CAMH services broaden their base, it raises the question of whether at some stage the separate individual professions within each team will begin to lose their former identity and metamorphose into a new kind of practitioner taking on characteristics of their colleagues from different professional backgrounds.

- In order for the CAMH policy imperatives to work there needs to be a vertical information cascade within the CAMHS tiered structure and horizontal lines of communication outside to the broader children and families services framework as well.

Chapter 6

Family and
Community Support

Learning objectives
»   Understand the impact social policy changes have had on protecting and promoting children's mental health.

»   Consider how family and community resources can be harnessed to help support the emotional well-being of children and young people.

»   Develop knowledge and skills in relation to family functioning and community development.

»   Understand the impact of traumatic issues or events such as war, genocide and forced migration on the emotional development of children.

Introduction

Children and young people suffering mental health problems usually do so in the context of a family or similar situation – there are usually other people nearby in close contact. The idea of supporting children indirectly by supporting parents/carers and other family members is not new but is gaining in social policy and therapeutic service responses. Family support is increasingly becoming a focus for intensive CAMH preventive or treatment work. This chapter will explore the social policy context of modern family life and consider the needs of families and strategies for relationship-building and therapeutic intervention. The importance of early intervention, cultural considerations, parent/carer support and community development will be highlighted.

The upward trend in CAMH problems and specific increases in young male suicides, school behavioural problems and female eating disorders provide examples of situations where issues about the focus of intervention and the form of intervention require serious attention. Are these manifestations of something inherently wrong with the modern family or are they the social consequences of the impact of free market economic expansion? In other words, should social workers be trying to help parents cope better with the emotional and behavioural needs of a new generation of children and young people, or help families and communities challenge the prevailing socio-economic structures that produce such negative effects? Or should they be trying to do both at the same time?

The social policy context

Unencumbered market economics and regimes have had a significant impact on social policy in the industrialised world and have contributed substantially to redrawing the role of the state, particularly with regards to the provision of welfare resources. As the limitations of capitalist laissez faire economics are revealed by unemployment and massive differences in wealth between countries so global opposition to the social, environmental and psychological consequences increases.

Social workers can assist in supporting and mobilising people who seek to liberate and empower themselves and orient their activities in providing assistance for one another and meeting their collective welfare needs (Dominelli 2002). Working with children and families where mental health and emotional well-being are at risk offers the opportunity to make a difference to how people feel about themselves and the society of which they are part. With marginalised and disenfranchised families this can be an important path towards reconnecting with their community, neighbours and other support systems. Feeling valued and cared for can be part of the social regeneration of a neighbourhood as important as its economic regeneration, with desirable impacts on children's mental health.

Equally, the widening gap between rich and poor highlights the needs of those families socially excluded, marginalised and disempowered, causing strong feelings of resentment, envy and anger. Increased numbers of mothers in work, the ageing of the population, rise in youth homelessness, increased reporting of domestic violence, child abuse and the prevalence of substance misuse are cited as evidence of the financial pressures and relationship strains put on modern family life. The social policy debate divides between those who blame lax child-rearing practices and the permissive 1960s, and those who cite the growth of individualism and the failure of capitalist economics to fulfil society's welfare needs.

Community developments

Racism and xenophobia have increased as European Union enlargement has accelerated migration, and armed conflict has precipitated increased numbers of asylum seekers. The consequent economic and social dislocation has prompted more refugee applications and illegal immigration to wealthier countries (Walker 2002). Impoverished communities in the UK have been incited to regard families fleeing persecution, ethnic cleansing and political oppression as an unwelcome burden and part of their economic problems. These changes in the socio-geographic texture of Europe are mirrored in other countries producing similar moral panics and hasty policy changes to tackle the consequences.

At the 2001 census over 3 million (5.5 per cent) of the 55 million people in Britain did not classify themselves as white. Half are South Asian (that is of Indian, Pakistani or Bangladeshi descent) and 30 per cent are Black. The rich diversity of Britain's minority populations reveals that nearly half of Britain's non-white population had been born in Britain, with three-quarters of these registered British citizens. The overwhelming majority of non-white children under 16 were therefore born in Britain.

Issues of citizenship and nationality, race and immigration provide the overarching context within legislation and public policy which sets the scene for racist and oppressive practice to go unchecked. The British Nationality Act (1948) provided legal rights to immigration which have served as a focal point for a continuing racialised debate about the numbers of Black immigrants and refugee/asylum seekers and the perceived social problems subsequently caused (Solomos 1989). The Race Relations (Amendment) Act (2000) came into force in 2001 extending the scope of the Race Relations Act (1976). The new Act strengthens the law in two ways that are significant to social work practice:

- It extends protection against racial discrimination by public authorities.

- It places a new, enforceable positive duty on public authorities.

Like the Human Rights Act (1998), the new Act defines a public authority very widely. Anyone whose work involves functions of a public nature must not discriminate on racial grounds while carrying out those functions. The most important aspect of the Act is the positive duty on local authorities because it gives statutory force to the imperative of tackling institutional racism. The new general duty replaces section 71 of the Race Relations Act 1976 with a tougher requirement on public authorities to eliminate unlawful discrimination and promote equality of opportunity and good race relations in carrying out their functions. Thus family support interventions must reflect anti-racist and anti-oppressive values as part of CAMH practice.

The Nationality, Immigration and Asylum Bill (2002) is the fourth piece of primary legislation attempting to reform the asylum system in ten years. Previous measures related to dispersal and support measures and were widely regarded as harmful to family and children's health because they resulted in sub-standard accommodation, isolation, discrimination and poverty (Dennis and Smith 2002; JCWI 2002). The new law proposes the establishment of accommodation centres housing about 3000 people in rural areas. Trying to maintain the emotional well-being of children in such places will be difficult due to the unsettling experience and high turnover of residents, while these children will be barred from opportunities to integrate and feel part of society (Walker and Akister 2004).

In addition, the new law proposes denying asylum seeking children the right to be educated in mainstream local schools. Such segregation could contravene the Human Rights Act 1998 and the UN Convention on the Rights of the Child 1989 because this is not in the best interests of the child and will very likely harm their development and mental health. Children who have suffered extreme trauma, anxiety and hardship need to feel safe, included and part of their new community in order to begin to thrive and rebuild their fragile mental health. There are serious doubts that the quality of education offered in accommodation centres would properly meet even basic standards of pedagogic practice (Walker 2003b).

Activity 6.1

o   Consider these two quotations:

They fuck you up, your mum and dad
They may not mean to, but they do
And fill you with the faults they had
And some extra just for you. (Philip Larkin)

Technology discloses man's mode of dealing with nature, the immediate process of production by which he sustains his life, and thereby also lays bare the mode of formation of his social relations, and of the mental conceptions that flow from them. (Karl Marx)

o   Now with a colleague discuss what they mean to you and which appeals to you most.

Defining the family

Before considering how to intervene in situations where a child or young person is suffering mental health problems it is important to consider their social context and not to make assumptions about how or who they live with. The word family can in itself be misleading if there are varied assumptions about what a family is. Traditional definitions were very narrow and reflected an era when a heterosexual couple married, had children and lived under the same roof. Nowadays this nuclear family stereotype is surprisingly resilient despite evidence of the diversity of different forms of family life. This is a popular conception of how the family is constituted that is more a reflection of how some traditionalists believe sexual, emotional and parental relationships ought to be structured rather than what is actually happening in real communities (Muncie *et al.* 1997).

In contemporary multi-cultural society with rich ethnic diversity combined with rapid sociological transformations there is a wide and complex variety of 'families' such as extended, kin group and lone parent. These can be further distinguished by parental partnerships that are same-sex couples, cohabiting, adoptive, fostering, separated, divorced, remarried and step-parents. Stretching the definition of family further can include the important role peers, friends, faith groups and local community figures perform in shaping and influencing family patterns of behaviour. We can therefore see that apparently simple concepts such as family are more complex the closer we examine them and so, therefore, are the ways to help. This is important in the context of finding ways of working that are relevant and acceptable to service users needing help with CAMH problems.

Any discussion of the family nowadays without incorporating the dimension of gender power would be considered inadequate, especially in the context of child and family social work where practitioners need to understand fully how masculine power is used in overt and covert ways to control, dominate and abuse partners and children. As public and professional debate constantly agonises over the emotional health of families and how to improve it, family therapy and family support are expanding their reach in the arena of family welfare policy and practice (Gorell Barnes 1998; Statham 2000). Both aspire to improving practice and engaging in evidence-based evaluation. Both are sometimes perceived as descriptions of therapeutic practice and service delivery format (Walker and Akister 2004).

Families and social workers

Early research into how social workers might experience using family therapy ideas in their work with families showed the following reasons for valuing such an approach:

- offers an open model of communication and sharing
- enjoyed by both family and social worker

- moves the focus of concern from the individual to the family with positive results

- offers a realistic way of working

- effective in problem-solving compared to other methods

- improves the quality of family life outside problem-solving. (Gorell Barnes 1998)

One of the problems social workers encounter in engaging with families in a statutory context and trying to employ family therapy methods is the threat they pose to families where the prospect of relationship changes is more overwhelming than the removal and institutionalisation of one of its members. It is possible to observe children with mental health problems increasing their symptoms during family therapy as the focus begins to shift towards other more upsetting problems hidden within the family. The pattern of contact with social services may have been one of child protection/childcare activity requiring the use of statutory powers to intervene. This 'resistance' to change is at the heart of all therapeutic paradigms as well as family support services. Unfortunately this can also confirm a partial systems view that an individual needs to be sacrificed or scapegoated by a dysfunctional family, rather than everyone concerned engaging in familial change.

However, social workers can use the concept of reframing the behaviour of a troubled child or young person and the family beliefs informing it as a means of illustrating the powerful protective forces at work inside families. In other words the acceptance by some individuals of being labelled as 'the problem' can be perceived as a means of protecting the family status quo. Suggesting to a family that the child's problem behaviour is serving a protective or loving function on behalf of other members delivers a strong message without a blaming connotation. This also testifies to the intrinsic strengths in a family who have developed such loyalty in one of their members, strengths which may have been temporarily lost sight of during the crisis (Gorell Barnes 1998).

Social workers using this notion will find it challenging in busy children and families teams where, despite government policy directives to the contrary, the climate is one of time constraints and resource shortages where investigation and assessment are the priority. This can create a reduction in expectations and a feeling of impotence and disempowerment in the worker that is invariably transmitted to clients. The family then have to acquire the variety of labels that trigger specialist intervention such as 'in need' or 'dysfunctional' where the opportunities for building on their strengths and resourcefulness are blighted. Both social worker and service user are thus restricted within circumscribed roles that militate against a positive partnership engaged in problem-solving activity.

Some family centres come closer to achieving the goal of offering a resource with a range of user-focused services such as advocacy, group work, support groups, individual counselling, and couple and family therapy. Such centres, it is argued, are better equipped to provide a more comprehensive service to disadvantaged users than for example, Tier 2 child and family consultation services staffed by professionals who have a narrower range of predominantly clinical skills (Reimers and Treacher 1995). Family centres are less stigmatising; they tend to have active representation from service users in the way they are run and, attended by clients who are motivated to attend, they can create the ideal conditions for effective therapeutic outcomes.

CASE ILLUSTRATION

The M family were referred to the childcare team following a period of increasing concern about the parents' capacity to cope with multiple problems including: unemployment, financial shortages, overcrowding, husband's violent temper, female teenager depressed and school refusing, and two under-fives demonstrating attachment difficulties. The case was allocated to a social worker who made an initial assessment and then combined this with the extensive history from the case record to produce an action plan. The evidence suggested that the family had never received consistent or coherent support, but a reactive service based on superficial negative risk assessments and anxieties generated by health and school staff.

Commentary

In order to make a difference and respond in another way rather than that anticipated by other people, including the family themselves, the social worker using a systems approach could begin by discussing options with all the family members present. This in itself would be unique because previously, for various reasons, the social work staff had only met with Mrs M. Taking the trouble to arrange a whole family meeting immediately changes the context for the social worker's visit. This permits each person to voice (or draw in the case of the under-fives) their perception of the family situation. This sets the scene for the work to follow and ensures that everyone has a stake in the process.

There are a number of ways forward once agreement has been reached about the practical ways of addressing the problems as defined by the family. Individual contact may need to be included, especially if there are concerns about abuse and/or domestic violence. Another worker can help in this respect with the double advantage of providing the caseworker with additional support and another resource for certain members of the family, e.g. a male social worker to meet with Mr M or a health visitor to do some parent modelling with Mrs M. A family centre could be contracted to do a number of sessions with various combinations of the family system, including extended family or friends.

A time-limited period of contact with a verbal or written agreement with a proper assessment and report at the end, composed in partnership with the whole family, demonstrates a different type of engagement with the M family. Using systems theory and family therapy techniques will help the allocated worker maintain a broad perspective of the family as an interactive system, rather than focusing narrowly on individual problems. Blame and scapegoating are avoided and the opportunities for change are maximised. Nevertheless, a professional social worker will need to anticipate a potential failure in this strategy and prepare for matters to worsen that require a more statutory/directive approach if risks increase and care diminishes.

Early intervention

Research on child poverty ranked Britain bottom in a comparison of the current 15 European Union countries with 32 per cent of children living in poor households (Micklewright and Stewart 2000). This is an important part of the equation of demand, needs and resources when evaluating provision and your role in supporting children and young people's emotional well-being. It has long been argued that early intervention is the key to effectiveness because it stops problems getting worse, when they become harder to tackle. It is less costly in terms of damage to children's development, family relationships, use of scarce resources and anti-social consequences in the long term (Bayley 1998). However, Eayrs and Jones (1992) have pointed out that the accumulated evidence for the effectiveness of early intervention programmes is not as optimistic as was once hoped. On occasion there is the possibility that such programmes can be damaging, de-skilling and undermining of parents' confidence (Walker 2002). This is particularly the case if parents feel coerced into attending programmes and when the quality of staff ability is low.

Other evidence suggests that early education interventions demonstrated that children from disadvantaged backgrounds were less at risk from developing mental health problems, maladjustment, school failure and delinquency after participating in these programmes which were delivered in an educational context (Sylva 1994). Some outcome research on primary prevention mental health programmes focused on school-based activities and concluded that positive changes were reported in social adjustment, academic performance and cognitive skills leading to a reduction in mental health problems in young people (Durlak 1998).

Much of the evidence supports the idea that the *location of family support* is clearly critical in engaging parents and children in the process of tackling CAMH problems. Schools are emerging as an acceptable and accessible non-stigmatising venue for individual or group-based activity where, for example, attached social workers using family support methods can engage in interprofessional work. The recent policy shift in education allowing extended schools to provide a deeper and broader range of services is evidence of the realisation that children do not learn when they are struggling with trying to maintain their emotional well-being and that if schools can promote and nurture emotional well-being, then children can learn. If children can learn then it is a most powerful early intervention to help prevent mental health problems progressing.

The purpose of intervention

The growing professional and public concern in recent years about the rising trends in children's emotional and behavioural problems has prompted health and social policy responses to the growing demand for CAMHS in the United Kingdom and elsewhere (Audit Commission 1998; Mental Health Foundation 1999; Micklewright and Stewart 2000; Rutter and Smith 1995; Singh *et al.* 2000; Walker 2001a). One of the issues raised is where and how to focus limited staffing and therapeutic resources to help families in trouble (DoH 1997a; DoH 1998b). A wider issue concerns the purpose of intervention in families – what outcomes are envisaged, how to evaluate them and whether it is family support or family therapy.

Family support appears in much government guidance and literature yet receives a low priority in statutory health and social care service provision in the United Kingdom. This is evidenced by a mixture of increasing pressure to improve child protection investigations, retrenchment in statutory preventive services, and the encouragement of charitable and non-governmental family support services (DoH 1999a). Meanwhile family therapy enjoys a privileged position within the regulatory United Kingdom Council for Psychotherapy and is developing a professional status distinct from its practitioner roots in social work, psychology and nursing. Therefore the professional status and client perception of both family therapy and family support are important issues to consider.

Fiscal and structural changes in the funding and organisation of social and health care are thus forcing choices about where to target finite resources to help families in need. Statutory workers bemoan the lack of time to practise preventively and at the same time are unable to employ therapeutic methods once CAMH problems arise because of the crisis-driven nature of cases which militate against establishing a safe, containing therapeutic relationship. Thresholds for eligibility criteria to services are so restricted that only the most worrying cases with high levels of risk tend to be accepted into statutory services.

Renewed recent interest in early intervention and preventive practice in the context of reliable evidence has enabled close examination of the challenges in assessing needs and demand against resource constraints (Thoburn et al. 1998; Tunstill 1996). Within government policy changes there is a possible ambivalence about the status and priority of family support work in the United Kingdom, and noted elsewhere (Hellinckx, Colton and Williams 1997). Family support may be perceived as something any well-meaning person or volunteer can provide while family therapy is elevated to the rarified status of advanced professionalism. Yet they both operate in very similar domains and can use similar therapeutic concepts with parallel processes and outcomes. More importantly, the family support worker may well have considerably more success at engaging and encouraging troubled young people than the supposedly more sophisticated therapist.

Activity 6.2

○ Get together with a colleague during a lunch break. Draw on large size paper a three-generation family tree (geneogram) of your families.

○ Now swap the papers and each in turn ask questions about the information revealed.

○ Discuss how this activity felt and consider what families might feel like when they are interviewed.

What is family support?

Renewed interest in early intervention and preventive social work practice in the context of robust evidence (Gardner 1998; Statham 2000; Thoburn et al. 1998; Tunstill 1996), together with rapid sociological change affecting the ability of parents to cope, has managed to keep the issue of family support for troubled children and young people highlighted. However the concept of family support is surrounded by different definitions and strategies. The Audit Commission (1994) defined family support as: 'any activity or facility provided either by statutory agencies or community groups or individuals, aimed at providing advice and support to parents to help them in bringing up their children' (p.46).

An important similarity between family therapy and family support is the way they inadvertently replicate another social structure – that of paternalism – which obscures the rights of children, especially in the area of CAMH (Walker 2002). Children's perspectives have rarely been explored in relation to the help they receive towards their emotional and mental well-being (Gordon and Grant 1997; Hill *et al.* 1995). Few studies have been undertaken with regard to therapeutic interventions with children and young people experiencing emotional and behavioural difficulties and whether they found the therapy helpful. This is a serious omission in the evidence base for practice improvement, and at variance with the contemporary interest in children's rights as service users.

Family therapy has evolved into definitions as simple as offering a view of problems as interpersonal rather than individual (Dallos and Draper 2000), or as comprehensive as Gorell Barnes (1998), who describes the activities as:

- encompassing a philosophy of relational events
- methods of description between people and their social context
- a relational approach to work with families
- a variety of therapeutic methods.

Some of the literature on family support describes ways of helping families (Hill 1999; Pinkerton, Higgins and Devine 2000; Sutton 1999). They provide the following common characteristics:

- using listening skills
- getting alongside families
- emphasising collaboration
- developing cultural awareness
- gathering information
- recognising positives in the situation.

An examination of these family support terms quickly shows similarities with skills considered important for family therapy training and accreditation, and will be familiar to those undertaking foundation level training in family support even though different vocabulary is employed. How far support or therapy directly address the social context, or succeed in doing so, is a moot point. The debate about the fit between family therapy practice and its application in social policy contexts has generated thoughtful contributions (Berger and Jurkovic 1984; Campbell and Draper 1985; Papadopoulos 2001; Sveaass and Reichelt 2001; Treacher 1995). The most recent contributions focus on the socio-political discourse generated around refugees and asylum seekers, and how these meta-contexts invariably intrude on the therapeutic encounter.

Families from areas of conflict will encounter family therapy or family support services, particularly when the effects of trauma manifest in CAMH problems. Without actively challenging and refuting the social policy context and media stereotyping that portrays these families as objects of pity or welfare scroungers, therapists and support staff will limit their helping potential. It could be argued that family support services, by their very nature, would be oriented more towards this social policy context, and are created specifically to address issues raised within it due to their often 'practical' focus.

But they may be missing important 'therapeutic' opportunities that are masked by too narrow a focus on human rights, legal or welfare benefit tasks. On the other hand, family therapists employing an inflexible therapeutic model, and concentrating on the intra-familial beliefs, behaviour and patterns of communication might be missing an important 'social' dimension to the family's experience and neglecting to find culturally competent ways of engaging them. In practice family support staff are very probably experienced by children and young people as therapeutic and family therapists can attend to practical matters without compromising therapeutic integrity.

The use of interpreters adds yet another complication, and communication becomes more and more difficult as each person in the process seeks to interpret others' beliefs whilst not necessarily making their own explicit. Family support staff using skilled interpreters could make remarkable progress with a young person's emotional well-being whereas the most skilled family therapist could find their work undermined by an interpreter out of touch with the purpose of the work.

Family support can be perceived as an overall aspiration within which particular models and techniques of practice are employed. These models and methods can be rooted in behavioural, psychodynamic or task-centred theories and focus on individuals, couples or the whole family. Family therapists using systems theory might also characterise their work in terms of a range of methods including for example, structural, psychoanalytic, systemic, cognitive-behavioural, solution-focused or constructionist. Equally, the focus can be on the individual, couple or whole family. Figure

6.1 illustrates the overlap and interconnectedness between the method employed, models of practice and the focus of intervention.

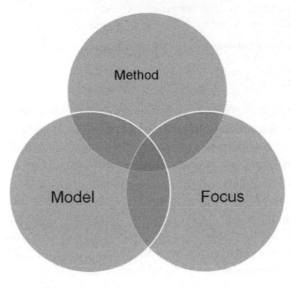

Figure 6.1 Method, model and focus

Within each overall mode of working there are a wide variety of techniques and approaches. So when terms such as family support and family therapy are used in multi-disciplinary professional contexts such as inter-agency meetings or case conferences it would not be surprising if participants made a number of different assumptions about what was actually being proposed or had already been tried in practice. Without clarification about what these terms mean the potential for confusion is high and increases the possibility that families receive mixed messages and conflicting advice from different staff they meet.

A major review of consumer studies of family therapy and marital counselling analysed a variety of research including large and small scale studies, individual case studies, specific therapeutic methodologies and ethnographic studies (Treacher 1995). It concluded that practitioners who neglected the service user perspective, and undervalued the personal relationship aspects of their family support work in favour of concentrating on inducing change, ran the risk of creating considerable dissatisfaction among service users. This reinforced findings from an earlier study into the effectiveness of family therapy that advised that advice and directive work needs to be balanced with reflective and general supportive elements (Howe 1989).

Activity 6.3

○ Reflect on the material above and think about the different situations and contexts in which you might consider using a family therapy or family support approach in your work with a troubled young person.

○ List the advantages and the disadvantages of your intervention.

Commentary

Family therapy is used in a variety of contexts, as we have noted earlier, and is perhaps more commonly associated with child and family problems where concerns have been expressed about the behaviour of an individual child. In therapeutic work it can also feature where a context of abuse, neglect, parental mental ill health or domestic violence requires an assessment of the impact on the child as well as efforts to promote a more protective environment. These can be addressed in a mixture of specialist resources, primary care interventions, or in statutory and voluntary contexts where psychodynamic approaches and systemic skills are used as an aid to decision-making and the preparation of official reports. Social workers have the basic skills required to adopt a competent approach in work that can prevent problems increasing or provide assessment for further intervention by other agencies or social work resources such as fostering or residential care.

As practice adjusts to an organisational climate where cost-effectiveness, audit and evaluation are expected to contribute to the growing evidence base, practitioners need to know what works in order to justify their intervention. One of the major problems in attempting to ascertain what works is in distinguishing the impact your particular intervention has had in the context of the multiple cultural influences on a child or young person's existence. They could be receiving a number of interventions from several agencies such as school, health visiting, youth offending – each of which or a combination of all could be having a significant effect. It is also the case that any or all of these could be contributing to a *deterioration* in the situation. Trying to isolate the particular impact your therapeutic work has had is very difficult, particularly if you avoid seeking feedback from the child or young person. Furthermore, it is argued that counselling or psychotherapeutic work is not even appropriate to evidence-based approaches to social work practice because, unlike medicine and experimental research, therapy is in a dynamic, interconnected relationship with clients, the nature of which cannot be subjected to conventional research methodology examining inputs and outcomes (Webb 2001).

The research evidence

There have been relatively few studies of family therapy employed in social work agency contexts. However, even within the confines of clinical practice it is clear that systemic therapy has established itself alongside some of the older and more orthodox methods and models of intervention as a reliable and acceptable approach. A meta-analysis of the findings of 163 published and unpublished outcome studies on the efficacy and effectiveness of marital and family therapy concluded that the clients did significantly better than untreated control group clients (Shadish *et al.* 1995). Based on a substantial literature search of the available research findings some clear findings (Friedlander 2001; Goldenberg and Goldenberg 2004) demonstrate:

- Compared with no treatment, non-behavioural marital/systemic therapies are effective in two-thirds of all cases.

- The efficacy of systemic, behavioural, emotionally focused and insight-producing therapies is established for marital and adolescent delinquent problems.

- Structural therapy appears to be particularly helpful for certain childhood and adolescent psychosomatic symptoms.

- There is evidence for the efficacy of systemic therapy in treating childhood conduct disorders, phobias, anxieties and, especially, autism.

Activity 6.4

o   You are considering commencing some direct work with a family in which there is a young person developing a depressive illness causing the parents and school a lot of concern.

o   However, you are not sure how to convince the family that this is worth trying and your manager is sceptical. How might you convince them?

Commentary

A major review of consumer studies of systemic therapy and marital counselling analysed a variety of research including large and small scale studies, individual case studies, specific therapeutic methodologies and ethnographic studies (Treacher 1995). These are particularly valuable sources of evidence because, whilst they do not have the same methodological rigour as 'clinical' research studies, they nevertheless reflect a more realistic experience of families in front-line working contexts (Walker and Akister

2004). The review concluded that practitioners who neglected the service user perspective and undervalued the *personal relationship* aspects of their family support work in favour of concentrating on inducing change, ran the risk of creating considerable dissatisfaction among service users. This reinforced findings from an earlier study into the effectiveness of systemic therapy in a social work context that advised that advice and directive work needs to be balanced with reflective and general supportive elements (Howe 1989). In particular the following conclusions are worth highlighting:

- Families needed an explanation of what therapy was about and how it differed from regular social service contact.

- Families felt they were being investigated, judged, manipulated and maligned and were unable to discuss issues they felt were important.

These studies point up the dilemmas faced by practitioners trying to employ therapeutic techniques in the context of a statutory remit which often includes a coercive element in family participation and an inspectorial/ monitoring element to the work. Assessment should include a therapeutic element but, in the context of determining whether a child is in need or child protection concerns, it is understandable if both parents and practitioners lose track of the purpose of such assessments. These dilemmas probably also reflect the constraints of time which impose artificial timescales and are inherently anti-therapeutic.

In either perception a number of roles may be prescribed which affect the emotional dynamics between the family and the social worker. This could range from parents *infantilising* themselves, resulting in behaviour that elicits an authoritative/parental response, through to aggressive/hostile behaviour that elicits a compliant or collusive response from the practitioner. These patterns of interaction need to be thoroughly understood in order to figure out the most appropriate way of using a competent approach. Fortunately, as a flexible approach, there are a wide range of options to select from, as we noted earlier. One of the significant conclusions to be drawn from considering the wider role of family support in contemporary social work practice is the impressive amount of activity, the variation in methods of intervention, and the worrying lack of systematic review of available research findings on which to build a reliable evidence base (Chalmers 1994; Webb 2001).

Family therapy and/or family support?

Does it matter what the work is called if everyone is satisfied? Wide status and pay differentials between qualified family therapists working in specialist CAMHS and family support workers employed by voluntary agencies do matter to staff. They often work with the same families and these differentials can cause envy, which will impact on relationships between staff in different positions. This must therefore impact on the work with clients or service users.

Equally, some families are intimidated by the concept of therapy, combined with the mental illness connotations and the stigma of CAMHS, which can be strongly influenced by a medical rather than social model of psychiatry. Other families are flattered by the opportunity to enter into such an experience and have no inhibitions about 'talking cures' and the culture of counselling or therapeutic ideas.

Innovative ways of responding to this need are required. Family support offers one way of bridging the gap between primary care responses and specialist family therapy input and the opportunity to engage with families who feel excluded from helping services. Bringing together different professionals in offering a more accessible, appropriate and acceptable service for troubled young people and their families is a timely response to a growing problem. Family support services can intervene early, over a short period of time, with an eclectic mix of practical and therapeutic activity. Professional rivalry and competitive fears of greater efficacy and role-blurring are challenged by evidence that paradoxically, the encouragement of generic interprofessional working actually reinforces boundaries between professions (Brown *et al.* 2000).

As family therapy continues to mature into a distinctive profession it is possible to see the mirroring of this phenomenon with teams of family therapists coming together from diverse professional backgrounds, while retaining their former values and knowledge base. There may be a degree of ambivalence about transforming from one professional role to another, with both advantages and disadvantages in maintaining a position of uncertainty (Walker and Akister 2004).

This is as true for staff moving from family support to family therapy, or the other way round. Experienced family support staff are able to integrate in family therapy teams as they share common skills base and theoretical assumptions. Social workers who have qualified after extensive training to become family therapists, and who are unable to secure a designated therapist post within a service, can work successfully in a family support service.

In CAMHS, non-urgent referrals have to join waiting lists to see family therapists. This prolongs family stress, amplifies symptomatology and hampers engagement with the therapist when the family are eventually offered an appointment. The clinic base, with its medical influence and often-psychiatric leadership, can deter referrers and families from properly engaging with help due to the stigma of mental illness associated with such resources. Their remoteness and detachment from their communities makes them intrinsically inaccessible and especially disconnected from socially excluded groups.

The following factors are worth bearing in mind if you embark on some direct work with a family or are involved in joint work with a therapist or support worker (Burnham 1986).

Factors that may help in working with families and communities

- *Good record keeping*
  Lack of record keeping can lead to aimless and repetitive work. It is perfectly acceptable to take notes during a meeting. Just explain that you want to be accurate and be able to think and reflect afterwards, in order to be more helpful to them. Using audio or videotape recording is ideal but requires extra time to set up and to view or listen to the material afterwards.

- *Technique*
  Skills development should never stop. Make sure you attend courses, in house or externally organised, workshops, interest groups. Read and learn about models of assessment and techniques. A common mistake is to use the correct technique but the wrong language. Families need to have information expressed in ways that fit better with their beliefs and culture.

- *Live supervision*
  One of the distinctive features of a family therapy model of practice which can be used in a variety of contexts for professional practice. Use a colleague or other professional in the room during a session, or behind a special one-way screen if provided. The observer can help supervise your work in action and enable you to be more effective both in the short-term and long-term development of your skills, experience and knowledge. Crucially, they can help you reflect on your practice.

- *Timing and pacing*
  Sensitivity is required to the speed at which a family is able to accommodate to an outsider. Some adapt quickly, others are more reserved and can only work slowly. Observation skills should be used to look for clues about the tempo a family uses in the early stages of work. The interval between sessions is an important factor to consider...a long gap between can in some cases be helpful if sessions are feeling stuck.

- *Proximity to the family*
  As with the concept of tempo, you must aim to assess the degree of proximity needed to adapt to a family situation. You will find that, for example, using a close, empathic style does not feel helpful in every case. You need to develop the ability to relate to families from a position of closeness, distance or a median point. The family will invariably give you clues about the distance they will tolerate.

- *Neutrality*
  This indicates a worker's ability to side with everyone and therefore no one in particular, in order to be most effective in helping them reach a resolution to their difficulties. In practice, however, this is a difficult position to maintain: for example, having to engage with one person in conversation during a family session or taking an important telephone call between sessions. A typical situation is where a worker finds themselves sympathising with one family member, perhaps a child who is being given a hard time and scapegoated. Recognising this is happening is crucial, and taking steps to realign with the rest of the family can be achieved by asking oneself the question 'What is the function in this family of this child being put in this position?'

- *Agency relationships*
  Developing your skills and knowledge in family therapy or working with families may produce difficulties in your relationships with colleagues who are envious of or hostile to your way of working. Conflict can be avoided or minimised by avoiding a competitive stance towards other methods of working, and seeking colleagues' views or advice helps diminish any impression of aloofness or superiority.

- *Professional network*
  Information sharing and clarity about who is doing what between different professionals can mitigate against families receiving

conflicting advice and support. Analysing the role and function of the various professional systems could also help shed light on how problems in the family developed. It may even be that a problem originates in the relationship between the family and another agency, e.g. disagreement with the school over a child's educational support can lead to non-attendance, isolation and the development of other problems within the child.

- *Causality*
  Disagreement over the causes of the identified problem between parents/children/professionals occurs frequently when attempting to help families. For example, is the problem organic or social? Is it school-based or within the family relationships? Is it to do with the parents relationship? Has the child got undiagnosed learning difficulties? Try not to take sides, it is usually more helpful to ask yourself: what is the function of this disagreement? What is being helped by maintaining this disagreement? Who would lose out if this disagreement were to stop and who would gain?

- *Goals*
  A family might agree about the nature of the problem but their respective aims about how to resolve it might be quite different. In the case of a child sexually abused by her stepfather and who, with her mother, had left home, it could become problematic because the mother's aim might be to return home and get the family back together eventually; whereas the child's aim is to build a separate life away from the stepfather. Work between mother and daughter might need to proceed at first to move things on, or help in the process of risk assessment.

- *Disadvantages of change*
  You might perceive a family's problems as unbearable, yet the family may have covert reasons for maintaining the status quo. The idea of change might be more frightening and upsetting than the problem identified. Then it is worth asking yourself the question or better still ask the family themselves: if this problem were to be resolved what other problem would remain to be tackled that is currently being obscured? For example, a problem between mother and teenage daughter might be resolved but in the process other issues are revealed and difficulties emerge in the parental relationship.

Key chapter points

- The widening gap between rich and poor highlights the needs of those families socially excluded, marginalised and disempowered, causing strong feelings of resentment, envy and anger. Increased numbers of parents in work, the ageing of the population, rise in youth homelessness, increased reporting of domestic violence, child abuse and the prevalence of substance misuse are cited as evidence of the financial pressures and relationship strains put on modern family life.

- Early intervention is the key to effectiveness because it stops problems getting worse and becoming harder to tackle. It is less costly in terms of damage to children's development, emotional well-being, family relationships, use of scarce resources and anti-social consequences in the long term.

- Family support can be defined as self-help or volunteer help with little statutory involvement, or it can mean a continuum of advice, support and specialist help geared to provide early preventive intervention. The intervention can be directed at individual parents, couples, the child, the whole family or in groups. It can consist of individual counselling, psychotherapy, groupwork, advice and information or the provision of practical help. Within the mix of interventions are the hallmarks of the family therapy paradigm that assumes problems are manifested within interpersonal relationships that are themselves part of a wider social context.

- Research into systemic practice can be considered compatible with the process and practice of the model itself. The use of supervision, videotape recording and family tasks offers a rich source of evidence with which to measure and analyse the impact of the therapy. Systemic theory also sits comfortably within new paradigms in the social sciences which seek to look beyond observed behaviours and recognise the importance of the meanings and beliefs created by families about their problems and attempted solutions.

- Social workers engaged in family support or family therapy are finding additional benefits to the intended outcomes of intervention. Therapists are helping families in the wider context while support staff are witnessing subtle changes in the quality of personal and community relationships and improvements in children's emotional well-being as a result.

- Family therapists have much to learn from families and from family support staff, without restricting themselves to expert roles as supervisors or consultants. Family support staff can equally learn much from therapists trained to high standards with focused theoretical parameters, and ethical and regulatory protection.

Part III

The Context of Social Work with Children and Young People

Chapter 7

The Organisational and Legal Framework

Learning objectives

»   Describe the four-tier model of CAMHS organisation and how these tiers link together.

»   Articulate the main legislative and policy framework for CAMHS.

»   Explain how CAMHS engages with and supports other children's services.

»   Understand the ways in which the Human Rights Act 1998 and the UN Convention on the Rights of the Child supports CAMHS.

Introduction

In 1997 the British House of Commons Health Committee fourth report on expenditure, administration and policy, focused on CAMHS. This took place in the context of demands from parents and staff in education, health and social work services overwhelmed by needs they were unable to meet (House of Commons 1997). The Committee noted the significance of mental health as one of five key areas in the Conservative government's Health of the Nation programme. It suggested that the Department of Health should adopt indicators and targets for children, including the setting of a target to reduce child suicides, and a target for the reduction of specific mental health disorders.

Later in 1997 the new Labour government pledged itself to change the National Health Service (NHS) internal market and lay the foundation for a new approach based on co-operation rather than competition between all stakeholders. The aim was to promote partnership as one of the key strategic commissioning objectives to deliver best outcomes for local populations from the resources available to them (DoH 1997c). Assembling the findings of three influential pieces of research and combining them with government policy statements enabled the design of a set of guidelines for CAMH service providers as shown in Figure 7.1 (Audit Commission 1998; HAS 1995; Kurtz 1996).

Relationships with commissioners

The service should be represented on a group that regularly advises commissioners and purchasers about arrangements for delivering comprehensive CAMHS.

CAMHS should have a plan which reflects an understanding of how the purchaser(s) perceives the contribution of this *specialist* service as part of the delivery of the *full* CAMHS.

Top-level trust planning

There should be an operational policy for CAMHS.

There should be a recognisable and separate budget for CAMHS.

There should be an awareness of the major elements of CAMHS expenditure.

Services should be child-centred and responsive to age-related and other particular needs, such as those of families from minority ethnic groups.

Services should have protocols for dealing with confidentiality.

Services should be provided in a welcoming environment, with buildings and rooms safe and suitable for children and young people.

There should be service level agreements to cover consultancy and advice for consultant colleagues in other specialities such as paediatrics. Agreements should ensure that the service provides regular and adequate input to children's homes, Emotionally and Behaviourally Disturbed (EBD) schools, secure units and to other groups of young people at particular risk.

There should be provision for adequate specialist mental health support to social workers, teachers, GPs and others.

CAMHS should be provided by a multi-disciplinary team or through a network. Health service personnel will make up only a part of the team – appropriate input from social services and education departments should also be maintained.

There should be a clear relationship with adult mental health services.

Operations

There should be an adequate information system geared specifically to CAMHS.

The service should offer a relevant range of interventions to suit different needs.

There should be clear referral channels to CAMHS which are appropriate to the referrer.

There should be a clear access route to day patient and inpatient services.

There should be a clear protocol for dealing with young people who present in crisis – including those who may deliberately harm themselves. There should be access to adequate and appropriately skilled 24-hour cover by mental health specialists for the child and adolescent population.

Waiting time for the first appointment for a non-urgent condition should be less than 13 weeks.

The service should identify topics for audit which should be undertaken regularly.

Appropriate training should be offered to CAMHS staff, including secretarial and reception staff.

Source: Audit Commission 1998

Figure 7.1 CAMHS service provider guidelines

Activity 7.1

○ Review the guidelines above and then investigate whether your local specialist CAMHS provider has operational protocols and systems that demonstrate implementation of the guidelines.

Commentary

The guidelines have been an important step towards establishing some commonality and equality in service provision. Mental health services for children and adolescents are generally poorly planned and historically determined rather than needs-led. Their geographical distribution is patchy and they are variable in quality and composition. The work they do often seems unrelated in strength or diversity to assessed population need. CAMHS comprise the specifically trained resources in CAMH available for a particular population. In 1995 CAMHS were found to be managed and delivered often in more than one health trust , and in more than one agency, thwarting attempts to co-ordinate care (HAS 1995). Services for the mental health of children and adolescents aim to:

- *promote* mental health in young people

- *prevent* problems occurring

- *treat* and manage problems and disorders that do arise so that their adverse impacts are minimised.

The national picture in CAMHS is still characterised by long waiting times and uneven distribution of specialist provision (DCSF 2008). Obscure access routes for service user pathways combine with excessive pressure on primary preventive services in health and social care, resulting in poor levels of inter-agency co-operation. The outcome is to create barriers to those most disadvantaged and socially excluded families requiring help. The government's *National Priorities Guidance, Modernising Health and Social Services* (1998), stated that one of its mental health objectives is to:

Improve provision of appropriate high quality care and treatment for children and young people by building up locally-based child and adolescent mental health services. This should be achieved through... improved liaison between primary care, specialist CAMHS, social services and other agencies. (DoH 1998b, p.17)

This was the first time that National Priorities Guidance was directed jointly at local authorities and health authorities. Local authorities were given the lead on children's welfare and inter-agency working. Local authorities and health authorities were to share lead on mental health and reducing health inequalities. Yet 12 years later CAMHS is still disjointed across the child development spectrum, and failing to meet the needs of older teenagers, and children and young people with learning difficulties – why is this?

Historically, there have been difficulties in collaboration in the area of CAMH which undermine the strategic aim of fostering closer working. These difficulties can be explained in terms of resource constraints combined with extra demands continually being placed on all statutory agencies. Other explanations emphasise, in addition, the different theoretical models underpinning working practices, the importance of personality factors and the capacity of senior managers to create an atmosphere of co-operation at all levels of the system (Pearce 1999).

For the time being the current organisational structure of CAMHS can be represented by Table 7.1 which illustrates the four tier progressive framework through which children and young people will be referred and the range of staff potentially involved.

TABLE 7.1 CAMHS TIERED FRAMEWORK: KEY COMPONENTS, PROFESSIONALS AND FUNCTIONS OF TIERED CHILD AND ADOLESCENT MENTAL HEALTH SERVICES

Tier 1. A primary level which includes interventions by:

- GPs
- health visitors
- school nurses
- social services
- voluntary agencies
- teachers
- residential social workers
- juvenile justice workers

CAMHS at this level are provided by non-specialists who are in a position to:

- identify mental health problems early in their development
- offer general advice – and in certain cases treatment for less severe problems
- pursue opportunities for promoting mental health and preventing mental health problems

Tier 3. A specialist service for the more severe, complex and persistent disorders. This is usually a multi-disciplinary team or service working in a CFCS or child psychiatry out-patient service, and including:

- child and adolescent psychiatrists
- social workers
- clinical psychologists
- community psychiatric nurses
- child psychotherapists
- occupational therapists
- art, music and drama therapists

The core Tier 3 CAMHS in each district should be able to offer:

- assessment and treatment of child mental health disorders
- assessment for referrals to Tier 4
- contribution to the services, consultation and training at Tiers 1 and 2
- participation in research and development projects

Tier 2. A level of service provided by uni-professional groups which relates to others through a network (rather than within a team)

These include:

- clinical child psychologists
- paediatricians, especially community
- educational psychologists
- child psychiatrists
- community child psychiatric nurses/ nurse specialists

CAMHS professionals should be able to offer:

- training and consultation to other professionals (who might be within Tier 1)
- consultation for professionals and families
- outreach to identify severe or complex needs which require more specialist interventions but where the children or families are unwilling to use specialist services
- assessment which may trigger treatment at a different tier

Tier 4. Access to infrequently used but essential tertiary level services such as day units, highly specialist outpatient teams, and inpatient units for older children and adolescents who are severely mentally ill or at suicidal risk

The most specialist CAMHS may provide for more than one district or region, and should be able to offer a range of services which might include:

- adolescent inpatient units
- secure forensic adolescent units
- eat disorder units
- specialist teams for sexual abuse
- specialist teams for neuro-psychiatric problems

Source: HAS 1995

Social workers, whether in statutory or voluntary organisations, may be involved at any of the four tiers of intervention, but the majority of non-specialists will be involved at Tier 1 and Tier 2. Social workers are employed at Tier 3 and 4, usually with advanced training and/or specialist qualifications in therapeutic work. Most children or adolescents with mental health problems will be seen at Tiers 1 and 2. All agencies should have structures in place to facilitate the referral of clients between tiers, and to maximise the contribution of CAMH specialists at each tier. The importance of multi-professional and inter-agency working cannot be over-emphasised in this area of work, and Chapter 6 has explored this in more detail.

Children's Trusts

The Children's Trust is a thematic partnership within the Local Strategic Partnership – the multi-agency partnership operating at local level and bringing together public, private, community and voluntary sectors to work together more effectively to promote better outcomes for local people. It is underpinned by the duties in section 10 (1) and (5) of the Children Act 2004 on local authorities and their 'relevant partners' to co-operate in the making of arrangements to improve well-being for local children. Well-being is defined as the five Every Child Matters outcomes: that all children should be healthy, stay safe, enjoy and achieve, make a positive contribution and enjoy economic well-being. These relatively new organisations are therefore crucial in the development of CAMHS.

In theory this should mean better integrated and outcome-focused ways of working on a whole range of issues, especially CAMH and emotional well-being, for example, having a specialist early intervention and prevention service organised around a central hub which both enables information to be shared and acts as the central referral point for all children and young people identified as having additional needs. It means having a strategy in place to reduce child poverty by targeting the most marginalised families and, through local schools, raising the aspirations and attainment of the whole family. The risk with such targeting is the potential for stigmatisation and feelings of persecution aroused in vulnerable households.

Arrangements established under section 10 of the Children Act 2004 aim to help drive and sustain Children's Trusts and in doing so:

- place a clear and measurably effective emphasis on narrowing the outcome gaps between children from disadvantaged backgrounds (for example, looked-after children) and their peers, while improving outcomes for all

- focus rigorously on prevention and early identification, including for those children and young people at risk of being harmed or falling into anti-social behaviour or crime

- involve and empower parents, and become more responsive to children and young people themselves

- ensure effective planning and commissioning of services and the flexible use of pooled budgets (or greater alignment) where that is the best answer locally

- lead to more integrated and strategic infrastructure planning, making best use of all available assets and funding streams to deliver facilities for children and young people's services, including through greater co-location; drive effective integrated working between all professionals working with children and young people

- support families in securing world-class health and well-being outcomes for their children, and tackle the problem of child poverty.

In 2008 new proposals extended the section 10 duty to co-operate to schools and schools forums, as well as sixth form and further education colleges; required all local areas to have a Children and Young People's Plan and extending ownership of the plan to all statutory 'relevant partners' represented on the Children's Trust Board; strengthened the statutory framework for Children and Young People's Plans, and established a statutory basis for Children's Trust Boards.

It remains to be seen whether these bold aims are realised and whether outcomes for disadvantaged children, young people and their families improve, gaps between vulnerable groups and their peers are narrowed, and significant moves have been made towards early intervention and prevention of children's mental health problems.

Activity 7.2

- Make sure that your team resources contain up to date copies of the latest legislative and practice guidance related to Every Child Matters.
- Invite a member of your agency legal department or a guest speaker to your next team/student group meeting to explain recent changes.

The creation of most Children's Trusts was expected to be achieved by the end of 2008, combining education and children's social services under one corporate director for children's services. By 2009 local authorities were expected to have completed the integration of these previously separate organisations. Evidence thus far suggests that each authority will adapt the process of change to local circumstances. There is no national blueprint so you may find yourself working in a *virtual trust* where staff and services integrate when and where necessary with the focus on co-ordination of front-line teams with maximum flexibility. Or you might work in a physically integrated space occupied by a range of staff from various agencies.

Reflecting the children's rights agenda, however, there is an explicit expectation that children and young people will be *actively consulted* about service development. Inspectors in future will be seeking evidence of how your service is reaching out to, and engaging with, young people in order to establish genuine communication about their needs. Several children's charities and independent organisations have track records of representing children and young people and will be valuable partners in future developments in this important area of practice. These are all part of the government's long-term aim to bring all commissioning for children's services together. Children's Trusts will be made up of the following key services:

- *Local education authorities* who provide educational welfare; youth services, special educational needs, educational psychology, childcare and early years education and school improvement.

- *Children's social services* who provide assessment and provision for children in need, family support, fostering residential and adoption services, advocacy, child protection and support for care leavers.

- *Community and acute health services* include community paediatricians, drug action teams, teenage pregnancy co-ordinators, CAMHS, health visiting and occupational therapy.

- *Youth offending teams* provide multi-disciplinary work with young people and their families to prevent offending.

- Connexions provide a multi-agency advice and guidance service for 13-19-year-olds.

- *The police service* have expertise in domestic violence, child protection, truancy and tracking missing children.

Legal framework

The legal framework for CAMH encompasses a wide spectrum of social policy including juvenile justice, mental health, education and children and family legislation. An important point is that the term 'mental illness' is not defined in law relating to children and young people. The variety of legal frameworks affecting them provide the context for work undertaken by a number of health and social care staff concerned about children and young people whose behaviour is described as disturbed or disturbing. The relevant legal and ethical issues for social workers are linked to practice principles and values best embedded in a psychosocial approach. Of particular interest to social workers in the context of empowering practice are the issues of consent and confidentiality. The Children's Legal Centre (2008) drew attention to a number of issues regarding the rights of children and young people who might have contact with agencies on the basis of their mental health problems:

- Lack of knowledge and implementation of legal rights for children and young people to control their own medical treatment, and a general lack of rights to self determination.

- Discrimination against children and young people on grounds of disability, race, culture, colour, language, religion, gender and sexuality which can lead to categorisation as mentally ill and subsequent intervention and detention.

- Unnecessary and in some cases unlawful restriction of liberty and inadequate safeguards in mental health and other legislation for children and young people.

- Inadequate assessment and corresponding lack of care, treatment and education in the criminal justice system.

- Use of drugs for containment rather than treatment purposes in the community, schools and in other institutions, combined with a lack of knowledge of consent procedures.

- Placement of children on adult wards in psychiatric hospitals.

- Lack of clear ethical guidelines for extreme situations such as force-feeding in cases of anorexia, care of suicide-risk young people and care of HIV positive or AIDS patients.

The organisational complexity

Children with mental health problems may move between four overlapping systems: criminal justice, social services, education and the health service. Children are not always helped by the appropriate service since this often depends on the resources available in the area at the time. It also depends on how different professional staff may perceive the behaviour of a particular child, and the vocabulary used by the service in which they work.

A youth offending team member may talk about a young person engaged in anti-social activity, a teacher about poor concentration and aggressive behaviour, and a social worker may perceive a needy, anxious, abused child. All are describing the same child.

CASE ILLUSTRATION

At a multi-agency meeting you find yourself considering the case of a young female, 14 years of age, with a history of self-harm and school refusal. She is described by her parents as 'moody' and 'uncommunicative'. The school nurse noticed old parallel cut marks on her arm when she administered a year-wide immunisation. The girl did not respond to questions about the marks. The police have been involved with her due to incidents of shoplifting and gang-related alcohol abuse. The teacher reports that she is hardworking but low on ability when she does attend lessons. As far as social services are concerned there has been sporadic contact with the family over the past few years with one younger brother sustaining one incident of non-accidental injury. There are four other children in the household and the father has a history of alcoholism and domestic violence. The task of the multi-agency team is to prepare an action plan, but first you have to work out what your role might be and anticipate what options other professionals are going to suggest.

The pathway of a child into these systems is crucial because the consequences for subsequent intervention can either exacerbate the behaviour or help to reduce it. Table 7.2 illustrates schematically potential agency responses to the same presenting problem. In this illustration the young person has been labelled *aggressive*.

TABLE 7.2 AGENCY RESPONSES TO THE SAME PRESENTING PROBLEM

Juvenile justice	Social services	Education	Psychiatry
Aggressive	Aggressive	Aggressive	Aggressive
Referral to police: decision to charge ⇓	Referral to social services ⇓	Referral to education department ⇓	Referral to child psychiatrist ⇓
Pre-sentence report completed ⇓	Social work assessment conducted ⇓	Educational psychology assessment ⇓	Psychiatric assessment ⇓
Sentenced to custody ⇓	Decision to accommodate ⇓	Placed in residential school ⇓	Admitted to regional inpatient unit ⇓
Labelled as *young offender*	Labelled as *beyond parental control*	Labelled as *having learning difficulty*	Labelled as *mentally ill*

Source: Malek 1993

The Crime and Disorder Act 1998 and the Special Educational Needs and Disability Act 2001 provide the legislative framework for youth justice and children with special educational needs. In both cases children and young people with mental health problems may find they are being inappropriately dealt with under these Acts. The Mental Health Act 1983, the Children Act 1989 and the Human Rights Act 1998 are currently the three significant pieces of legislation providing the context for social work practice in CAMH.

Mental Health Act 1983

In 2003 more than 270 children were detained under the Mental Health Act and placed in unsuitable adult psychiatric establishments, according to the Mental Health Act Commission (MHAC) (2004). The MHAC has recently expressed concern about the safety of children in adult psychiatric wards. The Mental Health Act 1983 is a piece of legislation designed mainly for adults with mental health problems and amongst other things, sets the framework for the assessment and potential compulsory admission of patients to hospital. The majority of children in psychiatric hospitals or units are informal patients. They do not have the same access to safeguards available to adult patients detained under the Mental Health Act 1983.

Children under 16 are frequently admitted by their parents even though they may not have wanted to be admitted. This is *de facto* detention. The number of children admitted to NHS psychiatric units has risen in recent years. In 1995 4891 children and young people under 19 were admitted in England. By 2000 the number had risen to 5788, an increase of 18 per cent (Walker 2003a). This is a worrying trend, which is also reflected in the adult statistics for compulsory admissions. Health and social care policy is meant to be shifting resources away from institutional-based provision to community care, but in the context of troubled young people the reverse appears to be the case.

Parts 2 and 3 of the Mental Health Act 1983 provide for compulsory admission and continued detention where a child or young person is deemed to have, or is suspected of having, a mental disorder. The mental disorder must be specified as mental illness, psychopathic disorder, learning disability or severe mental impairment. The Act does not refer to learning disability and, as with psychopathic disorder, it must be associated with abnormally aggressive or seriously irresponsible conduct. Full assessment and treatment orders under sections 2 and 3 require an application to be made by the nearest relative or a social worker approved under the Mental Health Act, together with medical recommendation by two doctors. Social workers have a role whether as ASWs or not in safeguarding the rights of children and young people at these rare and acute episodes in their lives. The sections of the Mental Health Act 1983 most likely to be used with children and young people are:

- *Section 2*: for assessment for possible admission for up to 28 days
- *Section 4*: for an emergency assessment for up to 72 hours' admission
- *Section 5 (2)*: for emergency detention by one doctor for up to 72 hours
- *Section 5 (4)*: for emergency six-hour detention when no doctor or social worker available
- *Section 3*: for inpatient treatment for a treatable disorder for up to six months.

Consent

Defining the capacity of a child to make her or his own decisions and consent to intervention is not easy especially in the area of child mental health. The concept of 'Gillick competent' arose following a landmark ruling in 1985 in the House of Lords. That ruling held that competent children under 16 years of age can consent to and refuse advice and treatment from a doctor. Since then further court cases have modified the Gillick principle so that if either the child or any person with parental responsibility gives consent to treatment, doctors can proceed, even if one or more of these people, including the child, disagree. The preferred term now is 'Fraser competent' after the presiding judge in those later cases.

The concept of competent refers to a child having the capacity to understand the nature, terms and consequences of proposed treatment, or the consequences of refusing such treatment, free from pressure to comply (Walker 2003b). In practice, children are considered to be lacking in capacity to consent, although this could be as a result of underestimating children's intelligence, or more likely, reflect an inability to communicate effectively with them. Courts have consistently held that children do not have sufficient understanding of death – hence the force feeding of anorexics and forcible blood transfusions for Jehovah's Witnesses.

Court of Appeal decisions have since overturned the principle that Fraser competent children can refuse treatment. Such cases were extreme and life-threatening situations involving anorexia, blood transfusion and severely disturbed behaviour. Importantly, the courts have indicated that any person with parental responsibility can in certain circumstances override the refusal of a Fraser competent child. This means that children under a care order or accommodated by the local authority even if considered not to have the capacity to consent, still retain the right to be consulted about proposed treatment. If a child is accommodated the social worker should always obtain the parents' consent since they retain full parental responsibility (Brammer 2003). If the child is under a care order the parents share parental responsibility with the local authority. Good practice requires the social worker in these situations to negotiate with parents about who should give consent and ensure that all views are recorded in the care plan.

Confidentiality

Children and young people require the help and advice of a wide variety of sources at times of stress and unhappiness in their lives. There are voluntary, statutory and private agencies as well as relatives or friends who they find easier to approach than parents. They may want to talk in confidence about worrying feelings or behaviour. The legal position in these circumstances is confused, with agencies and professional groups relying on voluntary codes of practice guidance. A dilemma frequently arises when children are considering whether a helping service is acceptable while the staff are required to disclose information to others in certain situations, for example, where child protection concerns are aroused.

The agency policies should be accessible to children and clearly state the limits to confidentiality. But in doing so many practitioners know they could be discouraging the sharing of important feelings and information. Social workers know only too well the importance of establishing trust and confidence in vulnerable young people and constantly have to tread the line between facilitating sensitive communication and selecting what needs to be passed on to parents, colleagues or to third parties. Ideally, where disclosure needs to be made against a young person's wishes, it is good practice to inform the young person in advance and give her or him the chance to disclose the information first.

The Data Protection Act 1984 and the Access to Personal Files Act 1987 give individuals the right to see information about them, with some limitations. Children 'of sufficient understanding' have the right of access except in certain circumstances. These are particularly relevant to social work and child mental health:

- where disclosure would be likely to cause serious harm to the child's physical or mental health
- where the information would disclose the identity of another person
- where the information is contained within a court report
- where the information is restricted or prohibited from disclosure in adoption cases
- where the information is a statement of special education needs made under the Education Act 1981.

Updates to the Mental Health Act 1983 came into force in 2008 with the Mental Health Act 2007. These included a single definition of mental disorder; changing the criteria for detention by abolishing the Treatability Test and introducing a new Appropriate Treatment Test. Importantly, changes also included a directive to ensure that age-appropriate services are available for any young person aged under 18 admitted to hospital. Broadening the professional groups that can take particular roles has concerned many social workers who fear their vital independent role, separate from the health service, has been weakened. Young people now have the ability to apply to court to change their nearest relative, and to ensure the right to an advocacy service when under compulsion.

New safeguards were also introduced for patients regarding electro-convulsive therapy, and a new provision to allow supervised community treatments. This allows a patient detained on a treatment order to receive their treatment in the community rather than as an inpatient. As a result of further changes, earlier referral to a mental health tribunal should occur. This introduces the inclusion of any period spent on section 2 to be included in the first six-month referral by hospital managers to the Mental Health Tribunal and retaining the right of the Secretary of State to reduce this referral period in the future.

Importantly, the UK at long last signed up in full to the United Nations Convention on the Rights of the Child. The United Kingdom government had maintained an opt out since 1991, which meant they did not fully accept responsibilities to asylum seeking children to appropriate protection and assistance. Now asylum seeking children have the same protection and access to services as other children, although such children are still subject to inhuman detention and financial constraints which adversely affect their mental health.

Children Act 1989

A child who is suffering with mental health problems may behave in ways that stretch their parents/carers' capacity to cope, which can result in the potential for significant harm. On the other hand a child who is being abused or neglected may come to the attention of professionals concerned initially about her/his mental health. The interactive nature of mental health and child abuse presents a considerable challenge for social workers tasked with conducting assessment work in child and family contexts. In terms of the Children Act social workers operate within deceptively clear guidelines. In practice, however, the provisions within the Act and subsequent practice guidelines have sought to bring simplicity to what are inevitably highly complex situations. The duties under the terms of the Children Act are straightforward and underpinned by the following principles:

- The welfare of the child is paramount.

- Children should be brought up and cared for within their own families wherever possible.

- Children should be safe and protected by effective interventions if at risk.

- Courts should avoid delay and only make an order if this is better than not making an order.

- Children should be kept informed about what happens to them and involved in decisions made about them.

- Parents continue to have parental responsibility for their children even when their children are no longer living with them.

The shift in emphasis heralded by the Children Act from investigative child protection to needs-led assessment for family support services is particularly significant for social workers engaged in work involving children's mental health. In harmony with a broad range of fiscal and social policy measures and neighbourhood renewal projects, it means family support is enjoying something of a renaissance, enabling social workers to practise psychosocial interventions. There is a specific legal requirement under the Act that different authorities and agencies work together to provide family support services with better liaison and a corporate approach (Brammer 2003).

Together with the four-tier integrated CAMHS structure, the framework is there to achieve better co-ordination and effectiveness of services to help any family with a child who has a mental health problem. This is made clear under the terms of section 17 of the Children Act, which lays a duty on local authorities to provide services for children in need. The definition of 'in need' has three elements:

- the child is unlikely to achieve or maintain, or to have the opportunity of achieving or maintaining, a reasonable standard of health or development without the provision for the child of services by a local authority or

- the child's health or development is likely to be significantly impaired, or further impaired, without provision for the child of such services or

- the child is disabled.

The Act further defines disability to include children suffering from mental disorder of any kind. In relation to the first two parts of the definition, health or development is defined to cover physical, intellectual, emotional, social or behavioural development and physical or mental health. These concepts are open to interpretation of what is meant by a 'reasonable standard of health and development', as well as the predictive implications for children having the 'opportunity' of achieving or maintaining it. However, it is reasonable to include the following groups of children within this part of the definition of in need and to argue the case for preventive support where there is a risk of children developing mental health problems:

- children living in poverty
- homeless children
- children suffering the effects of racism
- young carers
- delinquent children
- children separated from parent/s. (Ryan 1999)

Some children from these groups may be truanting from school, getting involved in criminal activities, or have behaviour problems at school and/ or home. Agency responses will tend to address the presenting problem and try an intervention apparently to address it. Assessment of the needs of individual children and families is often cursory, deficit-oriented and static. The Common Assessment Framework (2005) offers the opportunity for social workers, in collaboration with other professionals, to conduct more positive, comprehensive assessments that permit the mental health needs of children and adolescents to be illuminated.

Activity 7.3

○ At your next team/student group meeting present a case in which the assessment of a child or young person raised issues about whether the child was 'in need' as defined in the 1989 Children Act.

○ Ask the group to consider the information available and then to make an individual judgement.

○ Compare and contrast the different responses and discuss.

Section 47 of the Children Act gives the local authority a duty to investigate where they suspect a child is suffering or is likely to suffer significant harm. Guidance suggests the purpose of such an investigation is to establish facts, decide if there are grounds for concern, identify risk and decide protective action. The problem with CAMH problems is that this guidance assumes certainty within a time-limited assessment period. The nature of emotional and behavioural difficulties is their often hidden quality combined with the child's own reluctance to acknowledge them.

The interpretation of a child or young person's emotional or behavioural state is usually decided by a child and adolescent psychiatrist who may be brought into a section 43 child assessment order that has been sought following parental lack of co-operation. The social worker in situations like this, and in full care proceedings, has a crucial role in balancing the need to protect the child with the future consequences on them and their family of oppressive investigations and interventions.

In cases where the child's competence to consent to treatment, or capacity to express their wishes and feelings is impaired, it is likely that the Children Act 1989 should be used in preference to the Mental Health Act 1983. The Children Act does not carry the same stigma and consequences of the Mental Health Act, and it provides for a children's guardian to consider all the factors and act as an independent advocate in legal proceedings. The Children Act aimed to consolidate a number of childcare reforms and provide a response to the evidence of failure in children's services that had been mounting in the 1980s (DHSS 1985).

Professional social work practice was, prior to the Children Act 1989, perceived as intrusive, legalistic and biased towards child protection investigation. The new Act tried to redress the balance towards identifying needs and providing support to parents to prevent harm or neglect of children and young people. Contemporary debate about the Children Act is still concerned with how to translate the widely endorsed principles of the legislation into practical help for child welfare service users and providers (O'Hagan 1996). In the context of CAMH this requires social workers to optimise professional knowledge, skills and values in a very complex area of practice.

One of the distinctive roles for social workers in this context is that of advocate. This may seem contradictory in cases where the local authority is acting in the child's best interests, but in terms of establishing trust, respect and relationship building, supporting a complaint has benefit for staff involved in CAMHS. Section 26 of the Children Act provides for a complaints procedure through which children and young people can appeal against decisions reached by social workers. There are informal and formal stages to the procedure with an expectation that an independent person is included at the formal stages. When these procedures have been exhausted a judicial review can be applied for within three months of the decision being appealed against. The three grounds for succeeding with judicial review are:

- *ultra vires* – the social services department did not have the power to make the decision

- *unfair* – the decision was reached in a procedurally unfair manner, or by abuse of power

- *unreasonable* – all relevant matters were not considered, the law was not properly applied or there was insufficient consultation.

Human Rights Act 1998

The Human Rights Act (1998) came into force in 2000 and incorporates into English law most of the provisions of the European Convention on Human Rights. The Act applies to all authorities undertaking functions of a public nature, including all care providers in the public sector. The Human Rights Act supports the protection and improvement of the health and welfare of children and young people throughout the United Kingdom. *Article 3* concerns freedom from torture and inhuman or degrading treatment. Children and young people who have been subjected to restraint, seclusion or detention as a result of alarming behaviour could use this part of the Act to raise complaints.

Article 5 concerns the right to liberty, and together with *Article 6* concerning the right to a fair hearing, is important to children and young people detained under a section of the Mental Health Act, the Children Act or within the youth justice system. Social workers involved in such work must ensure that detention is based on sound opinion, in accordance with clearly laid out legal procedure accessible to the individual, and only lasts for as long as the mental health problem persists. In the context of youth justice work, particular attention needs to be paid to the quality and tone of pre-sentence reports which can be stigmatising. The formulaic structure of pre-sentence reports might not enable an assessing social worker, working under deadline pressure, to provide an accurate picture of a young person.

Article 8 guarantees the right to privacy and family life. Refugees and asylum seeking families can become entangled in complex legal procedures relating to citizenship and entitlement. This provision can be invoked when UK authorities are considering whether a person should be deported or remain in this country. Compassionate grounds can be used for children affected by the proposed deportation of a parent or in cases where a parent is not admitted. Social workers attuned to the attachment relationships of small children can use this knowledge to support Article 8 proceedings. In such circumstances the maintenance of the family unit is paramount.

Social workers involved in care proceedings or adoption work will have to consider very carefully whether such plans are in the best interests of the child but also are consistent with the child's rights under the Convention. For example, the Convention emphasises that care orders should be a temporary measure and that children should be reunited with their family as soon as possible, where appropriate. In the case of a parent with a mental health problem detained in a psychiatric hospital, the Convention could be employed by their children to facilitate regular visits if these have been denied.

Article 10 concerns basic rights to freedom of expression and, in the context of children's mental health, is a crucial safeguard to ensuring that practitioners work actively to enable children and young people to express their opinions about service provision. Social workers have an opportunity within this specific provision to articulate and put into practice their value principles of partnership and children's rights.

Article 14 states that all children have an equal claim to the rights set out in the Convention 'irrespective of the child's or his or her parent's or legal guardian's race, colour, sex, language, religion, political or other opinion, national, ethnic or social origin, property, disability, birth or other status'. This provision could be used to argue for equality of service provision and non-prejudicial diagnosis or treatment. Social workers need to ensure they are employing anti-racist and non-discriminatory practice as well as facilitating children and young people to:

- access information about their rights

- contact mental health services

- access advocates and children's rights organisations

- create children's service user groups.

The social work role

Social workers in a variety of work contexts in statutory or voluntary agencies, organised generically or in specialist teams, wherever they are likely to encounter children and young people as clients or carers, are potentially going to need to develop awareness and skills in CAMH practice.

Activity 7.4

○ Refer to the above material and consider in what ways the legal and organisational framework affects the role of social work in CAMH.

Commentary

In terms of the policy and organisational context, advice from the Children's Legal Centre (2008) is that social workers need to follow these principles when planning to intervene in the lives of children and young people on the grounds of disturbed or disturbing behaviour:

- *Informing* the child fully, consulting the child and taking her/his views and wishes into consideration.

- *Accepting* that in the absence of any specific statutory limitation, children gain the right to make decisions for themselves when they have 'sufficient understanding and intelligence'.

- *Respecting* in particular the child's independent right to consent or withhold consent to treatment as appropriate; and where a child is incapable of giving an informed consent ensuring that the parents' consent is sought, save in emergencies.

- *Ensuring* that any intervention is the least restrictive alternative, and leads to the least possible segregation from the child's family, friends, community and ordinary school.

- *Children* without the support of family or friends in treatment decisions should have access to independent visitors, advice and advocacy organisations. In the event of a parent wishing to override the child's refusal to be treated, a legal challenge may be justified if there is evidence that the parent is not acting in the best interests of the child.

A great deal of social work will, however, involve delivering or commissioning family support work linked to formal or informal assessment procedures designed to find out the best way of intervening to prevent children being removed from the care of their parents or deprived of their liberty. The signs and symptoms of mental health problems may not manifest clearly, or even if they do, alternative and sometimes punitive explanations for a young person's behaviour may obscure an underlying psychological problem.

It is important to locate the social work role in this area of practice in its wider policy and professional context. A useful way of doing this is to consider in general terms what the role of social work is in relation to other professionals working with children and families. What is it that makes social work unique and is not or rarely done by other agency staff? The first key difference is the *statutory power* enshrined in local authority practice contexts which always distinguishes the social work contribution to multi-agency working. The inherent capacity for compulsory sanction inevitably influences the nature of social work and affects the relationship with the service user. The second key difference is probably the training in wider *social science and social policy* perspectives which permits an understanding of oppressive and discriminatory processes in society. The third key difference is the explicit acknowledgement that community-focused interventions are a valuable means of *empowering individuals and groups*.

Together, these three elements can inform social work practice with children and adolescents who have, or are at risk of developing, mental health problems. A social model of mental health that encompasses these elements can help social workers challenge medical, institutional and punitive responses to distressed children. The social policy imperative for closer interprofessional working and reducing the barriers between staff in different agencies offers an opportunity to restate the core elements of effective social work practice.

Key chapter points

- The increase in the rate, volume and complexity of CAMH problems has caused government, health and social care agencies, and families to seek responses and to design sustainable policies to meet the increasing demand for services.

- CAMHS is characterised by long waiting times for specialist help, patchy distribution of resources, and variable quality and composition. Inter-agency co-operation is poor with a history of different theoretical models of practice, and structural barriers to improved collaboration. Recent changes including the National Service Framework, Children Act and Children's Plan guidance should improve practice.

- The legal framework for CAMHS encompasses juvenile justice, human rights, mental health, education and social services law. The issues of client consent and confidentiality are especially important in the context of children's rights principles. The link between child mental health and child abuse highlights the crucial role social workers have in understanding the legal contexts for informing assessment and intervention.

- Social work principles of empowering, service user-focused practice combined with a social model of human growth and development are valuable perspectives to bring to inter-agency work in this area of practice. A psychosocial model of practice rooted in wider social science theory enables social workers to maintain an anti-discriminatory stance and value community-based solutions to CAMH problems.

Chapter 8

Culture, Ethnicity and Diversity

Learning objectives

» Describe what is meant by culturally competent practice.

» Illustrate the importance of cultural identity to the mental health of children in a diverse society.

» Explain how understanding of oppression and discrimination influences contemporary practice.

» Understand the mental health needs of Black and ethnic minority families.

Introduction

The first decade of the twenty-first century marked the anniversary of the abolition of slavery, and in 2009 the inauguration of the first Black president of the United States. These are important milestones and a punctuation in the story of racism, discrimination and prejudice that has endured for centuries. Legislative and policy initiatives in the UK designed to ensure equality of opportunity for all citizens and stop racist abuse of Black people continue to develop. Yet all the recent evidence demonstrates significant disparities between the majority and minority communities in terms of employment, housing, educational attainment, wealth share and access to mental health services (Dwivedi 2002; Vostanis 2007). Overtly racist political parties and those with a covert ideology continue to thrive and foster suspicion, conflict and oppression between citizens.

Perhaps more worrying is the way that racist attitudes, beliefs and behaviour have been driven underground, obscured and disguised by the very measures designed to prevent them. Some people have learned to 'talk the talk' of anti-racism, to ensure they say the right things and go through the motions of anti-discriminatory practice while harbouring the opposite private feelings. A *neo-racism* can thus be detected where a false impression of equal opportunities can be created with well-meaning policies and working practices, while below the veneer of legislative protection Black people still experience abuse.

Children and young people face considerable challenges in maintaining their cultural integrity and emotional well-being in the face of institutional racism, homophobia, economic inactivity or enforced migration patterns (Dogra 2007). The consequences may lead to significant emotional and psychological problems expressed, for example, by high rates of school exclusion among African–Caribbean children (Okitikpi 1999), suicide and para-suicide of gay and lesbian young people (Trotter 2000) or unemployment among Bangladeshi youth (Jones 1996). The cultural assets of minority children regularly go unrecognised, denied or devalued within the wider community (Newman 2002).

It is crucial therefore that support offered by social workers includes opportunities for young people to celebrate their heritage and create links with other members of their cultural or social group. Children from migrant cultures are especially vulnerable to feelings of inferiority resulting in frustration, anxiety and poor school attainment (Spencer 1996). In the United States the promotion of resilience in Black communities is an important strategy aimed at developing cultural confidence and enhancing problem-solving capacities as a way of mitigating potential mental health problems (Reynolds 1998).

It is argued (Ackroyd and Pilkington 1999) that children do not have one essential identity, but switch identities in different situations and, subject to a diversity of cultural influences, can produce new identities. This is the case with Black and Asian children and young people influenced by the cultural norms of their white peers, whilst feeling pressured to maintain religious or cultural practices from elders. Social workers employing anti-racist and anti-discriminatory principles may simplistically try to reinforce apparent cultural norms which are not applicable, explain disturbed behaviour in terms of cultural features which are irrelevant, or miss emerging mental health problems (Walker 2005a).

The social work role in CAMHS offers practitioners the resources to maintain anti-racist principles in working with established Black communities as well as insights into the inner world of refugee and asylum seeking children and adolescents psychologically traumatised by war, ethnic persecution and profound losses. The importance of social care staff developing a culturally aware practice for working with children and young people cannot be overstated. If we are to truly reach them therapeutically and create the crucial relationship within which they can begin to understand themselves better, then we need to work hard at knowing them fully. By developing these informed, thoughtful relationships we can begin to address any emerging mental health problems or prevent them from starting.

Activity 8.1

○ Write down three key ways in which you can enhance your practice better to understand the emotional and mental health needs of Black and other ethnic minority children.

Commentary

This could mean adapting and developing your methods and models of practice to fit the child – not the other way round. Remember that every child is unique and time spent patiently getting to know the young person will be rewarded (Walker 2003a). It means resisting offering a *monotherapeutic* experience to every child or young person regardless of their unique characteristics. In so doing we can engage them and enable their needs to permeate our working practices more comprehensively. It means ensuring that we do not make general assumptions about a child or young person's home life, customs or beliefs from a cursory question or relying solely on information about religion, ethnic origin or family background (Hartley 2003; Kehily and Swann 2003; Parekh 2000). Challenging stereotypes and raising your awareness of how you might be perceived will help foster more authentic communication. The Royal College of Psychiatrists recommended the following as a way of improving service provision:

- Needs assessments are conducted as part of the commissioning process and representatives from minority ethnic groups and voluntary groups are involved in this process.

- Each locality develops a directory of all agencies and contact names who provide culturally sensitive services.

- Each service develops and implements a service delivery strategy for children from minority ethnic groups.

- Data collection systems are developed to provide accurate and useful information relating to, and for the use of, children and young people from minority groups.

- Staff training in cultural competence is incorporated into the personal development plans of individuals. (Malek and Joughin 2004)

A smaller world

Children and young people are developing psychologically in an external world in which the availability of information and the power it has to influence and shape their beliefs and feelings have never been greater. Control and manipulation of that information is being concentrated in a few hands, themselves closely identified with a narrow ideological doctrine that legitimates certain forms of behaviour, attitude and culture. Western developed countries led by the United States dominate the production, marketing and distribution of products representing brand names and iconic images aimed at maximising profit in the global marketplace (Hall 1993).

Children and young people are viewed as consumers and in this context the nature of their indigenous culture is seen as another part of their identity to be moulded in order to maintain cultural conformity. Young people's desperate need to fit in, be included and be the same as other children is exploited relentlessly by corporations propagating certain values that reinforce the consumerist culture of the early twenty-first century. This is harmful to their emotional well-being and psychological development.

What is culture?

Culture is a word that appears in everyday discourse – so much so that as with much common parlance it ceases to require any great effort at understanding what it means. We all seem to know what we are talking about when we mention culture. Yet the variety of definitions and interpretations of the word allow it an elasticity that is more a hindrance to clarity than a help. The increasing need to improve our therapeutic work with children and young people requires us to examine their changing cultural environment for evidence of how we might harness new ways of understanding them and their troubles (Walker 2005).

At a general level culture is associated with high art, refinement, superior taste, etc., or there is *popular culture* which is associated with the masses, low taste, tabloid media and TV soap operas. We can also acknowledge that there is a *therapy culture*, that is, something associated with western methods of responding to individual human psychological difficulties. Depending on the context it can be used as a term of criticism, implying that the problems of society are caused by the culture of therapy which posits people as victims and weak-willed (Furedi 2003; Masson 1988). Or it can be used in a benign sense illustrative of how advanced societies are becoming in attending to the stresses and pressures of modern life. What is certain is that those of us seeking to help troubled children and adolescents need to develop our understanding of how cultural influences affect, maintain and ultimately provide solutions to the psychological difficulties of young people (Walker 2005).

Culture in the anthropological sense has come to mean the way of life followed by a people. This concept developed as the history of western expansionism and colonialism encountered manifestations of difference around the world. These encounters prompted a reaction at several levels of consciousness. Politically there was a need to justify the appropriation of native land and resources, economically the imperial explorers required raw materials to service industrialisation, but *psychologically* there was a fear of difference that had to be rationalised. Hence the early attempts at racial categorisation and efforts to construct order from diversity and chaos in human lifeways.

Culture can also be defined in opposition to nature – the product and achievement of human beings representing a rising above of our natural instincts. In this sense human nature is typically understood as the opposite of culture. Culture can also mean the difference between humans and animals – the capacity to use language and complex communication to symbolise that which is not present (Jenkins 2002).

Thus the bearers of a culture are understood to be a collectivity of individuals such as a society or community. However, the cultural patterns that shape the behaviour of children and young people in groups should not be confused with the structure of institutions or social systems, even though there is a link between them. We can think of culture in one sense as the organisation of experience shared by members of a community including their standards for perceiving, predicting, judging and acting. This means that culture includes all socially standardised ways of seeing and thinking about the world; of understanding relationships among people, things and events; of establishing preferences and purposes; of carrying out actions and pursuing goals (Haralambos 1988; Jenkins 2002; Valentine 1976). As the history of the past three centuries demonstrates, the impact of western imperialism has reproduced its economic and political structures worldwide, resulting in the development of industrial societies in former agrarian countries that have disrupted cultural patterns with negative psychological effects.

Inequalities in the distribution of wealth among these newly developing countries has created expectations and increasing demands for fairer trade relationships. Globalisation combined with instant international communications has brought the consequences of these unequal relationships and the needs of poor nations closer to our attention than ever before. Thus developed nations are confronted with a variety of cultures with a common experience of exploitation and a need to reconcile conflicting feelings and responses. It is important that social workers acquire systematic knowledge about groups or categories of humanity who are more mobile and are attracted to western lifestyles of wealth, materialism and welfare.

Safeguarding children's culture

The evidence for the need to distinguish the different mental health needs of all children in a culturally diverse society and protect them from indirect or direct racist abuse is strong (Barter 1999; Blackwell and Melzak 2000; Chand 2000; Stanley 2001; Weaver and Burns 2001). For example, refugee and asylum seeking children, some unaccompanied, many affected by extreme circumstances, which include witnessing murder of parents or kin, dislocation from school and community, severing of important friendships and extended family support, loss of home, and prolonged insecurity. These experiences will probably trigger symptoms consistent with post-traumatic stress syndrome. This is manifested in a variety of ways, including: shock, grief, depression, anxiety, hyperactivity, self-harming behaviour, anger, aggressive behaviour, fear and guilt. Each individual child or adolescent will react differently according to variables such as:

- the context of their departure from the home country
- the family cohesion and coping capacity
- the child's own personality and predisposing psychological constitution
- proximity to extreme acts of murder or violence
- the child's developmental stage and history of transition.

Recent research is emerging that attempts to identify specific therapeutic orientations with improved outcomes for children and young people (Carr 2000; Fonagy and Roth 1997). A number of studies compared levels of stress in adolescents and family functioning across different national boundaries including Canada, the United States, Britain, Malaysia, India, Hong Kong and the Philippines (Bagley and Mallick 1995; Bochner 1994; Gibson-Cline 1996; Martin *et al.* 1995; Watkins and Gerong 1997). A meta-analysis of these studies found evidence to support the hypothesis that, while subjectively perceived levels of stress can vary significantly between cultures, the underlying causes of personal distress could be relatively similar between cultures (Bagley and Mallick 2000). This is useful information to consider when trying to practise in culturally competent ways that avoid racist stereotyping.

The strongest evidence for prediction of mental health problems in children and adolescents across cultures is that for general family stress (Bagley and Mallick 2000). Looked at more closely this includes the effects of physical, sexual and emotional abuse in the context of a climate of persistent negative family interactions. These findings are supported by other studies, which seek to illuminate and distinguish the particular factors influencing those children likely to develop mental health problems (Ackroyd and Pilkington 1999; Bagley and Young 1998; Kashani and Allan 1998; Vincent and Jouriles 2000). Social workers seeking to intervene effectively have to consider carefully the various ways potential mental health problems are thought about, understood and communicated in every family, in every culture.

In the early part of the twenty-first century the recent history of ethnic conflicts, population changes and poverty has prompted the emigration of refugee and asylum seekers towards the west. The more privileged and comfortable strata of western societies, as well as new urban communities in former agricultural economies, are facing the reality of desperately poor people who feel more and more marginalised and neglected. Resentment is a feature of the reaction of wealthier nations to inflows of dependent people and the realisation among refugees that they are not universally welcome.

There is a need therefore to render knowledge about difference and cultural diversity coherent in order to inform public attitudes and social policy, as well as to enhance therapeutic practice. One example of an inarticulate way of doing this is to attribute a culture or subculture to a broad variety of social categories. Hence we encounter relatively meaningless terms such as the culture of poverty, youth culture, pop culture, Black culture or drug culture. There is even a refugee culture that apparently explains the motivation of families from troubled or impoverished regions to take incredible risks to seek refuge and safety. This highlights the inadequacies in our contemporary ways of thinking and working practices around cultural competence.

Conceptualising culture

Cultural competence can initially be understood in the context of a desire to improve our practice in order to meet the needs of the growing multi-cultural and ethnically diverse society developing around us. It assumes that historical and orthodox assumptions about human growth and behaviour have served their purpose in meeting the needs of troubled children and young people in particular circumstances and at particular points in time. Now in the early stages of the twenty-first century changes are required to address and respond to the psychological and emotional problems of a modern generation of families and offspring who cannot be easily fitted into existing theoretical paradigms. There is increasing evidence for the need to refine and develop our methods and models of assessment and intervention so that they are more relevant and accessible to children and young people from a much wider range of backgrounds than was the case in the past (Madge 2001).

This is not to say that children and young people in the majority ethnic communities do not also require improved methods of help and support. They are being socialised and exposed to a quite different society than former generations. The pace of life, enhanced stressors, individualism and consumerism are blamed for producing heightened states of arousal and stimulation. Evidence has begun to emerge of genetic changes, the development of new illnesses and of course a range of new risk factors to their mental health, especially the availability of cheap psychoactive drugs and greater access to alcohol. Depictions of family life in children's literature, for example, has changed dramatically in the past 40 years from misleading idyllic paternalistic havens of safety and security to the grim reality of poverty, child abuse, divorce, mentally ill parents and personal and institutional racism (Tucker and Gamble 2001).

Holliday (1999) takes up this notion by trying to distinguish between large culture and small culture, in which he emphasises the need to move beyond the orthodox definition of culture as related to ethnicity, national and international characteristics. Small also is distinct from subculture, which is normally taken to mean something within and subservient to large culture. Small culture in Holliday's meaning is a way of understanding many cultures in all types of social grouping which may or may not have significant ethnic, national or international qualities. Thus the apparent patterns and characteristics of cultures reveal on closer inspection the variations and variability within and between cultures in reciprocal patterns of influence.

Understanding ethnicity

Ethnicity requires some clarification as another term that can be used in a variety of contexts but without much thought as to its meaning. Its use alongside the term culture can cause confusion especially when the two become almost synonymous. This is because there is no easy definition, but we at least need to know the complexities of the use of the term ethnicity because it perhaps reflects something deeper and more ambivalent about the way we internally manage difference and otherness. Part of the problem lies in mixing up birthplace with ethnic identity. A white person born in Africa and a Black person born in Britain can be defined by their ethnic grouping and place of birth (Walker 2005).

Thus the white person is African and the Black person British, or White African and Black British. Further confusion has historically prevailed due to the way the official census data has been collated. In the UK since 1951 the methods of data collection have altered from just recording the country of birth, to the birthplace of parents, to 1981 when there was no question on ethnicity. In 1991 a question on ethnicity offered a range of categories and in 2001 there were further changes to account for citizens with dual or mixed heritage.

The term 'race' is now generally accepted to be redundant as a meaningful scientific category; however, *the idea of race* as a general descriptor of assumed national, cultural or physical difference persists in society (Amin *et al.* 1997). The concept is embraced at the policy level with legislation such as the Race Relations Act in the UK and institutions such as the Equality and Human Rights Commission in the UK. Legislation such as the 1989 Children Act, the 2004 Children Act and Children's National Service Framework, which contextualise work with children and young people, expects practitioners to take account of a child's religious persuasion, racial origin and cultural and linguistic background, without adequate guidance as to what is meant by 'race' or 'culture'. The issue becomes more complex when we consider census data that shows the increase in numbers of children from dual and mixed heritage backgrounds and consider the particularly complex set of problems they can encounter.

Scientific work in the nineteenth and twentieth centuries attempted to conceptualise race and classify people in different countries according to their supposedly inherent superiority or inferiority. Similar comparisons were made on the basis of gender and class which permitted the tolerance of inequalities based on innate biological differences. A eugenics movement was inspired by these findings whose aim was to improve the genetic stock of the human race by eradicating people with less than perfect genetic dispositions. In the latter part of the twentieth century advances in genetic research were able to dismiss these earlier notions of racial hierarchies, classifications and the supposed link between biology and behaviour (Kohn 1995; Walker 2005).

However, vestiges of these outdated concepts still survive at the popular level as people try to understand where they fit into an ever-shrinking world where much more is known about other countries, customs and culture. Cheap air travel, faster communication and the creation of refugee and asylum seekers from troubled areas are bringing images, experiences and feelings to our collective consciousness. Skin colour, language and religion are still interpreted as signifiers of more profound differences in abilities and outlook, as well as being used to justify discriminatory practices or outright racism. For some people the notion of white superiority is barely below the surface, especially in the context of a colonial history and latterly immigration.

The incredible cultural diversity in the United Kingdom belies populist notions of an Anglo-Saxon *monoculture*. This is a clear example of an economically successful country that benefits from immigration while perpetuating xenophobia and racist hysteria reflected in the popular media and in more subtle ways in some mainstream political parties. It is important to understand the specific manifestations of cultural differences in every country rather than try to prescribe a universal explanatory theory. We need therefore to find an explanation for racial inequalities that can attend to the social construction as well as to the individual internal construction of difference and the link with cultural competent practice in CAMH.

Emotional well-being and culture

The link between race, ethnic identity and inequality has been repeatedly established in terms of its effect on wealth, status and power. These socio-economic and other environmental variables are recognised as risk factors for the development of CAMH problems. The data shows that, for example, Black and other ethnic minority young people and adults charged with anti-social behaviour are more likely to receive punitive or custodial disposals in the criminal justice system rather than community options geared to a better understanding of their causality. High levels of psychological problems are reported from male and female Black populations within young offender institutions. Socially constructed notions of racial difference thus remain a potent basis for identity and affecting our sense of sameness and difference (Bilton *et al.* 2002). This has led to frequent criticisms of the discriminatory and stereotyping attitudes of police officers, teachers and the legal system.

In considering the various ways in which children's mental health is understood it is useful to consider some of the orthodox theoretical and research-based evidence on human growth and development as part of the standard repertoire of guidance available. Social workers are expected to have a sound grounding in these subjects to help inform all aspects of their work with a range of child and adolescent age groups. The theories were more fully explored in Chapter 2 but in this context some of the classic authors and contemporary literature need to be reviewed critically as part of a professional and theoretical discourse that is notable for its lack of culturally competent concepts. They illustrate the way conventional child development is conceptualised offering a normative model of childhood that assumes a *universalist* application when it should be used as a limiting starting point requiring adaptation and amendment as you begin the process of engagement with your client.

A good starting point is in a sense where some of the theories end. Wherever the emphasis is placed on the spectrum of the nature versus nurture debate and any explanation for human behaviour in the literature, you need to be clear where *you place yourself* as a practitioner. Not for the purpose of trying to prove a theory right or to convince yourself of the correct explanation for the behaviour of a child or young person, but to make more explicit your own personal bias. This is not a weakness but a strength. A practitioner knowing where they stand and understanding there are other perceptions and beliefs about a child's development, and adopting an inquisitive, culturally flexible stance, will be acting more in the child's best interests. Rather that, than trying to defend the indefensible or answer the unanswerable.

Recent advances in genetic research and refinement of developmental instruments for assessing children and young people's emotional and behavioural health have concluded that to regard nature and nurture as separate and independent is an oversimplification. A more helpful answer to what shapes children and adolescents' mental health is *both* nature and the environment or, rather, the *interplay* between the two. Thus it is crucial to incorporate an understanding of culture and the way it can shape both your perception of a child and young person's psychological difficulties and affect that young person's perception of themselves.

The multi-disciplinary complexion of many staff groups working with CAMH problems and the structural/organisational changes towards more inter-agency and interprofessional working mean that a variety of social workers will be familiar with the orthodox developmental theorists. These suffice as a baseline starting point from which to modify and improve upon so that they maintain their relevance in a rapidly changing multi-cultural society.

For example, young people in social withdrawal, a phenomenon reported on since 2004 in Hong Kong, are those who seclude themselves at home for a protracted period of time and reject most forms of contact and relationship with the outside world (Wong 2009). It is an echo of the phenomenon of *hikikomori* (social withdrawal), which can be traced back to the mid 1980s in Japan. These *hikikomorians* or youth with *hikikomori* (a condition) are usually males in their twenties (who may comprise nearly a million) living mostly in urban outskirts of densely populated Japanese cities (Wong and Ying 2006). The developmental transition from adolescent to adult can include periods of social shyness, awkwardness and several attempts at leaving home and achieving independence. The phenomena of the socially withdrawn youth in western households can elicit images of computer-obsessed males conducting social relationships via the Internet. Yet in another cultural context this is causing high levels of concern (Suwa *et al.* 2003).

Activity 8.2

○ Select a recent piece of work from your caseload in which you assessed a family from a different ethnic community from your own.

○ Now reflect on the similarities and differences in your use of developmental theory compared to another family assessment.

Commentary

The ideas of Freud, Klein, Piaget, Eriksen, Skinner, Bowlby and others may feel attractive, sensible, logical or contradictory, anti-instinctive or confusing. They can help or hinder the process of your work; the important point is that by employing a resource you permit the adoption of some intellectual rigour to the way your work is organised (Beckett 2002; Mills and Duck 2000). This can provide a starting point in your family assessment, a framework within which the selection of assessment and intervention methods and models can take place. Crucially, it will enable a more systematic process to proceed in a recognisable direction or provide a knowledge base to discuss ideas put forward by other staff. This will be helpful in supervision, case conferences, legal proceedings or report writing contexts. However, these theoretical resources and frameworks need to be enhanced and improved to make them more useful to a modern social work practice. Sometimes it is helpful to acknowledge that there is no clear-cut explanation, or that there are multiple interpretations for a child's emotional and behavioural problems that are concerning others. The ethnic and cultural identity of a young person for whom there is much concern may well be a minor aspect of their difficulties – or it could be the most significant and crucial aspect.

Social workers can especially utilise theoretical concepts from social policy and sociology to add to their framework of explanation. This distinguishes your contribution from most other agency staff in child mental health work. The combination can be powerful, adding weight to professional arguments and providing authority for interpretations (Walker 2005). They can also be burdensome and confusing and should therefore always be used cautiously. They enable a social model of mental health to be acknowledged alongside others and therefore more readily advance a culturally competent practice. The choice is again vast in the area of sociology alone. Marx, Durkheim, Mills, Parsons, Popper, Habermas and others offer a rich and diverse knowledge base (O'Donnell 2002). The important point is that the chosen theoretical preference can be identified and acknowledged, and a plan can proceed consistently within that premise.

The importance of reflective practice whilst undertaking culturally competent work with children and adolescents cannot be emphasised enough. In the process of using measures of human growth and development it is crucial. This is because children and young people are constantly changing, as are their circumstances. Your assessment could be out of date within weeks, reliant on too few factors or based on inaccurate referral information. This requires a high level of concentration and alertness to changes that will be unique and unpredictable, as well as changes that appear to conform to a predictable developmental transition. Such changes may have nothing to do with your intervention and some may have everything to do with it. The key is in appreciating that developmental issues are significant and require you to have a good grasp of them (Thompson and Thompson 2002).

Human growth and development theoretical resources should be seen as part of a wide spectrum of potential, rather than deterministic, interactive causative factors in the genesis of CAMH problems. Some social psychologists criticise the emphasis on normative concepts in child development theories and suggest enhancing the judging, measuring approach towards one that embodies context, culture and competencies (Woodhead 1998).

The mosaic of diversity and difference

Culture defines accepted ways of behaving for members of a particular society. But such definitions vary from society to society leading to misunderstanding and a failure to engage therapeutically in a helping relationship. Klineberg (1971) offered an example of just such a misunderstanding. Amongst the Sioux Indians of South Dakota it is regarded as incorrect to answer a question in the presence of others who do not know the answer. Such behaviour would be regarded as boastful and arrogant and an attempt to shame others. In addition the Sioux regard it as wrong to answer a question unless they are absolutely sure of the correct answer. A white American teacher in a classroom of Sioux children and unaware of their culture might easily interpret their behaviour as a reflection of ignorance or hostility. In a therapeutic context we can imagine our reaction to exploratory questions which resulted in a silent response with consequent interpretations of resistance with further attention being paid to that area. An understanding of the role of certainty and respect on the other hand could open up creative possibilities for engagement.

Culture is not static; it is an organic living entity with an external and internal presence. Any attempt to define it is bound to be provisional because people – and more especially children and young people – are developing rapidly at many levels of physicality and consciousness. They do so in an equally fast changing and bewildering societal context that sets the scene for our understanding of culture. It is possible, however, to select some common characteristics that can help us think about the concept of culture in a more useful way that enables us to focus our therapeutic efforts to the best advantage of children and young people:

- Culture is definitely human: it is the characteristic way that humans do things, rooted in our capacity for complex communication and reflexive relationships.

- It carries within it implications of controlled development and change. Culture is the medium within which human individuals grow and become competent.

- Culture is also a matter of differentiating human collectivities, and their characteristic patterns of behaviour, one from another. It is important to understand the different ways in which child and adolescent development is conceptualised by diverse communities. (Jenkins 2002)

In western industrialised countries there is a less clearly defined division between childhood and adolescence compared with developing countries. The change is more pronounced and shorter in countries where there is less tradition of further and higher education and greater sharing of domestic or agricultural labour between adults and younger family members. There is an assumption in western industrialised countries that adolescence has been stretched so that it covers a much greater time span than in previous generations. This is cited as a cause of much problematic behaviour and psychological problems in contemporary young people (Rutter 2005).

There is also evidence of the earlier onset of puberty in the more affluent societies and delays in the onset of menarche has been reported in girls who are exceptionally physically active (Beckett 2002). On the other hand children from non-western countries or whose parents were raised there will have expectations and experiences based on a very different time span. Parents may have been married at the age of 12 or 13 and perhaps have served as soldiers in civil wars, or been responsible for the care of several younger siblings. This can be a cause of stress in multi-generational immigrant families.

Globalisation and young people's identity

The term globalisation has begun to feature in the literature, reflecting profound shifts in the economic and social patterns of relationships between the richer industrialised countries and the poorer developing countries. It involves closer international economic integration prompted by the needs of capitalism, but also has demographic, social, cultural and psychological dimensions (Midgley 2001; Pieterse 2004). Consistent with the link between the social context of CAMH problems, it is therefore important to consider the global context in terms of the challenges for building culturally competent practice.

Critics of globalisation argue that its impact is to maintain unequal power relationships between the richer and poorer countries so that patterns of wealth and consumer consumption in Europe and North America can be sustained. This involves the exploitation of labour and other resources in poorer countries thereby preventing them achieving a diverse and equitable economic and social structure within which health and social welfare programmes can develop. The consequences of globalisation are being noticed in the way traditional social care systems are taking on the characteristics of business ethics and commercialism (Dominelli 1999; Mishra 1999). One of the side effects of this process is the standardisation and conformity required for consumer consumption patterns in order to maximise profit. The consequence is the steady and inexorable erosion of traditional markers of indigenous cultural identity combined with the elevation of global branding (Walker 2005).

This critique of the latest phase of capitalist development echoes earlier concerns about the impact on economic growth and subsequent erosion of traditional government policies of full employment and social welfare (Bailey and Brake 1980; Corrigan and Leonard 1978). A failure to develop social welfare services fully, or to have them subjected to the gyrations of speculative global financial markets, invariably corrodes the quality and the depth of services designed to reach children and families in personal and culturally appropriate ways. This means that services are pared to the minimum, oriented towards crisis intervention and designed in the narrowest terms to conform with inflexible eligibility criteria that limits access. These features are inconsistent with culturally competent practice that aims to spread accessibility, improve acceptability and enrich our creative potential to respond to a diverse society.

The paradox of globalisation is that as new varieties of cultural expression are encountered and celebrated there is an underlying impulse to impose a sameness by the powerful western nations on the developing nations. Thus at a supranational level there is a parallel process occurring of the individual rejection of difference by the powerful countries with the technology and military capacity to influence the majority powerless countries. This must both steer and reinforce the latent fear of *the other* inside individuals who then feel they have permission to reject Black and ethnic minority families. This contradiction is further illuminated by government policies against racism while at the same time resorting to draconian measures to control the immigration of refugees and asylum seekers.

The globalisation of culture produces deeply contradictory states for individuals and groups with consequences for the development of an integrated sense of self. Hence we observe the way Black youth are regarded as predisposed to violence and disorder resulting in persecutory oppression and aggressive reactions which are interpreted by police as evidence of anti-social predisposition. On the other hand Black athleticism and success in international sport produces a celebratory image masking denigratory undertones (Briggs 2002). White youth can be seen and heard imitating Black youth culture in terms of dress and accent, while African–Caribbean youngsters, for example, learn the patois of their grandparents, and celebrate Rastafarianism by wearing dreadlocks, which some regard as a hostile anti-establishment stance. Young Asian women are torn between the aspirations of their white peers for sexual independence and socialisation and the expectations of some parents for social restrictions and arranged marriage. These conflicts and pressures are the genesis of emotional and psychological problems.

Culturally competent practice

Dilemmas in trends towards cultural competence have been highlighted by reference to the practice of forced/arranged marriages and dowry, genital mutilation of children and harsh physical punishments condoned by some societies (Midgley 2001). These practices can be used to counter the argument for respecting ethnic and cultural diversity and support the notion of universal values as the basis for competent practice. Ethnic rivalries and the pride in national identity on which they are based also sit uneasily with culturally competent aspirations of international collaboration and mutual understanding.

An estimated 20,000 girls under 15 years of age are considered to be at risk of female genital mutilation, with 11,000 highly likely to have already experienced it. The psychological consequences include: acute trauma, low self-esteem, genital phobia and anxiety/depression (DoH 2007).

However, rather than seek answers to these difficult issues in an introspective way, this emphasises the need for social workers to reach out to the international community with service users, to continue to debate, discuss and strive for ways to discover solutions. In the area of CAMH we need to understand the impact such practices and the beliefs on which they are based are having on the mental health and emotional development of those adults promoting them and the children and young people experiencing them.

Cultural competence has been defined as developing skills in assessing the cultural climate of an organisation and being able to practise in a strategic manner within it. It has also been broadened to include any context in which workers practise in order to permit effective direct work at many levels (Baldwin 2000; Fook 2002). Whether at the strategic organisational level or the direct interpersonal level we can actively resist those pressures to conformity and routinised practice that in often discreet and inconspicuous ways can undermine efforts to practise in culturally competent ways. The requirements of social justice demand vigilance and creativity in order to contribute towards an emancipatory practice that can liberate both workers and service users from prescribed practice orthodoxies. Such practice is the antithesis of stereotyped, one-dimensional thinking and is characterised by:

- a commitment to standing alongside oppressed and impoverished populations

- the importance of dialogic relations between workers and service users

- orientation towards the transformation of processes and structures that perpetuate domination and exploitation. (Leonard 1994)

These characteristics are in harmony with culturally competent practice. They do not imply that therapists should reject statutory practice for the voluntary sector, childcare for community work or psychodynamic theories for advocacy. These simplistic oppositional devices do not help us manage the complexities and dilemmas in seeking different practice orientations (Healy 2002). The possibilities for creative practice within organisational constraints are there. They may be limited and subjected to pressures of time but in the personal relationship with service users and particularly children and adolescents with mental health problems, the rewards are unquantifiable for both worker and client. Even introducing a small change in practice can have a much larger disproportionate and beneficial impact.

Working together – learning together

There is growing interest in the development of multi-disciplinary and interprofessional working in order to maximise the effectiveness of interventions to meet the diverse needs of multi-cultural societies and service users (Magrab *et al.* 1997; Oberheumer 1998; Tucker *et al.* 1999). The characteristics of such work apply in a framework familiar to health and social care staff. It begins with assessment then proceeds through decision-making, planning, monitoring, evaluation and, finally, to closure. It is argued that this common framework offers the optimum model for encouraging reflective practice to be at the core of contemporary work (Taylor and White 2000; Walker 2003b). Reflective practice offers the opportunity to shift beyond functional analysis to making active links between the value base, policy-making process and the variety of interventions conducted.

> Activity 8.3
>
> o Consider with a colleague how your agency guidelines and practices enhance or hinder your work with young people in the modern, culturally diverse society.
>
> o Together, discuss how you both might support each other in future work to improve your cultural competence.

Commentary

Combining reflective practice with culturally competent practice, we have the opportunity to make a major contribution towards responding to the social policy aspiration of inclusion and anti-oppressive practice. In so doing we can facilitate closer co-operation between professionals coming into contact with vulnerable families on a shared agenda of challenging institutional and personal discrimination (Eber, Osuch and Redditt 1996;

Sutton 2000; VanDenBerg and Grealish 1999). Drawing together the elements of practice that can contribute towards a model of culturally competent care means it is possible to define cultural competence as a set of knowledge-based and interpersonal skills that allow individuals to understand, appreciate and work with families of cultures from other than their own. Five components have been identified comprising culturally competent care:

- awareness and acceptance of cultural difference

- capacity for cultural self-awareness

- understanding the dynamics of difference

- developing basic knowledge about the family's culture

- adapting practice skills to fit the cultural context of the child and family.

These are consistent with other work which critiques the historical development of cross-cultural services and offer a model of service organisation and development designed to meet the needs of Black and ethnic minority families (Bhugra 1999; Bhugra and Bahl 1999; Dominelli 1988). Culture has been defined as the sets of shared cultural perspectives, meanings and adaptive behaviours derived from simultaneous membership and participation in a multiplicity of contexts such as geographical, religion, ethnicity, language, race, nationality and ideology. It has also been described as the knowledge, values, perceptions and practices that are shared among the members of a given society, and passed on from one generation to the next (Leighton 1981). Four particular theories have been identified in modern systemic practice that attempt to harmonise systemic theory with cultural competence:

- *Ethnic focused* – this stresses that families differ but assumes that the diversity is primarily due to ethnicity. It focuses on the commonality of thoughts, behaviour, feelings, customs and rituals that are perceived as belonging to a particular ethnic group.

- *Universalist* – this asserts that families are more alike than they are different. Hence, universalist norms are thought to apply to all families.

- *Particularist* – this believes that all families are more different than they are alike. No generalisations are possible; each family is unique.

- *Multi-dimensional* – this goes beyond the one-dimensional definition of culture as ethnicity, and aims at a more comprehensive and complex definition of culture that embraces other contextual variables. (Falicov 1995)

An attempt to elaborate a theoretical framework for multi-cultural direct work with troubled children and young people suggests that an overarching theory needs to be employed that permits different theoretical models to be applied and integrated. A synthesis between different methods and models of practice offers a more comprehensive way of achieving this. In this way, both client and worker identities can be embedded in multiple levels of life experiences with the aim of enabling greater account being taken of the client's experience in relation to their context. The power differentials between worker and children and adolescents are recognised as playing an important role in the therapeutic relationship. Clients are helped by developing a greater awareness of themselves in relation to their different contexts resulting in therapy that is contextual in orientation and can, for example, draw upon traditional healing practices (Sue, Ivey and Penderson 1996).

Ethnocentric, and particularly Eurocentric, explanations of emotional and psychosocial development are not inclusive enough to understand the development of diverse ethnic minority groups. Failure to understand the cultural background of families can lead to unhelpful assessments, non-compliance, poor use of services and alienation of the individual or family from the welfare system. By using an anti-discriminatory, empowerment model of practice social workers are ideally placed to work with other professionals in multi-disciplinary contexts to enable the whole team to maintain a focus on culturally competent practice (Walker 2005). For example, the increased demand for help from parents and children themselves suffering the effects of mental health problems has prompted policy initiatives to invest in and reconfigure CAMHS provision in more acceptable and accessible ways.

However, in order to be effective all staff need to address the different belief systems and explanatory thinking behind emotional or psychological symptoms. Skills and values are required to articulate these concepts in such diverse teams. Challenging crude stereotypes, questioning implicit racism and simply ensuring that other staff stop and think about their assumptions can help. Combined with respectful consideration of indigenous healing practices within diverse populations this can optimise helping strategies. The traditional psychiatric methods and models of therapeutic practice have failed to take full account of cultural factors but contemporary literature is attempting to catch up. The following areas offer guidance to enhance your communication skills:

- Families may have different styles of communicating fear, grief, anxiety, concern and disagreement.

- Emphasis should be placed on listening with the goal of understanding the family's perspective.

- Care should be taken to explain to the family the agency culture.

- Steps should be taken to recognise and resolve conflicts which occur between the cultural preferences, understandings and practices recommended by professionals.

- Communication is enhanced if you can demonstrate sensitivity towards the family's cultural values.

- Appreciating the family's cultural understanding of the problem will help build a trusting relationship. (Whiting 1999)

CASE ILLUSTRATION

A family of Iraqi asylum seekers fled the country before the recent US and British invasion in 2003. The father, Mohammad, had worked in the petroleum industry. Mohammad claims he was tortured and had death threats made against his wife and three children who are of Kurdish origin. The children are all under eight years of age and his wife Shirez is a nursery teacher. Some of the children speak very little English. The family have been relocated to a small town where there are very few Iraqis, or any families from Middle Eastern countries. The local Housing Department has referred the family to your office following reports of racist attacks in the bed and breakfast hostel where they have been housed in emergency accommodation. A teacher has called your team four times in the past fortnight expressing concern about one of the children who is wetting and soiling in class, provoking bullying from other children.

Commentary

Your first task is to begin the process of assessment by constructing a visual map of all the people, agencies and services connected to this family. You will find it helpful then to make contact with as many as you can within a realistic timescale to start to plan your response. This information-gathering exercise will enable you to begin to evaluate the different agendas and perceptions of other staff working with or concerned with the family. Your priority is to establish meaningful contact with the family and gain factual evidence of racist incidents for possible criminal prosecution against the perpetrators, as well as offering a caring, sympathetic relationship. Bear in mind that the family are likely to be highly suspicious of your motives and will require a lot of genuine evidence that they should trust you. Their naturally defensive behaviour may come across as hostile/uncommunicative and you need to deal with this in a non-confrontational manner.

A translator/interpreter should accompany you, having been fully briefed beforehand about your task, the different roles each of you holds and to assess their suitability for this particular task. Do not assume that every interpreter is the same, and try to evaluate their beliefs/attitudes and whether there may be ethnic or religious differences between them and the family. For a variety of reasons they might be inappropriate for this task despite having the right language skills. Strict translation of words and terms will be unhelpful, therefore time needs to be spent on the interpretation of the interpretation. Right from the start you can better engage with the family by:

- enabling everyone to have their say
- sensitive questioning to enable expression of feelings
- reinforcing the integrity of the family system
- noting patterns of communication and structure.

Having established a helping relationship a holistic perspective enables you to locate the family system within a wider system of agencies, resources and a local environment that is generally hostile. Your networking skills can mobilise the statutory agencies to provide what is required to attend to the immediate areas of concern and clarify roles and responsibilities. A case conference or network meeting can put this on a formal basis with an action checklist for future reference to monitor the plan. One option may be to plan some family sessions together with a colleague from another agency such as health or education. This could combine assessment and intervention work to ascertain medium-term needs whilst using therapeutic skills to help the family establish their equilibrium. The key is to enable them to re-establish *their* particular coping mechanisms and ways of dealing with stress, rather than trying to impose an artificial solution. Maintaining a systems-wide perspective can help you evaluate the factors and elements building up to form a contemporary picture of their context. Working with them as a family and demonstrating simple things like reliability and consistency will provide them with an emotional anchor – a secure enough base to begin to manage themselves in due course (Elliot 2007).

The evolution of culture

What the above tells us is that the subjects of culture, race and ethnicity are evolving all the time as society changes and develops according to demographic changes, advances in social science research and the personal internal psychic changes happening as a result of external modifications to the environment – and vice versa. We can observe that previous assumptions about superiority, normality and behaviour among different peoples have been discarded. Thus we need to hold in mind a provisional understanding of what is at present acceptable as terms and descriptions to describe the diversity of populations. These may not be suitable in the changing landscapes of the future (Alibhai-Brown 1999).

Restricted conceptualisations of culture as a set body of information, something to be learned in order to understand a child or young person better, offer a static model for engaging with all troubled children. It is more useful to think of culture as a process for generating frameworks of perception, a value system and a set of perspectives. Knowledge about culture is not something external to be found, memorised and then utilised. Cultural competence is therefore best understood as engaging in the process of transaction where difference is encountered and we try to evolve our meaning-making skills (Tseng 2002).

A prescribed, normative and superficial notion of large cultural difference leads to an exaggeration of those differences resulting in the psychological concept of 'other' reduced to a simplistic, easily digestible or exotic or degrading stereotype (Holliday 1999). An example from ethnographic research in Southall, West London, revealed that people there had a sophisticated understanding of culture and community. When asked what was meant by culture it became clear that a person could speak and act as a member of a Muslim community in one context, in another take sides against other Muslims as a member of the Pakistani community, and in a third count himself part of the Punjabi community that excluded other Muslims but included Hindus, Sikhs and even Christians (Baumann 1996). Thus a more enlightened concept of culture accepts it is a dynamic, ongoing group process which operates in changing circumstances to enable group members to make sense of and operate meaningfully within those circumstances. For social workers it offers a way of illuminating the full inter-cultural complexity of children and adolescents' lived experience.

Key chapter points

- Cultural competence can initially be understood in the context of a desire to improve social work practice in order to meet the needs of the growing multi-cultural and ethnically diverse society developing around us. Historical and orthodox assumptions about child development need to change to address and respond to the psychological and emotional problems of a modern generation of families.

- Children and young people face considerable challenges in maintaining their cultural integrity in the face of institutional racism, homophobia, economic inactivity or migration patterns. The consequences may lead to significant emotional and psychological problems. The cultural assets of minority children regularly go unrecognised, denied or devalued within the wider community. Children from migrant cultures are especially vulnerable to feelings of inferiority resulting in frustration, anxiety and poor school attainment.

- Social workers can utilise theoretical concepts from social policy and sociology to add to their developmental framework of assessment and explanation for CAMH problems. They enable a social model of mental health to be acknowledged alongside others and therefore more readily advance a culturally competent practice.

- Culture is a constantly evolving entity with an external and internal presence. Any attempt to define it needs to be provisional because children and young people are developing rapidly at many levels of physicality and consciousness. They do so in an equally fast changing and bewildering societal context that sets the scene for our understanding of culture.

- Globalisation maintains unequal power relationships between the richer and poorer countries so that patterns of wealth and consumer consumption in Europe and North America can be sustained. The consequence is the steady and inexorable erosion of traditional markers of indigenous cultural identity combined with the elevation of global branding.

- Combining reflective practice with culturally competent practice, social workers have the opportunity to make a major contribution towards the social policy aspiration of inclusion and anti-oppressive practice. It is possible to define cultural competence as a set of knowledge-based and interpersonal skills that allow individuals to understand, appreciate and work with families of cultures from other than their own.

- Ethnocentric, and particularly Eurocentric, explanations of emotional and psychosocial development are not inclusive enough to understand the development of diverse ethnic minority groups. Failure to understand the cultural background of families can lead to unhelpful CAMH assessments, non-compliance, poor use of services and alienation of the individual or family from the welfare system.

Chapter 9

Understanding Spirituality and Religion

Learning objectives

» Understand the meaning of religion and spirituality as dimensions of emotional well-being.

» Actively consider how to practise in CAMHS in a way that values and respects children and young people's beliefs.

» Incorporate an understanding of the importance of religious and spiritual practices to child and adolescent development.

» Adapt assessment and therapeutic interventions to embrace the diversity of personal and family belief systems.

Introduction

Religion and spirituality are dimensions of mental health and emotional well-being which must be actively considered in order to practise in a useful way. The principles underpinning the psychosocial helping relationship offer a complementary model to build on the capacity for healing that is associated with religious and spiritual experience. They also fit with the concept of personal growth and social justice enshrined in a modern, progressive social work practice. The subject of religion and spirituality has not featured strongly in much of the classic social work literature until quite recently. Perhaps it touches on too many sensitive issues for some social workers or contradicts their personal constructs about society, the causes of problems and the solutions. However, it is a subject of great importance to many children and young people whether they are atheists, agnostics, believers, evangelists or fundamentalists. As part of their lived experience we need to engage in this area and investigate ways in which we can use it to help with mental health problems and emotional well-being.

Religion and spirituality can either be equated or seen as quite distinct concepts. Spirituality, it is argued, refers to one's basic nature and the process of finding meaning and purpose whereas religion involves a set of organised, institutionalised beliefs and social functions as a means of spiritual expression and experience (Carroll 1998). Religion and spirituality have traditionally been separated in their application to an understanding of the human condition in education and training contexts and by qualified social workers. It is as if the human desire and need for recognition in the physical realm and the importance of material worth has to be privileged over all other influences – particularly those that impinge on the realm of the unconscious and psychological. Some go further and suggest that religions typically act to increase anxiety rather than reduce it, or that they are an instrument of oppression and control over women and the poor (Guerin 2002; Sinha 1998).

On the other hand the often criticised Islamic codes of the Qur'an on closer inspection reveal equal rights prescribed for Muslim women in terms of property, education inheritance and employment, far in advance of western statutes. Critics of Catholic teachings regarding female fertility might also applaud the work of Socialist priests in South American dictatorships who are inspired by their Liberation Theology to fight for the emancipation of oppressed people. The complexities and subtleties of different cultural manifestations of relationship dynamics are lost on those relying on religious media stereotypes and deliberately obscured by those seeking to exploit them. The central features of spirituality have been described as:

- *meaning* – the significance of life and deriving purpose in existence

- *transcendence* – experience of a dimension beyond the self that opens the mind

- *value* – standards and beliefs such as value truth, beauty, worth, often discussed as ultimate values

- *connecting* – relationships with others, God or a higher power and the environment

- *becoming* – a life that requires reflection and experience including a sense of who one is and how one knows. (Martslof and Mickley 1998)

These spiritual needs can be understood in psychological terms as well. The conventional literature available to social workers can be used to explain these ideas in many ways using evidence from orthodox science and theories that have stood the test of time and served professionals well. Yet there is a lingering doubt perhaps that on deeper reflection the concepts of faith, purpose and the search for meaning are inadequately quantified in the language of scientific certainty that asserts they are just thought processes or embroidered survival needs. Even in this age of evidence-based practice we know that to ignore our intuitions and gut feelings risks denying us and the children and young people we aspire to help a most valuable tool.

It cannot be coincidental that the further the human race moves towards scientific and rational certainty, aided by the bewildering power of computers and technology able to explore and manipulate the biological foundations of life using genetic research, that people seem more determined than ever to seek answers to fundamental questions about existence whether from organised religions or alternative forms of spirituality. Jung believed that therapists needed to recognise the relevance of spirituality and religious practice to the needs and workings of the human psyche. He suggested that a psychological problem was *in essence* the suffering of a soul which had not discovered its meaning – that the cause of such suffering was spiritual stagnation or psychic sterility. 'Religions are psychotherapeutic systems in the truest sense of the word, and on the grandest scale. They express the whole range of the psychic problem in mighty images; they are the avowal and recognition of the soul, and at the same time the revelation of the soul's nature' (Jung 1978 p.223).

Jung's concept of archetypes suggests that unconscious components of the psyche are revealed through dreams and fantasies at critical points of internal conflict. This transcendent process mediates between oppositional archetypes in order to produce a reconciling symbol. This experience enables children and young people to achieve gradual individuation and the revelation of the self. Some of the central experiences of individuation, such as the hero's journey, the metaphor of death and rebirth or the image of the divine child are paradigms of religious experience (Nash and Stewart 2002). They migrate into myths, fairy stories and legends, as we shall see later, and are therefore accessible for work with troubled children and adolescents.

Activity 9.1

o   Take some time to reflect on your own personal belief systems, religion and/or spirituality.

o   Think about how these beliefs or non-beliefs have shaped and informed your social work practice.

      ◦   Note the disadvantages as well as the advantages.

Commentary

A sense of religion or spirituality has the capacity to inhibit or enhance culturally competent therapeutic work with children or young people. You may feel that an over-reliance on beliefs of this nature is symptomatic of a denial defence and a fatalistic outlook in your clients (Walker 2005). On the other hand you may believe that having faith in something outside themselves permits a child or young person to experience a sense of purpose and greater good that can enhance a therapeutic intervention. As a social worker you may also have religious beliefs or a sense of spirituality that helps you in your therapeutic work. It might also hinder your work if you encounter an atheistic belief system in a young person or a religious affiliation that contradicts your own. The evidence, although yet to be fully developed, does suggest that spirituality has a protective function against developing psychological problems. Children and young people who possess such a sense of spirituality are considered more resilient in the face of traumas, including sexual abuse, and less prone to mental health and adjustment problems in adolescence (Resnik, Harris and Blum 1993; Valentine and Feinauer 1993).

Religion and belief

The relevance to modern social work practice of religion and spirituality must not be underestimated as they form a part of the covert or overt belief systems of children and young people that will to a larger or lesser extent impact on your contribution to their emotional well-being. This is not to say that only those who have a religious faith or a belief in spirituality will be affected. The impact of *not believing* or of having firm ideas about the absence of spiritual feelings can be just as important. What is relevant is the existence of the ideas of religion, gods and spirituality in society and how individuals and families orientate to them – or not. Most cultures can trace back into deep history evidence of their ancestral heritage and the ways early civilisations sought to explain the world around them. These tend to involve the intervention of a supreme being or power with the capacity to control the natural elements vital for the survival of the species.

    We can understand how, without the tools to predict the climate and manipulate food production methods, primitive people thousands of years ago felt vulnerable and frightened by natural phenomena. Seeking explanations for unpredictable events, good or bad, was perfectly natural.

These ancient understandings echo throughout history. They form part of the fabric of world heritage. They have evolved and changed, or in some cases stayed more or less the same (Walker 2005). Settlers in developed countries embrace unorthodox and ancient customs while some native cultures in developing regions absorb modern theological concepts and spiritual practices. There are pockets of Christianity in strict Islamic states and places where minority religious beliefs are persecuted. Thus for many children and young people these frightening experiences will already at this young age have become embedded in their psychological lives ready to be aroused in the future.

The age of enlightenment and the scientific paradigm provided an alternative set of explanations for why things happened as they did. This started a perennial tension between rationalism and religious divinity symbolised in the creationist versus evolutionist debate about the origins of humanity. The polarisation of these two ideas should intrigue the inquisitive practitioner – the need to find extreme opposites to charge an argument or debate might mask deeper ambivalence that is too uncomfortable to bear. In the same way that certain religions seek to claim a single truth or denounce others as *heretical* should serve as useful material for engaging with certain children and young people:

- What meaning does this have for the child's temperament or problem-solving skills?
- What are the advantages and disadvantages for holding such profound beliefs?

The certainty of a person's belief could be measured by the depth of their mixed feelings and/or their absolute terror of the other point of view. Here again we encounter the concept of the other – the opposite which is not part of us and must be avoided, rejected or overwhelmed. In earlier centuries countries went to war and mass murders took place with official sanction on the strength of one's religious beliefs. The history of modern societies has been shaped as much by the religious struggles of previous stages of development as by the economic and political forces motivating people to embark upon social change or revolution. To try to understand these processes better, psychosocial practice would look for the interactive nature between religious development and political and economic movements – how each influences the other. Social workers might formulate an explanation based on the primitive insecurities driving those individuals leading these mass movements and ideologies. One or the other or a combination of the two offers us a therapeutic understanding of these powerfully important contexts within which individual children and young people evolve their own psychic road map.

Today the world is said to be constructed into geopolitical blocks based on economic power and geographical position. But there are equivalent and much more complex *theo-political* blocks which have the capacity to invoke strong feelings and mass change in whole nations or significant sections of them. The large contemporary range of known religions and sects offers evidence of the incredibly rich tapestry of religious material available to incorporate within our comprehension of the enormous culturally diverse world our clients inhabit. It also demonstrates the potential for inter-faith rivalries and the fertile seed bed for those charismatic figures seeking to influence young people towards a religious and spiritual certainty that claims priority over all others. As with any strong belief, when it turns into obsession it has the potential for great destructiveness.

Culture and spirituality

The decline of organised religious expression in the western world has been documented in recent years and to some extent is blamed for the increasing prevalence of emotional and behavioural problems in children and young people, a generation supposedly without moral guidance or social values, according to reactionary pundits. But what is less well documented is the evidence that experiences of the sacred or spiritual remain widespread especially among children (Cobb and Robshaw 1998). Evidence suggests a strong underlying belief system in young people in the concept of spirituality – even by avowed atheists. Spirituality goes beyond the narrow definition of religion and offers a different and arguably *more difficult* paradigm within which to understand the troubles of children and young people. There are identifying characteristics that can help us in our therapeutic work but with such diverse meanings and interpretations that it is hard to be certain about what spirituality is, how it can be defined and whether there are universally accepted categories (Swinton 2003).

We are in effect entering an aspect of children's experience that transcends description and is difficult to express adequately in words. The very nature of the spiritual is inexpressible because it springs from the innermost depths of the human experience. If we are to engage with the religious and spiritual aspects of children and young people's culture then we need to find a way of accessing this rich reservoir of material within which important therapeutic work is ready to be done. The orthodox medical model, whether employed by clinicians or adhered to by parents/carers, may frame a child's psychological difficulties in a biopsychosocial formulation that encapsulates all the intrinsic and extrinsic variables thought to explain the problem. But when working in a culturally competent manner we need to consider the various ways different cultures conceptualise psychological problems and if that means using a spiritual explanatory framework then so be it.

The recent ban on girls wearing the hijab at school in France has served to illustrate the potential destructiveness in the underlying tensions between the former colonial countries and their legacies of immigration and cultural diversity. The French state education system reflects the secular model of society created in the aftermath of the revolution. The strict separation of religion from the state has provided the context in which the wearing of the hijab is perceived as a religious symbol and therefore disallowed in school. Following the French example some schools in the UK have also banned the wearing of the hijab. For some girls this may represent an attack upon their religion and result in considerable anxiety and depression. Evidence suggests that the wearing of the hijab in western societies is a complex act involving a desire to remain within their tradition and to challenge it at the same time while also seeking to create a space for equality (Ghuman 2004).

If a child or young person, from whatever culture, has a belief system that accepts and takes account of a spiritual dimension then, rather than *pathologising* this, a social worker needs to reflect on how this meaning may be affecting the problem concerned. It could be part of the problem, it could be maintaining the problem, it could be stopping matters getting worse or it could offer a way out of the problem. Resisting the impulse to make untested and unfounded assumptions may be hard but bearing uncertainty and keeping open all possibilities will be more helpful in the long run. Spirituality can be seen as an intra, inter and transpersonal experience that is shaped and directed by the experiences of individuals and of the communities within which they live out their lives (Swinton 2003).

An example to illustrate this is provided by the development of the Family Group Conference approach to child welfare in New Zealand which is based on a cultural-religious indigenous concept among Maori people emphasising the relationship between celestial and terrestrial knowledge. The origin of the Family Group Conference was, according to Maori belief, a rebellious initiative by the children of Ranginui the great Sky Father, and Papatuanuku, the matriarch Earth Mother. Protected in a darkened cocoon by their parents the children desired freedom to explore the outer limits of the universe. The family conference that was convened included close and distant relatives and grandparents who were all regarded as part of a single spiritual and economic unity (Fulcher 1999). Thus each Maori child's cultural identity is explicitly connected to their genealogy or *whakapapa*.

The Family Group Conference is now being incorporated into mainstream child protection and adult mental health services in the UK, where extended family members are invited to participate in care planning.

Child development

Children and young people have the capacity to conjure feelings of faith and hope when experiencing emotional and psychological distress. Myths, legends and fairy stories as part of their early child development offer a rich source of material to draw from and enlist in direct work. Fairies often act in a healing capacity in mythology, or appear as agents between the world of human affairs and the invisible forces of nature (Williams 1997). They possess powers in advance of mortals, achieving superhuman tasks, but they can also run into trouble and sometimes rely on assistance from humans to succeed.

The Oedipus legend demonstrates the way that counselling and therapeutic practices can make use of legends, fairy stories and myths. In this example the legend serves to illustrate the unconscious struggles taking place in a child's development. Fairy stories in particular can be used to engage children when conventional ordinary dialogue is inadequate or unsuccessful at promoting therapeutic engagement and process. If we accept that childhood tales form a building block in the construction of the child's fantasy world and therefore their personality development then this offers an opportunity to understand the variety of meanings and influences contained therein at many levels. Myths are poetic tales explaining why the world is the way it is and why people behave the way they do. They usually involve gods and goddesses or spirits. Legends are stories about events that may or may not have taken place a long time ago.

The fairy realm is a central aspect of cultures all over the world yet until very recently mainstream school and young person's literature reflected a narrow spectrum of examples from a Eurocentric base. Classic tales read in classrooms or appearing in popular culture on television or in annual pantomimes such as Jack and the Beanstalk, Cinderella or Puss in Boots can neglect the rich diversity of stories from around the world. Aladdin, for example, while incorporated into mainstream pantomime is actually one of the *Arabian Nights* stories told over 1001 nights by Sheherazade to King Shahryar, part of a lost collection of Persian tales from circa AD 850.

Specific fairies are identified with spiritual qualities of flowers and herbs, echoing back to a time when humans were more connected to the land and nature. In mainly agricultural and developing countries where industrialisation has not fully trampled over traditional beliefs and practices, the link between the spiritual and earthly realms is closer (Reed 2002). Centuries of traditional practices have been passed on. From a narrow western perspective this might seem backward, ignorant or downright dangerous if faith is put in spiritual or herbal remedies for the treatment of serious illness. Yet in recent years there has been an explosion of interest in developed countries in natural remedies, herbalism and complementary medicine.

There are studies of folklore contained in holy books such as the Qur'an, Torah and Bible where proverbs, parables and surah are used to convey powerful religious truths (Dundes 2003). There is increasing evidence of the power of faith as an important variable in the prognosis for a variety of medical conditions and alternative or complementary medicine is increasingly being incorporated in public health provision. Homeopathic and herbal medicines are a huge business and, at the very least, testimony to people's appetite for solutions that are unconventional and perhaps more mystical than orthodox scientific cures.

Activity 9.2

○ In partnership with a colleague consider the question: Is there a point at which a child develops a sense of spirituality?

○ How can you use western orthodox developmental theories to explain or challenge your assumptions?

Commentary

One of the central tenets of religious belief is that of death and a belief in an afterlife. Jung considered that belief in an afterlife was important for mental health whereas Freud suggested it was an unhealthy denial. In the context of the rise in self-harming behaviours and suicide rates among young men and the life-threatening risks in anorexia nervosa it is clear that the subject of death and its connection with belief or lack of belief in an afterlife must be an important variable. The terms intrinsic and extrinsic religiousness have been coined in order to define the complexities behind religious belief more closely. Intrinsic religiousness is characterised by a young person extending their beliefs beyond acts of worship into every aspect and behaviour in their life. It is foundational to their concept of self. However, a young person with extrinsic religiousness is motivated by a self-serving instrumental approach to life that uses religion to provide status and social support. It has been compared to a neurosis in the sense that it is a defence against anxiety whereas intrinsic religiousness makes for positive mental health (Paloutzian 1996).

Until about the age of ten children are generally understood to be unable to grasp abstract concepts. If we accept the more abstract and non-literal aspects of religion then it follows that before that age religious education in schools is failing to connect with children. This has to some extent been acknowledged in studies examining difficulties in establishing in-school educational programmes aimed at tackling social exclusion and using religious studies as a means to enhance cultural respect (Jackson 2004; Larsen and Plesner 2002). Recent evidence suggests that religious education in schools is now a focus for policy makers seeking to increase understanding and respect between children of different religions or world views that foster knowledge about and respect for freedom of religion or belief as a human right (Jackson 2003). It is argued that older school children can demonstrate *metacultural* competence in classroom discussion about different religions by developing their ability to handle new and unfamiliar cultural material with skill and sensitivity (Leganger-Krogstad 2000).

However, this relies on a narrow definition of religious development and cognitive capacity. Perhaps the concept of spiritual development enables us to begin to understand that such a process begins at a much earlier stage of development when children are trying to make sense of the multiplicity of sensations and experiences bombarding them. The cognitive complexity in religious language is more a barrier to children's spiritual expression, and in order for us to understand it better we need to learn how to listen to the language of children and young people, within which is ample spiritual expression. Studies of children's spirituality using cross-cultural and multi-faith samples confirm the profound nature of spirituality and that spirituality is not only about what children talk about but also how they talk, act or feel about all sorts of things (Coles 1990; Hay 1990). It is important to bear the following points in mind when seeking to assess whether religion and spirituality are relevant to your work with a child or young person:

- Don't initiate discussion about religion – this will invariably elicit learned facts rather than the natural associated images and metaphors actually used by children.

- Accept that children may spontaneously introduce religious or spiritual concepts consistent with heightened states of awareness similar to meditational experiences.

- Create accepting conditions and an open environment to encourage the child to speak freely without censure or dismissal.

- Respect and value the child's religious beliefs and statements in order to reinforce the validity of expressing a personal point of view.

- In some situations you can initiate discussion about spirituality as a way of demonstrating that the conventional secular taboo which suppresses these matters can be challenged. This may encourage the child to share their most private and confusing thoughts in other areas of life.

Research in the area of development and spirituality has produced a useful three-stage model of faith development that can be matched against developmental stages to enable you to orientate your therapeutic process conceptually:

TABLE 9.1 FOWLER'S STAGES OF CHILDREN'S FAITH DEVELOPMENT

Stage	Age	Characteristics
One	3–7	Children live in worlds of fantasy; images, mood, story, action and examples. To move out of this, they need to develop rational thinking and a distinction between fantasy and reality
Two	7–11	Mythic-literal stage. Story is of central importance; fairness and justice are central concerns. Children may become convinced of their exceptional goodness/badness
Three	11–18	Synthetic-conventional faith. To reach this, children need good personal relationships and more awareness of the larger environment

Source: Fowler, Nipkow and Schweitzer 1991

Psychology, religion and spirituality

The western model of psychological illness tends to ignore the religious or spiritual aspects of the culture in which it is based. However, Eastern, African and Native American cultures tend to integrate them (Fernando 2002). Spirituality and religion as topics in general do not feature often in the therapeutic literature, yet they can be critical components of a child and young person's psychological well-being, offering a source of strength and hope in trying circumstances. Children for whom family and faith backgrounds are inseparable may need encouragement to feel comfortable in multi-faith settings. You need to address this dimension as part of the constellation of factors affecting children and adolescents, bearing in mind the positive, and sometimes negative, impact spiritual or religious beliefs might have on their mental health. It is well understood that children communicate about feelings and experiences more easily through responses to stories. Direct work that allows them to use their *imaginations* and access their own spirituality through stories can be liberating.

The therapeutic value of western individualistic concepts is incomplete in attempting to alleviate suffering and alienation for those young people whose origins reflect a more humanitarian philosophy characteristic of collectivist and land-base cultural groups. Beatch and Stewart (2002) in their work with Aboriginal communities in the Canadian Arctic show how significant problems related to depression, addiction and family violence are linked with cultural loss through colonisation, environmental destruction and assimilation of western influences. Aboriginal healing includes strengthening cultural belonging, identity and community-based self determination. Indigenous outlooks indicate a preference for ecological systems, holistic processes, belonging at the community level and reliance on traditional beliefs and values. A culturally competent approach embracing this context requires practitioners using counselling and psychotherapeutic skills to adapt and synthesise their work with prevailing indigenous ideas in order to maximise effectiveness.

Multiple caregiving of young children in Australian aboriginal culture has attracted concerns based on western notions of attachment theory and the need for secure attachment relationships with primary carers. However, this concept is inappropriate when we consider that research has demonstrated that Aboriginal children can sustain and thrive with multiple attachment figures that are wholly consistent with societal norms (Yeo 2003). Indeed, there are sometimes lengthy absences by parents, related to important sacred initiations or religious ceremonies necessary for the child or young person's spiritual development. These findings resonate with research in the UK and elsewhere studying the developmental progress of Black children raised in single parent households with multiple attachment figures (Daycare Trust 2000).

In South American countries the influence of the Catholic church and family planning combined with poverty, a history of military dictatorships and a culture of *machismo* has produced a culture of extreme social inequality where children can easily drift into prostitution, child labour or become homeless. In these conditions authoritarian family structures create a climate where domestic violence thrives (Ravazzola 1997). Here Liberation Theology translates Christian concepts into activity that challenges the prevailing order, offering hope of better circumstances and prospects through revolutionary struggle. Children and young people can thus link religion with empowerment and liberation from inequitable and socially unjust conditions.

Activity 9.3

○ Review the material above and consider whether it is possible to draw together the knowledge, theories and ideas from diverse communities and define some common characteristics.

Commentary

Children and young people may well wonder about religion and spirituality either directly or indirectly. They may encounter friends, family members or others for whom such beliefs are an intrinsic part of their lives. In our work as social workers these people may well enter into the conversations and reflections ventilated by children. This could trigger an interesting exploration by the child or adolescent about the meaning of life or a search for the answer to the question: what is religion? Your own perspective and theoretical orientation will guide you in considering how to respond:

• Do you take this literally or metaphorically?

• Do you enable the client to speculate, describe their hidden fears about such matters or suggest an interpretation that seeks to address underlying dilemmas or conflicts around the issue?

The following list attempts to bring forward a definition or to describe the common characteristics of religions around the world:

• They look for the something else or somebody beyond the world of senses and scientific measurement. This something or somebody controls all.

• They have great figures, men of vision who seem to perceive the something else more than other people.

• They all express themselves in the written word trying to encapsulate what they believe in.

• Each religion gives to its own people advice on how to behave and what to do to draw close to the something else or somebody.

• Religions are often practised by people coming together in common worship at special places.

• Religions often bring people together at special times for particular celebrations.

• All religions hold special funeral ceremonies and grapple with the problem of whether there is life after death. (Whiting 1999)

The inner world of the child

Research findings that explored the concept of spirituality with several groups of school-age children, some of whom held deep religious convictions and others who belonged to no formal religion, discovered that it is rare to come across a child who does not have at least an *implicit spirituality*. Even in the most resolutely secular boy evidences of spiritual sensitivity emerge, sometimes through self-contradiction, allusive metaphor or through Freudian slips of the tongue. Our task is not to detect the presence of spirituality, but to understand how it becomes suppressed or repressed during the process of growing up (Hay 1990).

Four core qualities of spiritual experience have been identified: awareness, mystery, value and meaningfulness/insight. They are often assumed to be consistent with positive life-affirming experiences. However, children who experience wonder, awe and mystery can quickly become distressed and fearful – even terrified if a secure and stable main carer is not available to contain those negative feelings. Many religions contain concepts of hell and punishment which could trigger profound feelings of despair that are experienced as completely overwhelming physically and psychologically.

Sin is defined variously in many religions and for a child or young person comes with the sense of failing to be satisfactory, for example, from early toileting experiences through to exam performance or adolescent sexuality. The sense of sin and failure is quickly transformed into guilt and shame resulting in feelings of depression, distress and despair unless there is some balancing influence. Children and young people without this balancing experience and with deficits in their environment and personal temperament are likely to develop mental health problems at the time or later on in life. It is easy for children to feel that they are failing or cannot fit easily into the world. This is the opposite of spiritual experiences of value, insight and relatedness. A persistent sense of sinfulness or failure prevents the development of healthy relationships (Crompton 1996).

This is illustrated in the story of the Hindu god Krishna, who was very naughty as a small boy. When he was accused of eating dirt, his foster mother Yasoda ordered him to open his mouth. When he did so she became terrified at the sight she beheld, revealing as it did the eternal Universe. Krishna understood that such knowledge would be harmful to Yasoda so he erased her memory of all she had witnessed. This tale illustrates how awareness and closeness to the divine can be potentially overpowering or harmful. A sense of connection to the supreme being in religion can be mediated through a connection with nature and the environment.

If children witness the harm being done to the environment or face the threat of war, they can become very anxious. What do children and young people make of the increasing deterioration of their environment and lurid tabloid tales about the greenhouse effect and extreme weather events? Do they see this as the retribution of a powerful god punishing humanity for spoiling a once pristine planet offered to us as a habitat? And are those teachers and parents lecturing them about the virtues of conservation and recycling instilling a sense of guilt masquerading as virtue?

Children involved in war as victims or forced combatants are deprived of the enjoyment of spiritual rights. Research demonstrates the severe and enduring mental health problems experienced by refugee and asylum seekers from areas of conflict (Hodes 2000). Social workers can utilise spiritual beliefs in helping children recover from dehumanising and traumatising atrocities by enabling the expression of terror and fearfulness through reconnecting them with their prevailing religious constructs, which may have been abandoned. However, some of these children may have a strong sense of guilt inherited from a religious belief system that blamed humanity for the death of Jesus. The death of parents, siblings or close relatives may have resonated with these inherent guilt feelings, compounding them into a persecutory frame of mind. Therapists need to be careful with evoking a religious construct that could inadvertently exaggerate already troubling feelings.

The link between spirituality and psychosocial practice is emphasised if we enlist an understanding of spirituality that suggests it is the outward expression of the inner workings of the human spirit. In other words it is a personal and social process that refers to the ideas, concepts, attitudes and behaviours that derive from a child, a young person's or a community's interpretation of their experiences of the spirit. It is intrapersonal in that it refers to the quest for inner connectivity and it is interpersonal in that it relates to the relationships between people and within communities. And it is transpersonal in so far as it reaches beyond self and others into the transcendent realms of experience that move beyond that which is available at a mundane level (Swinton 2003).

Therapy and cultural belief

Therapeutic work with children and young people will amongst other things address the belief system of the individual and/or their family. Belief in this sense usually means exploring the client's beliefs about their problem as the start of establishing a helping relationship. The client may believe that their problem/s are the result of divine intervention – a punishment for a sin or misdemeanour of some kind. Among some cultures there is a potent belief system that spirits can possess people and make them unwell or be invoked to help them with a problem. In the case of a child or young person who is causing concern among teachers, social workers or health professionals there may be a simple diagnosis or assessment of the cause of the problem but this may not fit with the family's beliefs about the cause.

However, belief also relates to religion and spirituality. If you are unable or unwilling to explore this aspect of belief then you may be missing a vital component of the individual or family's overall belief system about how the world works and how problems arise and, more importantly, what is likely to be effective treatment (Walker 2005). The key is to open communication and seek a greater depth to your understanding of the way the family works. An example from *The Arabian Nights* illustrates one of the central themes in fairy tales that are common to many cultures and relate directly to children's experiences and beliefs about the power adults hold over them. 'The Fisherman and the Jinny' tells the story of a poor fisherman who hauls in his net four times. The first three times there is no catch but on the fourth occasion he hauls up a copper jar which when opened reveals a huge jinny (genie) that threatens to kill him. Thinking very quickly the fisherman starts to flatter the jinny, telling him how powerful and strong and clever he is. The jinny feels good about this. Then the fisherman asks the jinny to demonstrate his powers of transformation by changing into a mouse. This he does and as quick as he can the fisherman grabs the mouse and pushes it into the copper jar which is sealed and thrown back into the sea.

The story illustrates to a child precisely those feelings of powerlessness and awe when faced with an adult figure who can behave in a threatening oppressive manner. The transformative capacity can be seen as representative of adults who can change quickly in their mood but who are also in some way dependent on the child's behaviour. Ultimately it might give a child hope to learn through the story that through persistence and hard work a reward is possible although the reward (in this example the copper jar) turns out to be tainted. Finally a child is shown that with a sharp wit and quick thinking a powerful threatening figure can be brought down to size and contained safely. This might relate to a parental figure, school bully or a sibling.

There is the potential for a rich and sophisticated understanding of the interplay between psychosocial principles and a more explicit acknowledgement of a spiritual dimension to child and adolescent psychological health. Epidemiological studies provide a raft of orthodox explanations for emotional and behavioural problems encountered by children and young people but they neglect the possibility that difficulties may occur from responses to their *spiritual environment*. Recently the popular diagnostic manual of mental illnesses included the category of spiritual disorder for the first time (DSM IV; American Psychiatric Association 1994). However, the implication was that this area represented a threat to a young person's psychological health – overlooking the positive effects of spiritual health. This ought to provoke our curiosity and at the very least enable us to reflect on the constructs and assumptions that informed this new development in the influential psychiatric literature.

The notion of a special place has been identified in research with children that signifies a potent context for reflection. It may be a church, mosque, synagogue, temple or even a tree, or gang den. The association children and young people have with this special place can be interpreted as an actual or desirable place within themselves seeking peace and contentment. The issue of place has not been explored at any depth in the literature in this area, and further research with children and young people into rituals, creativity and social action is needed.

In a developed spirituality, affinity with particular places, expressing one's creativity, participation in rituals or being involved in social action may be merely outward signs of some deeper internal processes of feeling connected with others, including a god or other deity (Crisp 2008). Using this concept therapeutically opens up another avenue for practitioners who seek to explore the inner world of children and young people. It can relate to the notion of the secure attachment base or even a fantasy of returning to the womb and an infantile state. Older children may feel this concept is beneath them and will be most resistant to exploring this special place but younger children who maintain a more active sense of imagination and magic may be more open to working in this psychic space.

A recurring theme associated with relationship issues as the source of some problems is that of trust. Children learn the benefits of developing trusting relationships but also the hurt and pain of a betrayal of trust. These can be related to parental abuse or neglect or a school friend's disclosure of a promised secret. Thus trust contains an element of hope in something intangible beyond a reassurance or school yard bargain. If children can connect with a sense of trust in some kind of transcendent benevolent power such as a god then this too can be a fruitful area for exploration of their own vulnerability, limitations and dependence (Crompton 1996).

The importance of spirituality is illustrated when we appreciate for example that spirituality is the cornerstone of the Aboriginal identity. Australian aboriginal spiritual tradition places the origin of each Aboriginal clan in its own land. These clans hold deep spiritual links with their lands which were formed in Dreamtime. The ancestral creative beings that travelled across the continent at the beginning of time established land boundaries between different Aboriginal clans and the sacred sites. Ritual obligations and religious ceremonies are carried out at these sites in order to reinforce the bond Aboriginal people feel to their lands. If they move from the land or it is taken from them they lose their cultural identity and self-esteem (Yeo 2003). Psychological problems have been linked with the Australian government policy of forced removal of people from Aboriginal lands (Human Rights Commission 1997).

A powerful argument is advanced by several authors who recommend incorporating a more explicit acknowledgement of the role that religion and spirituality can play in our work. A recent study found that the cost of not taking religious and cultural beliefs into account resulted directly in lack of attendance at specialist CAMH services. Insisting on holding certain support sessions on set days and times meant that some Muslim children could not benefit from appointments because they were expected to attend mosque after school (Jayarajan 2001).

Activity 9.4

○   Consider how often religion and spirituality are mentioned in relation to your clients in general.

○   Are these aspects or non-aspects of their lives taken into account when undertaking assessment and reviewing strengths and resources?

○   How active are you in mentioning these topics when engaging in work with children and young people?

The concept of postmodernism and its reductionist thesis for deconstruction of scientific or non-empirical certainties has gained significance in social work and should be placed alongside other intellectual resources with which we can analyse the context of children and young people's lives. The thesis is challenged by an appeal to that which is ignored or rendered silent. In essence it is argued that because postmodernism emphasises separation and groundlessness in a context whereby *every prevailing orthodoxy* is questioned, people are paradoxically developing an appetite for community and connection. Moules (2000) suggests that we exist beyond our cultural creation and interpretations and need to learn from diversity connection through variety – to learn from the uncertainty of knowledge but not to deny any knowledge.

In order to respond to this dilemma and enable social workers to harness positive aspects of religion and spirituality in their work a theory of multi-cultural therapy has been advanced that offers a multi-dimensional paradigm to guide practice (Raval 1996; Sue *et al.* 1996). The authors suggest that:

- It is necessary to have a meta-theory of counselling and psychotherapy to allow different theoretical models to be applied and integrated where possible.

- Both counsellor and client identities are formed and embedded in multiple levels of life experiences and contexts, therefore treatment should take greater account of the child or young person's experience in relation to their context.

- The cultural identity development of the counsellor and client, and the wider power differentials associated with this, play an important role in the therapeutic relationship.

- Multi-cultural counselling and therapy effectiveness is enhanced when the counsellor uses modalities and defines goals consistent with the life experiences and cultural values of the client.

- The theory stresses the importance of multiple helping roles developed by many cultural groups and societies. Apart from the one-to-one encounter aimed at remediation in the individual, those roles often involve larger social units, system intervention and prevention.

Multi-cultural counselling and therapy helps the child or young person develop a greater awareness about themselves in relation to their different contexts. This results in practice that is contextual in orientation and which is able respectfully to draw on traditional methods of healing with a spiritual or religious dimension from many cultures. Paul Tillich (1963) alluded to this when he described something called *theonomy*, meaning the *pursuit of culture under the impact of spiritual presence,* a liberal humanism with an underlying spiritual depth.

It is perhaps a paradox that the decline of organised religion in white western societies combined with the consequences of previous imperialist expansion throughout the world has produced a growing culturally diverse population among which are large numbers of devout religious communities with highly developed spiritual belief systems that organise social behaviour. Pundits, politicians and policy makers are quick to pronounce on the state of young people and increases in anti-social behaviour among disaffected and disadvantaged young white people, frequently blaming the absence of religious values and moral standards. Yet they are at the same time witnessing a growth in ethnic minority religious and spiritual affiliation resulting in social, psychological and educational attainment. Modern, progressive social work practice aspires to understand and support both groups of children and young people to help them make sense of their beliefs or lack of them in terms of vulnerability or resistance to mental health problems.

Key chapter points

- The relevance of religion and spirituality must not be underestimated as they form a part of the covert or overt belief systems of children and young people that will to a larger or lesser extent impact on your work.

- Most cultures can trace deep evidence of their ancestral heritage and the ways early civilisations sought to explain the world around them. These tend to involve the intervention of a supreme being or power, with the capacity to control the natural elements vital for the survival of the species.

- The history of modern societies has been shaped as much by the religious struggles of previous stages of development as by the economic and political forces motivating people to embark upon social change or revolution. A psychosocial model offer us an interpersonal and intrapsychic therapeutic understanding of these powerfully important contexts within which individual children and young people evolve their emotional well-being.

- The western model of psychological illness tends to ignore the religious or spiritual aspects of the culture in which it is based. However, Eastern, African and Native American cultures tend to integrate them. Spirituality and religion can be critical components of a child and young person's psychological well-being, offering a source of strength and hope in trying circumstances. This dimension is part of the constellation of factors affecting children and adolescents, bearing in mind the positive and sometimes negative impact spiritual or religious beliefs might have on their mental health.

- Four core qualities of spiritual experience have been identified: awareness, mystery, value and meaningfulness/insight. They are often assumed to be consistent with positive life-affirming experiences. However, children who experience wonder, awe and mystery can quickly become distressed and fearful – even terrified if a secure and stable main carer is not available to contain those negative feelings. Many religions contain concepts of hell and punishment which could trigger profound feelings of despair that are experienced as completely physically and psychologically overwhelming.

- There is the potential for a rich and sophisticated understanding of the interplay between social work principles and a more explicit acknowledgement of a spiritual dimension to child and adolescent psychological health.

- Children are creative in providing a potent context for reflection – it may be a church, mosque, synagogue, temple or even a tree or gang den. Using this concept therapeutically opens up another avenue for practitioners who seek to explore the inner world of children and young people.

Conclusion

Be a realist – demand the impossible.
Ernesto 'Che' Guevara

Introduction

Despite at least ten years of renewed interest and activity in the development of services for children and young people at risk of developing or experiencing mental health problems and threats to their emotional well-being, a recent National Review reported several worrying findings in late 2008:

- unacceptable variation in service provision

- administrative and organisational barriers to holistic planning

- long-standing problems for particularly vulnerable children. (DfCSF 2008)

The review called for the creation of initial training, local commissioning boards and improved transition to adult services. A National Advisory Council was set up to help progress improvements, but this Council has no power of enforcement; it is only an advisory body without teeth or power to effect change really to improve services for troubled children and young people. These findings should be of no surprise to professional social work staff who have spent considerable time and energy in advocating better service provision in this neglected area, but it is no less disappointing.

This book echoes the review findings and offers evidence and resources to progress matters and assist practitioners to make a difference to the lives of individuals, families and communities affected by CAMH problems. This final chapter will consider and reflect upon a diverse range of knowledge and research evidence from some of the leading practitioners in this complex area of work, in order to try to collate and summarise important data to help inform your understanding and practice. These questions have been posed to help us focus on some core practice issues:

What are the causes of CAMH?

Rutter (2005) raises a number of cautions and caveats about the interpretation of research data and taking too simple a view of what are, intrinsically, very complex, often inter-related causal factors in relation to young people's mental health. He identifies two fundamental aspects of causation that should not be confused:

- *individual differences*: in the liability to develop difficulties, in the course of those difficulties and in the extent to which they recur

- *group differences*: as, for example, between the sexes (asking why a certain increase is greater amongst men than women) or between different ethnic groups.

Outcome research must also look at the influence of the context and environment on an individual; at why a susceptibility to difficulty actually translates into, for example, a mental health problem or anti-social act. Researchers must watch for the interplay between risk factors: causal effects don't necessarily add up and most causes are multi-factorial. When considering causal hypotheses, researchers typically identify the risk indicator and ask how it operates. Rutter notes that parental loss is associated with depression, but it is the *impaired parenting* that follows the loss that triggers the depression, not the loss itself. Other considerations when posing causal hypotheses are:

- *Relative position versus absolute effects* – education is a protective factor but is it helpful in itself or just within one's immediate peer group?

- *Social selection versus social influence* – is the key factor the environment, or the factors that lead people into that environment?

- *Genetic versus environmental mediation* – studies show that both parental education and parental depression influence the likelihood of mental health outcomes for children and in both the genetic effect will be mediated by the environment.

What could constitute plausible hypotheses for the increase in mental health problems among the young? The UK has seen an increase in family disruption, in educational expectations and demand for scholastic credentials, in major decision-making (e.g. drugs, sex) and in prolongation of financial dependence on parents. Environmental factors could include greater cultural conflict, media images at odds with reality, toxins and pollutants, greater affluence and a decline in social cohesion and responsibility. To counterbalance these, society offers more attentive support opportunities, both targeted (family support, youth justice, less tolerance of child abuse) and universal (health visitors, pre-school provision). The following opportunities to prevent problems developing and foster early intervention are:

- *universal* – health visitors; pre-school provision; school
- *community* – attention to sexual health; attention to availability of drugs and alcohol
- *targeted* – avoidance of youth incarceration wherever reasonable; focus on evidence-based practice and its availability
- *family support interventions* – better responses to child abuse/ neglect; greater status and rewards for childcare.

Until relatively recently the different theoretical approaches to understanding the origin of children's mental health problems existed in isolation from each other. When brought together they were more likely to lead to competitive discussion and rivalry than thoughtful reflection and critical analysis. The polarised nature versus nurture debate is largely in the past and the inter-relationships between those factors associated with child developmental outcomes are now widely acknowledged to be complex. We have moved far away from assuming that factors associated with risk are necessarily the direct cause of problems. Likewise we no longer consider risk factors alone without also taking into account factors that promote resilience in children and young people. Simplistic statements that promote single causes of mental health problems in children, whether it be the role of diet, poverty, genes or other relevant associated factors, are misleading (Jezzard 2005).

Is there a consensus emerging on the causes of CAMH problems?

- Individual differences are important: people react differently to similar stimuli that can be social, biochemical or environmental. Some of these individual differences may be genetically influenced.

- Nature versus nurture is a false dichotomy – too many factors intervene to alter possible or probable causal pathways. Our genes merely determine predispositions, not precise outcomes.

- We need to take far more seriously the associative connections that undoubtedly exist between mind and body, which seem to be stronger than many suppose.

- What children eat (nutrition) and our perceptions of and reactions to stress (cortisol and its aftermath) undoubtedly affect the biochemistry of their brains and bodies in fundamental ways. This is likely to affect behaviour patterns and control mechanisms (impulsivity).

- When identifying solutions, it is vital to differentiate between the predicament/environment of a particular individual and that of the group (age, area, socio-economic status, ethnicity).

- The origins of mental health issues in adults will invariably lie in past experiences.

- Socio-economic status can have a profound impact on individual behaviour, for a range of different reasons, and these must be assessed carefully.

- Mental health problems and disorders can be viewed as the outcome of impaired, delayed or otherwise inhibited normal healthy development, as a rational yet often dysfunctional reaction to a difficult or challenging context, and as a dysfunctional, more extreme manifestation of an otherwise normal and functional state of mind.

What follows is an attempt to explore in greater depth the overlap between different professional perspectives, whether it is possible to synthesise some of these and explore the potential for further agreement in understanding the possible causes of mental health problems and prospects for emotional well-being in young people.

Time trends and vulnerability to mental health problems

Adolescence might be better understood less as a discrete event and more as a period during which earlier difficulties that may have been either hidden or manageable hitherto become exposed or re-exposed. If adolescence is turbulent largely because of the identity crisis elicited by the physical, neurobiological and hormonal changes, one can suppose that a robust pre-adolescent sense of self will provide some protection. The pre-teen years (8–12 years) are increasingly understood to be a crucial time for the crystallisation of identity that, from about the age of eight, encompasses gender, social acceptability and competence.

Children take their view of themselves, informed by their treatment within the family, and test this on the world outside (friends, peers and teachers). Their stronger bodies and more reflective and capable minds provide the chance to improve their range of skills and competence. But if they have no mother or father on whom to model themselves, if their self-image at the start of this period is negative or is undermined during this important stage, if they have few opportunities to develop interests and skills that fuel pride or to practise autonomy, or if they have poor relationship and attachment experiences, then their ability either to do well in school or to form good friendships can be compromised, with potentially devastating consequences. Even those who have no special problems face more intense academic, social and commercial pressures that can shake self-belief.

Resilience and risk factors – a critical assessment

Resilience is an important theoretical concept as it encompasses the complexity of causal factors. It acknowledges, for example, the influence of both social and environmental factors and individual differences and identifies what helps individuals to cope and what increases the risk that they will not. It also accepts that a particular, perhaps unexpected, event, when added to other earlier or concurrent difficulties apparently coped with, can trigger a behavioural or emotional crisis, while as an isolated event it may not have done so. Resilience arises out of a belief in one's own sense of agency, the ability to deal with change and a repertoire of social and problem-solving skills (Rutter 2005).

Having a sense of agency and a coherent narrative of personal history that makes sense of the world are both necessary for the formation of a sound identity. The resilience framework does not, however, address causation in depth. This raises a danger that the associated protective and risk factors are given undue prominence in policy, with the more telling underlying causal factors or relationships, contextual influences and implications insufficiently appreciated. Personal characteristics that protect individuals (secure attachment, average to high intelligence, good communication, planning and problem-solving skills, humour, reflective capacity, religious faith and easy temperament) are largely inter-related.

A secure attachment will encourage easy communication, reflection and, because the future (based on past experience) feels safe, the inclination to think ahead, sequence actions, plan and develop a 'can-do' approach to anticipated problems. If a child is not securely attached, s/he is more likely to feel that their very sense of self is under threat. Living in and for the moment, s/he will have little room for reflection, and consequently less space to feel concern for others (which is crucially important for the development of a rounded and whole personality).

Risk factors include features such as poverty, low IQ, poor educational achievement, harsh discipline, parental conflict and a poor environment. Poverty is likely to be problematic not in itself, but because the stresses it creates can lead to poor parenting. It might, however, also be possible that where parents as individuals have deep relationship difficulties, poor capacity for reflection and empathy, volatile reactions to perceived threat and profound self-doubt, this contributes to poor educational outcomes, intermittent work patterns and consequential inadequate income flow.

Simply increasing family income, without addressing individual and family experiences, relationships and interactions (e.g. family violence or serial partnering) that can trigger disengagement and poverty, may not reduce the social, health and educational problems that are typically associated with low income. In the context of mental health, protective factors help to deliver feelings of security, significance and connection, whereas risk factors tend to contribute towards the opposite: feelings of insecurity, insignificance and isolation. Such feelings can lead young people to form negative views of themselves, and it is these beliefs which underlie much mental distress.

How much does food and diet affect behaviour and emotional well-being?

There is considerable public and professional interest in what role food has in mitigating mental health problems or in exacerbating latent predisposition. But focusing exclusively on food and diet is inadequate in pursuing solutions to multiple and complex emotional and mental health problems in young people. There is growing interest in the effect of diet on behaviour in the national debate on school dinners, but nutritional improvements at one meal a day only during term time will not be a panacea for dealing with classroom disruption. Naturally, hungry children will concentrate less well, as will those fired up on sugar.

Those not receiving essential nutrients may be more impulsive or think more slowly, and mood, application and thinking processes may improve when recommended proportions of fatty acids are present in the diet. Dietary improvements could have an exponential effect on learning, given that much learning is incremental, and could help children to 'catch up' optimally on some aspects of development during periods of neural plasticity, when the brain is programmed to be receptive to stimuli and restructure.

In addition, if the debate also encourages families to cook more fresh food and eat together more frequently, this could help children to feel more cared for, and so raise their confidence and competence further. Nevertheless, it is hard to see how diet might offset totally the effects of early and prolonged harsh discipline, serial family disruption, trauma or neglect. Disruptive behaviour has many different causes because young children have few ways to express complex feelings such as frustration, boredom, anger, fear, dejection, jealousy and a need for attention. Some equally troubled children become excessively quiet and diligent, and these should not be ignored. Multiple causes demand multiple interventions.

What is the role of stress and threat and the propensity to retreat to a place of safety?

Many researchers highlight the impact of severe and prolonged stress and difficulty on young people's psychosocial and physiological development across a wide range of functions. Children can feel threatened in different ways: events may threaten their sense of who they are (identity and status), of what they can do (self-efficacy, self-esteem) and their physical or emotional security (when events or people are unpredictable and their behaviour is intimidating or threatening). Young children will feel these uncertainties more intensely partly because they are more dependent and need to rely on patterns, routines and parents to help them feel safe and cared for.

It is also partly because their sense of self is emergent, therefore not robust, and partly because they cannot easily anticipate change, imagine how they will cope or know from experience how things can improve over time. Children find many ingenious ways to neutralise their fears and protect their self-respect (such as lying and cheating, being disruptive and not listening). Some of these responses can be seen as 'difficult' or not in their longer term interest and can start a pattern of behaviour that becomes increasingly dysfunctional, off-putting and abnormal.

How much does neglect affect identity, the sense of self, 'individuation' or capacity for mentalisation?

Over recent decades, professionals have become increasingly aware of and concerned about the physical and psychological effect of abuse on children, especially sexual abuse, more latterly physical abuse and, to a lesser extent, emotional abuse (as a consequence of neglect). Largely because prolonged and serious neglect is now rare, tends to occur behind closed doors and any damage may not show immediately, it has not been easy to conduct research. But if neglect at home persists, even if it is less severe, the cumulative damage may become significant. Fonagy *et al.* (2005) use the term 'mentalisation' to describe the capacity to interpret the behaviour of others (and oneself) in terms of mental states (beliefs, wishes, feelings, desires) – in short, the ability to recognise that other people have minds. They observe that the experience of both trauma and neglect inhibit the natural development of this capacity because the individual reverts to a more infantile state of mental functioning.

Attachment and neglect: how do these affect brain development?

Neglect is different from trauma in that trauma relates to an event while emotional neglect characterises the relationship and tends to be ongoing. During early brain development there are sensitive periods during which particular experiences dovetail with pre-programmed stages of brain maturation. As Glaser (2005) argues, the complex interconnections between different areas of the brain, each with its own timetable for critical periods of maturation, contribute to the varied outcomes and developmental complications of early detrimental experiences. For infants, some developments require particular environmental influences, such as safe handling, responsive gaze and intimate talking.

From the available research, the conclusion is that neglect and failure of environmental stimulation during critical periods of brain development may lead to permanent deficits in cognitive abilities. The infant brain is programmed to expect stimuli to be presented in a 'safe, nurturing, predictable, repetitive, gradual' way, attuned to the developmental stage. The right kind of sensitive attention also helps the caregiver to regulate the infant's arousal and impulses, to help cope with, often intense, frustration or distress. Glaser (2005) says, 'Such deficits (in self-regulation) may only become apparent later, when the child is expected to have matured for that particular task and these deficits may then become manifest by aggression or hyper-vigilance' (p.112) An important implication of this understanding is that those parents who themselves felt threatened by their environment or carer in their infancy and childhood may be unable to move beyond this, experiencing a non-compliant child as a threat.

To what extent do overall levels of mental health problems really reflect the general state of 'well-being' of the adolescent population?

There is evidence in some studies for increases in positive features such as competence, as well as negative ones such as mental health problems. Are adolescents getting more extreme, rather than getting worse overall? That is, are some doing much better while others are doing much worse? For example, it could be argued that only addressing problem behaviour is not a real measure of 'well-being'. Further analysis of trends in both negative and positive behaviours and experiences needs to be undertaken.

Maughan (2005) studied problems at the age of 15, to test what differences might exist in prevalence between different age groups, but if we look back at primary school age children over the same period, do we see the differences emerging there too? Further analyses addressing these issues are required. This means we should consider different types of causes depending on whether this is really an adolescent problem or a problem of earlier childhood that just expresses itself in adolescence. Problems that originate in earlier childhood might point more firmly to parenting issues and early socialisation, whereas problems that arise only in adolescence may be a result either of parenting or of issues arising in adolescence (like school or peer group transitions) or of some interaction between them. Are adolescents more vulnerable to societal changes than younger children, perhaps?

Several types of mental illness are characterised by an apparent incapacity to feel shame and guilt – an absence of moral sensitivity. Fonagy (2005) refers to a study that found four and a half-year-olds who had been fearless as infants experienced no guilt, so fearlessness could be an indicator of difficulties ahead. Interest is growing in how children develop moral awareness. It is therefore relevant to consider the possibility that problems arise where interactions that encourage moral development are either absent or inadequate.

The capacity for reflection is a necessary prerequisite for moral and 'appropriate' human engagement, or mental health. Fonagy has argued that awareness of one's thoughts and feelings arises through a process of having been thought about and cared for by someone who recognises and responds respectfully to these. If a child's presence, views or feelings are either ignored through neglect, or in the majority of cases misunderstood and misrepresented (even the most sensitive caregiver is insensitive to the child's state of mind in over 50 per cent of occasions), a growing child may be unable to trust his experience of himself, be unable to recognise or manage his emotions (and therefore recognise emotions in others) or, in certain cases, may feel he does not exist.

Prospects and possibilities

In response to an earlier independent review of CAMHS Young Minds, the children's mental health charity, highlighted a serious lack of skilled workers to treat the one in ten children suffering severe mental health problems. They concluded then that CAMHS provided inadequate services, particularly to children with learning difficulties and older teenagers. Mental health cannot and should not be left to overloaded specialists. All professionals working with children should be trained so they have the expertise to assess and identify problems as they arise. Recent research found that over 80 per cent of 7–13-year-olds said they would go to their teachers for help and support if they had a problem, rather than a health professional (Young Minds 2003). At the same conference Julia Mason, Deputy Chief Executive of Young Minds said:

> We are not calling for everyone to become a therapist but to simply understand the role they can play in spotting mental health problems at an early stage. It's key that young people have someone they can turn to who they can trust and knows how to support them. Young Minds is pressing for all people who work with children to have some training on mental health as part of their core professional development.
>
> Teachers, youth workers, social workers and health visitors should be trained to support children in distress, understand normal child development and know when and how to refer children to specialist practitioners. Training for professionals who provide support in the first years of a child's life is particularly important. The foundation of good mental health starts in these early years and is a critical stage of development.

The following impressive advice came from one of the most renowned and internationally acclaimed child psychiatrists some time ago. It is a measure of his humility and integrity that he acknowledged the limitations on his own profession and had no qualms about focusing our attention on the priority for effective intervention:

> The greatest chance of positive change in children with conduct problems and emotional difficulties consistent with early signs of mental health problems lies mainly in improvements in their family circumstances, positive peer group relationships, and good school

experiences, and less in direct contact with specialist child psychiatric services. (Rutter 1991)

As well as concentrating on early intervention it is important to re-evaluate how services for troubled young people are designed. Currently there is precious little active involvement for service users – children and young people themselves. This must change quickly if services are going to respond to needs in effective and meaningful ways. Another hindrance to improvement is that the views of children and parents are largely absent from evaluative research, particularly with lone parent families, gay and lesbian parents, and step-parents.

There is also very little systematic incorporation of culture and ethnicity as factors influencing parenting styles, on disability and the particular issues facing parents with disabled children who may have emotional and behavioural problems, and on gender influences within families and within professional groups. Further studies which pay attention to normative models of parenting in the community would counter this bias by identifying skills that lead to successful parenting – focusing on what went right rather than what went wrong (Walker 2003b). Anti-racist practice demands attention to the family life cycle/course of Black and other ethnic minority families focusing on transitional points, strengths and acceptable support (Kemps 1997).

Children are also not a homogeneous group. The age ranges from childhood to adolescence incorporates several developmental stages which would suggest attention being paid to the design of developmentally appropriate methods of intervention. It is important in this context to continue the task of finding out what works best for which children in what circumstances, and to link this with why some children fail to develop mental health problems even in highly disadvantaged situations.

Children are sometimes thought of as empty vessels waiting to be filled up. They are considered by some to be miniature adults. Services for children and young people's mental health have consequently often been based on adult concepts, models and practices. This has led to paternalistic, patronising practices that unwittingly disempower children and stifle their creativity and wisdom. It is still a relatively radical idea to think that children and adolescents are different from adults in fundamental ways that require different ways of conceptualising their problems and providing appropriate services in response.

Society is still at the beginning of a process of understanding childhood and adolescence in terms that are relevant to them, rather than to carers/ parents or adult dominated institutions. That understanding can only come from more involvement from children and young people in research, in the design of the research, and in the process of the research. The job of adults is to facilitate and support them in gaining more control over their lives, and social workers are ideally placed to fulfil that role in empowering, participatory practice.

Activity final

- Reflect on the above conclusions and recommendations.

- Think about what you can do as an individual to realise some of those aspirations.

- Write down three practical, achievable changes you can make in your everyday work to begin the process.

- Lobby your manager, local council, director of children's services, MP, secretary of state and the prime minister to improve service provision.

- Don't ever give up on troubled children and young people.

References

Achenbach, T.M. (1991) *Manual for the Child Behaviour Checklist 4–18 and 1991 Profile.* Burlington, VT: University of Vermont Department of Psychiatry.

Ackroyd, J. and Pilkington, A. (1999) 'Childhood and the construction of ethnic identities in a global age.' *Childhood 6,* 4, 443–454.

Adams, R., Dominelli, L. and Payne, M. (1998) *Social Work: Themes, Issues and Critical Debates.* Basingstoke: Macmillan.

Adams, R., Dominelli, L. and Payne, M. (2002) *Critical Practice in Social Work.* Basingstoke: Macmillan.

Aggleton, P., Hurry, J. and Warwick, I. (2000) (eds) *Young People and Mental Health.* London: Wiley.

Ainsworth, M., Dichar, M., Waters, E. and Wall, S. (1978) *Patterns of Attachment: A Psychological Study of the Strange Situation.* New York: Erlbaum.

Alderson, P. (2000) *Young Children's Rights.* London: Jessica Kingsley Publishers.

Alibhai-Brown, Y. (1999) *True Colours: Public Attitudes to Multiculturalism and the Role of the Government.* London: Institute for Public Policy Research.

Alvarez, A. (2005) 'Perspectives on the causes of mental health problems in children and adolescents.' Young Minds Symposium, London: Institute for Public Policy Research.

American Psychiatric Association (1994) *Diagnostic and Statistical Manual of Mental Disorders,* 4th edn (DSM IV). Washington, DC: American Psychiatric Association.

Amin, K., Drew, D., Fosam, B., Gillborn, D. and Demack, S. (1997) *Black and Ethnic Minority Young People and Educational Disadvantage.* London: Runnymede Trust.

Andersen, H.C. (1913) *Hans Christian Andersen's Fairy Tales.* London: Constable.

Anderson, K. and Anderson, L. (eds) (1995) *Mosby's Pocket Dictionary of Nursing, Medicine and Professions Allied to Medicine.* London: Mosby.

Angold, M. and Costello, P. (1993) 'Depressive comorbidity in children and adolescents: Empirical, theoretical, and methodological issues.' *American Journal of Psychiatry 150,* 1779–1791.

Appleby, L., Cooper, J. and Amos, T. (1999) 'Psychological autopsy study of suicides by people under 35.' *British Journal of Psychiatry 175,* 168–174.

Arcelus, J., Bellerby, T. and Vostanis, V. (1999) 'A mental health service for young people in the care of the local authority.' *Clinical Child Psychology and Psychiatry 4,* 2, 233–245.

Audit Commission (1994) *Seen But Not Heard.* London: HMSO.

Audit Commission (1998) *Child and Adolescent Mental Health Services.* London: HMSO.

Audit Commission (1999) *Children in Mind: Child and Adolescent Mental Health Services.* London: HMSO.

Bagley, C. and Mallick, K. (1995) 'Negative self perception and components of stress in Canadian, British and Hong Kong adolescents.' *Perceptual Motor Skills 81,* 123–127.

Bagley, C. and Mallick, K. (2000) 'How adolescents perceive their emotional life, behaviour, and self-esteem in relation to family stressors: a six-culture study.' In N. Singh, J. Leung and A. Singh (eds) *International Perspectives on Child and Adolescent Mental Health.* Oxford: Elsevier.

Bagley, C. and Young, L. (1998) 'The Interactive Effects of Physical, Emotional and Sexual Abuse on Adjustment in a Longitudinal Cohort of 565 Children from Birth to 17 years.' In C. Bagley and K. Mallick (eds) *Child Sexual Abuse – New Theory and Research.* Aldershot: Ashgate.

Bailey, R. and Brake, B. (eds) (1980) *Radical Social Work Practice.* London: Edward Arnold.

Baldwin, M. (2000) *Care Management and Community Care.* Aldershot: Ashgate.

Barclay, P. (1982) *Social Workers: Their Role and Tasks.* London: NISW/ Bedford Square Press.

Barnes, M. and Warren, L. (1999) *Paths to Empowerment.* Bristol: Policy Press.

Barter, C. (1999) *Protecting Children from Racism and Racial Abuse – a Research Review.* London: NSPCC.

Baumann, G. (1996) *Contesting Culture.* Cambridge: Cambridge University Press.

Bayley, R. (1998) *Transforming Children's Lives: The Importance of Early Intervention.* London: Family Policy Studies Centre.

Beatch, R. and Stewart, B. (2002) 'Integrating Western and Aboriginal Healing Practices.' In M. Nash and B. Stewart (eds) *Spirituality and Social Care.* London: Jessica Kingsley Publishers.

Beckett, C. (2002) *Human Growth and Development.* London: Sage.

Berger, M. and Jurkovic, G. (1984) *Practising Family Therapy in Diverse Settings.* San Francisco: Jossey-Bass.

Bhugra, D. (1999) *Mental Health of Ethnic Minorities.* London: Gaskell.

Bhugra, D. and Bahl, V. (1999) *Ethnicity: An Agenda for Mental Health.* London: Gaskell.

Bhui, K. and Olajide, D. (1999) *Mental Health Service Provision for a Multi-Cultural Society.* London: Saunders.

Bilton, T., Bonnet, K., Jones, P. *et al.* (2002) *Introductory Sociology.* Basingstoke: Palgrave Macmillan.

Blackwell, D. and Melzak, S. (2000) *Far from the Battle but Still at War – Troubled Refugee Children in School.* London: The Child Psychotherapy Trust.

Bochner, S. (1994) 'Cross-cultural differences in the self-concept: A test of Hofstede's individualism/collectivism distinction.' *Journal of Cross-Cultural Psychology 2,* 273–283.

Bowlby, J. (1979) *The Making and Breaking of Affectional Bonds.* London: Tavistock.

Bradshaw, J. (ed.) (2001) *Poverty: The Outcomes for Children.* London: Family Policy Studies Centre/ESRC.

Brammer, A. (2003) *Social Work Law.* Harlow: Pearson Education.

Brearley, J. (1995) *Counselling and Social Work.* Buckingham: Open University Press.

Brearley, P.C. with Hall, M.R.P., Jeffreys, P.M., Jennings, R. and Pritchard, S. (1982) *Managing Risk and Uncertainty in Social Work: A Literature Review: Risk and Ageing.* London: Routledge and Kegan Paul.

Briere, J., Elliott, D.M., Harris, K. and Cotman, A. (1995) 'Trauma Symptom Inventory: Psychometrics and association with childhood and adult trauma in clinical samples.' *Journal of Interpersonal Violence 10,* 387–401.

Briggs, S. (2002) *Working with Adolescents: A Contemporary Psychodynamic Approach.* Basingstoke: Palgrave Macmillan.

Broidy, L.M., Nagin, D.S., Tremblay, R.E. *et al.* (2003) 'Developmental trajectories of childhood disruptive behaviors and adolescent delinquency: A six-site, cross-national study.' *Developmental Psychology 39,* 2, 222–245.

Brown, B., Crawford, P. and Darongkamas, J. (2000) 'Blurred roles and permeable boundaries: The experience of multidisciplinary working in community mental health.' *Health and Social Care in the Community 8,* 6, 425–435.

Burnham, J. (1986) *Family Therapy.* London: Tavistock.

Butrym, Z. (1976) *The Nature of Social Work.* London: Macmillan.

Calder, M. (2007) *Understanding, Assessing and Engaging with Young People Who Self-Harm.* Lyme Regis: Russell House Publishers.

Campbell, D. and Draper, R. (eds) (1985) *Applications of Systemic Family Therapy.* London: Grune and Stratton.

Caplan, G. (1961) *Principles of Preventive Psychiatry.* London: Basic Books.

Carr, A. (2000) *What Works with Children and Adolescents? A Critical Review of Psychological Interventions with Children, Adolescents, and Their Families.* London: Routledge.

Carroll, M. (1998) 'Social work's conceptualization of spirituality.' *Social Thought: Journal of Religion in the Social Sciences 18,* 2, 1–14.

Central Council for the Education and Training of Social Workers (1989) *Paper 31. Rules and Requirements for the Diploma in Social Work.* London: CCETSW.

Chalmers, I. (1994) 'Assembling the Evidence.' In P. Alderson, S. Brails, I. Chalmers *et al.* (eds) *What Works? Effective Social Interventions in Child Welfare.* Barkingside: Barnardos.

Chand, A. (2000) 'The over-representation of black children in the child protection system: Possible causes, consequences and solutions. *Child and Family Social Work 5,* 67–77.

Children's Legal Centre (2008) *Young People and Medical Treatment – Fact Sheet.* Colchester: Children's Legal Centre.

Christiansen, E. and James, G. (eds) (2000) *Research with Children, Perspectives and Practices.* London: Falmer Press.

Clarke, L., Bradshaw, J. and Williams, J. (2001) *Family Diversity, Poverty and the Mental Well-being of Young People.* London: Health Education Authority.

Cobb, M. and Robshaw, V. (1998) *The Spiritual Challenge of Health Care.* Edinburgh: Churchill Livingstone.

Coles, R. (1990) *The Spiritual Life of Children.* New York: Random House.

Conners, C.K. (1997) *Conners Rating Scale for ADHD.* New York: Conners.

Cook, W.L. (2000) 'Understanding attachment security in family context.' *Journal of Personality and Social Psychology* 78, 2, 285–294.

Cooper, P. (ed.) (1999) *Understanding and Supporting Children with Emotional and Behavioural Difficulties.* London: Jessica Kingsley Publishers.

Copley, B. and Forryan, B. (1997) *Therapeutic Work with Children and Young People.* London: Cassell.

Corby, B. (2000) *Child Abuse – Towards a Knowledge Base*, 2nd edn. Buckingham: Open University Press.

Corby, B., Millar, M. and Pope, A. (2002) 'Out of the frame.' *Community Care*, September, 40–41.

Corrigan, P. and Leonard, P. (1978) *Social Work Practice under Capitalism: A Marxist Approach.* London: Macmillan.

Coulshed, V. and Orme, J. (1998) *Social Work Practice: An Introduction*, 3rd edn. London: Macmillan/BASW.

Crisp, B. (2008) 'Social work and spirituality in a secular society.' *Journal of Social Work 8*, 4, 363–375.

Crittenden, P.M. (1999) 'Danger and Development: The Organization of Self-protective Strategies.' In J. Vondra and D. Barnett (eds) *Monographs for the Society for Research on Child Development* 64, 145–171.

Crompton, M. (1996) *Children, Spirituality and Religion.* London: CCETSW.

Dallos, R. and Draper, R. (2000) *An Introduction to Family Therapy.* London: Open University Press.

Data Protection Act (DPA) (1998) London: Information Commissioner's Office/HMSO.

Davies, M. (1981) *The Essential Social Worker: A Guide to Positive Practice.* Aldershot: Arena.

Davies, M. (ed.) (1997) *The Blackwell Companion to Social Work.* London: Blackwell.

Davis, H. and Spurr, P. (1998) 'Parent counselling: Evaluation of a community child mental health service.' *Journal of Child Psychology and Psychiatry 2*, 3, 178–190.

Davis, H., Spurr, P., Cox, A., Lynch, M., Von Roenne, A. and Hahn, K. (1997) 'A description and evaluation of a community child mental health service.' *Clinical Child Psychology and Psychiatry 2*, 2, 221–238.

Davis, J., Rendell, P. and Sims, D. (1999) 'The joint practitioner – a new concept in professional training.' *Journal of Interprofessional Care 13*, 4, 395–404.

Daycare Trust (2000) *Ensuring Equality.* London: Daycare Trust.

DeBell, D. and Walker, S. (2002) *Evaluation of the Family Support Service in Norfolk CAMHS.* Cambridge: Anglia Polytechnic University.

Dennis, J. and Smith, T. (2002) 'Nationality, immigration and the Asylum Bill 2002: Its impact on children.' *Childright 187*, 16–17.

Department for Children, Schools and Families (2008) *Children and Young People in Mind: The Final Report of the National CAMHS Review.* London: HMSO.

Department for Education and Employment (1998) 'Towards an interdisciplinary framework for developing work with children and young people.' Childhood Studies Discipline Network Conference presentation: Cambridge: Robinson College.

Department for Education and Skills (2003) *Every Child Matters: Change for Children.* Nottingham: DfES.

Department for Education and Skills (2005) *Common Core of Skills and Knowledge for the Children's Workforce.* Nottingham: DfES.

Department for Education and Skills and Department of Health (2004) *National Service Framework for Children, Young People and Maternity Services.* London: Department of Health.

Department of Health (1989) *The Children Act.* London: HMSO.

Department of Health (1992) *Health of the Nation Strategy.* London: HMSO.

Department of Health (1995) *Child Protection: Messages from Research.* London: HMSO.

Department of Health (1997a) *Developing Partnerships in Mental Health.* London: HMSO.

Department of Health (1997b) *Innovations Fund. Specific Mental Health Grant.* London: HMSO.

Department of Health (1997c) *The New NHS: Modern, Dependable.* London: HMSO.

Department of Health (1998a) *Disabled Children: Directions for Their Future Care.* London: HMSO.

Department of Health (1998b) *Modernising Mental Health Services: Safe, Supportive and Sensible.* London: HMSO.

Department of Health (1999a) *LAC circular (99) 33. Quality Protects Programme: Transforming Children's Services 2000–01.* London: HMSO.

Department of Health (1999b) *National Priorities Guidance for Children's Services.* London: HMSO.

Department of Health (1999c) *The Health Act.* London: HMSO.

Department of Health (2000) *Framework for the Assessment of Children in Need and Their Families.* London: HMSO.

Department of Health (2001) *National Service Framework for Mental Health.* London: HMSO.

Department of Health (2007) *Statistical Study to Estimate the Prevalence of Female Genital Mutilation.* London: HMSO.

Department of Health and Department for Education and Employment (1996) *Children's Service Planning: Guidance for Inter-Agency Working.* London: HMSO.

Department of Health and Department for Children, Schools and Families (2004) *Children Act.* London: HMSO.

Department of Health and Department for Children, Schools and Families (2005) *Common Assessment Framework.* London: HMSO.

Department of Health and Social Security (1985) *Social Work Decisions in Child Care.* London: HMSO.

Dimigen, G., Del Priore, C., Butler, S., Evans, S., Ferguson, L. and Swan, M. (1999) 'Psychiatric disorder among children at time of entering local authority care.' *British Medical Journal 319*, 675–676.

Doel, M. and Marsh, P. (1992) *Task-centred Social Work.* Aldershot: Ashgate.

Dogra, N. (2007) 'Cultural Diversity Issues in Working with Vulnerable Children.' In V. Postanis (ed.) *Mental Health Interventions and Services for Vulnerable Children and Young People.* London: Jessica Kingsley Publishers.

Dominelli, L. (1988) *Anti Racist Social Work.* Basingstoke: Macmillan.

Dominelli, L. (1999) 'Neoliberalism, social exclusion and welfare clients in a global economy.' *International Journal of Social Welfare 8,* 1, 14–22.

Dominelli, L. (2002) *Anti-Oppressive Social Work Theory and Practice.* Basingstoke: Palgrave Macmillan.

Dulmus, C. and Rapp-Paglicci, L. (2000) 'The prevention of mental disorders in children and adolescents: Future research and public-policy recommendations.' *Families in Society: The Journal of Contemporary Human Services 81,* 3, 294–303.

Dundes, A. (2003) *Fables of the Ancients? Folklore in the Qur'an.* New York: Rowman and Littlefield.

Durlak, J. (1998) 'Primary prevention programmes for children and adolescents are effective.' *Journal of Mental Health 7,* 5, 454–469.

Durlak, J. and Wells, A. (1997) 'Primary prevention mental health programs for children and adolescents: A meta-analytic review.' *American Journal of Community Psychology 25,* 2, 115–152.

Dwivedi, K.N. (2002) *Meeting the Needs of Ethnic Minority Children,* 2nd edn. London: Jessica Kingsley Publishers.

Early Childhood Education Forum (1998) *Quality and Diversity in Early Learning.* London: National Children's Bureau.

Eayrs, C. and Jones, R. (1992) 'Methodological issues and future directions in the evaluation of early intervention programmes.' *Child Care Health and Development 18,* 15–28.

Eber, L., Osuch, R. and Redditt, C. (1996) 'School based applications of the wraparound process – early results on service provision and student outcomes.' *Journal of Family Studies 5,* 83–99.

Egan, G. (1998) *The Skilled Helper,* 2nd edn. Pacific Grove, CA: Brooks/Cole.

Elliot, V. (2007) 'Interventions and Services for Refugee and Asylum-Seeking Children and Families.' In V. Postanis (ed.) *Mental Health Interventions and Services for Vulnerable Children and Young People,* London: Jessica Kingsley Publishers.

Fagin, C.M. (1992) 'Collaboration between nurses and physicians; no longer a choice.' *Academic Medicine 67,* 5, 295–303.

Falicov, C. (1995) 'Training to think culturally: A multidimensional comparative framework.' *Family Process 34,* 373–388.

Falloon, I. and Fadden, G. (1995) *Integrated Mental Health Care – A Comprehensive Community-Based Approach.* Cambridge: Cambridge University Press.

Feeney, J.A. (2003) 'The Systemic Nature of Couple Relationships: An Attachment Perspective.' In P. Erdman and T. Caffery (eds) *Attachment and Family Systems.* New York and Hove: Brunner Routledge.

Ferguson, H. and Lavalette, M. (2004) 'Beyond power discourse: Alienation and social work.' *British Journal of Social Work 33,* 1005–1024.

Fernando, S. (2002) *Mental Health, Race and Culture,* 2nd edn. Basingstoke: Palgrave.

Fieldhouse, R. (1996) *A History of Modern British Adult Education.* Leicester: National Institute of Adult and Continuing Education.

Firth, M., Dyer, M. and Wilkes, J. (1999) 'Reducing the distance: Mental health social work in general practice.' *Journal of Interprofessional Care 13,* 4, 335–344.

Fombonne, E. (1995) 'Depressive Disorders: Time Trends and Possible Explanatory Mechanisms.' In M. Rutter and D. Smith (eds) *Psychosocial Disorders of Youth.* New York: Wiley.

Fonagy, A. and Roth, A. (1997) *What Works for Whom? A Critical Review of Psychotherapy Research.* London: Guilford Press.

Fonagy, P. (2005) *Perspectives on the Causes of Mental Health Problems in Children and Adolescents.* Young Minds Symposium. London: Institute for Public Policy Research.

Fonagy, P., Target, M., Cottrell, D., Phillips, J. and Kurtz, Z. (2005) *What Works for Whom? – A Critical Review of Treatments for Children and Adolescents.* London: Guilford Press.

Fook, J. (2002) *Social Work – Critical Theory and Practice.* London: Sage.

Fortune, S., Sinclair, J. and Hawton, K. (2005) *Adolescents' Views on Prevention of Self-harm, Barriers to Help-Seeking for Self-harm and How Quality of Life Might be Improved: A Qualitative and Quantitative Study.* Oxford: Centre for Suicide Research, University of Oxford.

Fowler, J., Nipkow, K.E. and Schweitzer, F. (eds) (1991) *Stages of Faith and Religious Development: Implications for Church, Education and Society.* New York: Crossroads Press.

Freeman, I., Morrison, A., Lockhart, F. and Swanson, M. (1996) 'Consulting Service Users: The Views of Young People.' In M. Hill and J. Aldgate (eds) *Child Welfare Services: Developments in Law, Policy, Practice and Research.* London: Jessica Kingsley Publishers.

Friedlander, M.L. (2001) 'Family Therapy Research: Science into Practice, Practice into Science.' In M.P. Nichols and R.C. Schwartz (eds) *Family Therapy: Concepts and Methods,* 5th edn. Boston, MA: Alleyn and Bacon.

Fulcher, L.C. (1999) 'Cultural origins of the contemporary group conference.' *Child Care in Practice 6,* 328–339.

Furedi, F. (2003) *Therapy Culture.* London: Routledge.

Furlong, A. and Carmel, F. (1997) *Young People and Social Change.* Buckingham: Open University Press.

Furniss, T. (1991) *The Multi-professional Handbook of Child Sexual Abuse.* London: Routledge.

Gale, F., Hassett, A. and Sebuliba, D. (2005) *The Competency and Capability Framework for Primary Mental Health Workers in CAMHS.* London: NCSS.

Galpin, D. (2009) 'Who really drives the development of post-qualifying social work education and what are the implications of this?' *Social Work Education 28,* 1, 65–80.

Garner, D.M., Olmsted, M.P., Bohr, Y. and Garfinkel, P.E. (1982) 'The Eating Attitudes Test: Psychometric features and clinical correlates.' *Psychological Medicine 12,* 871–878.

George, C. and Solomon, J. (1996) 'A representational model of relationships: links between caregiving and attachment.' *Infant Mental Health Journal 17,* 3, 198–216.

Ghaziuddin, M. (2005) *Mental Health Aspects of Autism and Asperger Syndrome.* London: Jessica Kingsley Publishers.

Ghuman, P. (2004) *Double Loyalties: South Asian Adolescents in the West.* Swansea: University of Wales Press.

Gibson-Cline, J. (ed.) (1996) *Adolescence: From Crisis to Coping.* London: Butterworth-Heinemann.

Giddings, F.H. (1898) *The Elements of Sociology.* New York: Macmillan.

Gillick v Wisbech and W Norfolk AHA (1986) AC112.

Glaser, D. (2005) 'Perspectives on the causes of mental health problems in children and adolescents.' Young Minds Symposium, London: Institute for Public Policy Research.

Goldenberg, I. and Goldenberg, H. (2004) *Family Therapy – An Overview.* Pacific Grove, CA: Thomson Learning.

Goodman, R. (1997) *Child and Adolescent Mental Health Services. Reasoned Advice to Commissioners and Providers.* Discussion Paper no. 4. London: Maudsley Hospital.

Goodman, R. and Scott, S. (1997) *Child Psychiatry.* London: Sage.

Gordon, G. and Grant, R. (1997) *How We Feel: An Insight into the Emotional World of Teenagers.* London: Jessica Kingsley Publishers.

Gorell Barnes, G. (1998) *Family Therapy in Changing Times.* Basingstoke: Macmillan.

Gowers, S., Bailey-Rogers, S., Shore, A. and Levine, W. (2000) 'The health of the nation outcome scales for child and adolescent mental health (HoNOSCA).' *Child Psychology and Psychiatry Review 5,* 2, 50–56.

Gowers, S.G., Harrington, R.C., Whitton, A., Beevor, A., Lelliott, P., Jezzard, R. and Wing, J. (1998) *HoNOSCA: Brief Report on the Research and Development.* London: CRU.

GSCC (2005a) *Post-qualifying Framework for Social Work Education and Training.* London: GSCC.

GSCC (2005b) *Specialist Standards and Requirements for Post-qualifying Social Work Education and Training – Children and Young People, Their Families and Carers.* London: GSCC.

Guerin, S. (2002) *Aggression and Bullying.* Leicester: British Psychological Society.

Gunnell, D., Weherner, H. and Frankel, S. (1999) 'Sex differences in suicide trends in England and Wales.' *Lancet 353,* 556–557.

Hacking, I. (1999) *The Social Construction of What?* London: Harvard University Press.

Hadfield, J. (1975) *Childhood and Adolescence.* London: Penguin.

Hagel, A. (2004) *Time Trends in Adolescent Well-being.* London: Nuffield Foundation.

Hagell, A. and Newman, T. (1994) *Persistent Young Offenders.* London: Policy Studies Institute.

Hall, S. (1993) 'Culture, community, nation.' *Cultural Studies 7,* 3, 16–29.

Hallett, C. and Birchall, E. (1992) *Coordination and Child Protection – A Review of the Literature.* London: HMSO.

Haralambos, M. (1988) *Sociology-theses and Perspectives.* London: Unwin Hyman.

Harris, P. (2007) *Empathy for the Devil: How to Help People Overcome Drugs and Alcohol.* Lyme Regis: Russell House Publishers.

Harrison, R., Mann, G., Murphy, M., Taylor, A. and Thompson, N. (2003) *Partnership Made Painless – A Joined Up Guide to Working Together.* Oxford: Aiden Group.

Harter, S. (1985) *Manual for the Self Perception Profile for Children.* Denver, CO: Denver University.

Hartley, J. (2003) *A Short History of Cultural Studies.* London: Sage.

Hay, D. (1990) *Religious Experience Today: Studying the Facts.* London: Mowbray/Cassell.

Healy, K. (2002) *Social Work Practices – Contemporary Perspectives on Change.* London: Sage.

Health Advisory Service (1995)*Together We Stand: Thematic Review on the Commissioning, Role, and Management of Child and Adolescent Mental Health Services.* London: HMSO.

Hellinckx, W., Colton, M. and Williams, M. (1997) *International Perspectives on Family Support.* Aldershot: Ashgate.

Henderson, P. and Thomas, D. (1987) *Skills in Neighbourhood Work.* London: Allen and Unwin.

Hendrick, H. (1997) 'Constructions and Reconstructions of British Childhood: An Interpretative Survey 1800 to Present.' In A. James and A. Prout (eds) (1997) *Constructing and Reconstructing Childhood.* Basingstoke: Falmer.

Hendrick, H. (ed.) (2005) *Child Welfare and Social Policy, An Essential Reader.* Bristol: Policy Press.

Hennessey, E. (1999) 'Children as service evaluators.' *Child Psychology and Psychiatry Review 4,* 4, 153–161.

Herington, S. (2007) *Extraordinary Enigmas.* Hereford: St Margaret's Press.

Hetherington, J. and Baistow, R. (2001) 'Supporting families with a mentally ill parent: European perspectives on interagency cooperation.' *Child Abuse Review 10,* 351–365.

Heyman, I., Fombonne, E., Simmons, H., Ford, T., Meltzer, H. and Goodman, R. (2001) 'Prevalence of obsessive-compulsive disorder in the British Nationwide Survey of Child Mental Health.' *British Journal of Psychiatry 179,* 324–329.

Higham, P. (2009) *Post Qualifying Social Work Practice.* London: Sage.

Hill, M. (1999) *Effective Ways of Working with Children and Their Families.* London: Jessica Kingsley Publishers.

Hill, M., Laybourn, A. and Borland, M. (1996) 'Engaging with primary-age children about their emotions and well-being: Methodological considerations.' *Children and Society 10,* 129–144.

HMSO (1968) *Local Authority and Allied Personal Social Services* (Cmnd 3703). London: HMSO.

Hodes, M. (2000) 'Psychologically distressed refugee children in the United Kingdom.' *Child Psychology and Psychiatry Review 5,* 2, 57–67.

Holliday, A. (1999) 'Small cultures.' *Applied Linguistics 20,* 2, 237–264.

Home Office (2008) *Crime in England and Wales.* London: HMSO.

HoNOSCA (2010) Health of the Nation Scales for Children and Adolescents. Available at www.liv.ac.uk/honosca, accessed March 2010.

House of Commons (1997) *Health Committee Report into Child and Adolescent Mental Health Services.* London: HMSO.

Howarth, J. (2002) 'Maintaining a focus on the child?' *Child Abuse Review 11,* 195–213.

Howe, D. (1989) *The Consumer's View of Family Therapy.* London: Gower.

Howe, D. (ed.) (1999) *Attachment and Loss in Child and Family Social Work.* Aldershot: Ashgate.

Howe, D., Brandon, M., Hinings, D. and Schofield, G. (1999) *Attachment Theory, Child Maltreatment and Family Support.* Basingstoke: Macmillan.

Howe, G. (1999) *Mental Health Assessments.* London: Jessica Kingsley Publishers.

Howlin, P. and Rutter, M. (1987) 'Living with impairment: The effects on children of having an autistic sibling.' *Child: Care, Health and Development 14,* 395–408.

Human Rights Commission (1997) *Bringing Them Home, Report of the Inquiry into the Separation of Aboriginal and Torres Strait Islander Children from Their Families.* Sydney: HR and EOC.

Hutchings, J., Nash, S., Smith, M. and Parry, G. (1998) *Long-term Outcome for Pre-School Children Referred to CAMH Team for Behaviour Management Problems.* Bangor: School of Psychology, University of Wales.

International Association of Schools of Social Work and International Federation of Social Workers (2001)*The Ethics of Social Work Statement of Principles.* IASSW General Meeting, Geneva.

Jackson, R. (2003) (ed.) *International Perspectives on Citizenship, Education and Religious Diversity.* London: Routledge Falmer.

Jackson, R. (2004) 'Intercultural education and recent European pedagogies of religious education.' *Intercultural Education 15*, 1, 3–14.

James, A. and Prout, A. (eds) (1997) *Constructing and Reconstructing Childhood*. Basingstoke: Falmer.

Jayarajan, U. (2001) *The Demographic Profile of the Children and Young People Referred to Birmingham CAMHS*. Birmingham: Birmingham Children's Hospital Trust.

JCWI (2002) *Joint Council for the Welfare of Immigrants' Response to the White Paper Secure Boarders, Safe Haven: Integration with Diversity in Modern Britain*. London: JCWI.

Jenkins, R. (2002) *Foundations of Sociology*. Basingstoke: Palgrave Macmillan.

Jensen, A.L. and Weisz, J.R. (2002) 'Assessing match and mismatch between practitioner-generated and standardized interview-generated diagnoses for clinic-referred children and adolescents.' *Journal of Consulting and Clinical Psychology 70*, 158–168.

Jezzard, B. (2005) 'Perspectives on the causes of mental health problems in children and adolescents.' Young Minds Symposium, London: Institute for Public Policy Research.

Jones, T. (1996) *Britain's Ethnic Minorities: An Analysis of the Labour Force Survey*. London: Policy Studies Institute.

Jordan, B. (1990) *Social Work in an Unjust Society*. Hemel Hempstead: Harvester Wheatsheaf.

Joy, I., van Poortvliet, M. and Yeowart, C. (2008) *Heads Up – Mental Health of Children and Young People*. London: New Philanthropy Capital.

Jung, C.G. (1978) *Psychological Reflections*. Princeton, NJ: Bollingen.

Kanner, L. (1943) 'Autistic disturbances of affective contact.' *Nervous Child 2*, 217–250.

Kashani, J. and Allan, W. (1998) *The Impact of Family Violence on Children and Adolescents*. London: Sage.

Kearney, P., Levin, E. and Rosen, G. (2000) *Alcohol Drug and Mental Health Problems – Working with Families*. London: NISW.

Kehily, J. and Swann, J. (2003) *Children's Cultural Worlds*. London: Wiley/OUP.

Kemps, C. (1997) 'Approaches to Working with Ethnicity and Cultural Issues.' In K. Dwivedi (ed.) *Enhancing Parenting Skills*. London: Wiley.

Kemshall, H. (1993) 'Assessing competence: Process or subjective inference? Do we really see it?' *Social Work Education 12*, 1, 36–45.

Kendall, P. (2000) *Childhood Disorders*. Hove: Psychology Press.

Kent, H. and Read, J. (1998) 'Measuring consumer participation in mental health services: Are attitudes related to professional orientation?' *International Journal of Social Psychiatry 44*, 4, 295–310.

Klineberg, O. (1971) 'Race and IQ.' *Courier 24*, 10.

Kohn, M. (1995) *The Race Gallery*. London: Jonathan Cape.

Kovacs, M. (1992) *Child Depression Inventory*. New York: Pearson.

Kurtz, Z. (ed.) (1992) *With Health in Mind – Quality Review Series on Mental Health Care for Children and Young People*. London: SW Thames Regional Health Authority.

Kurtz, Z. (1996) *Treating Children Well: A Guide to Using the Evidence Base in Commissioning and Managing Services for the Mental Health of Children and Young People*. London: Mental Health Foundation.

Kurtz, Z. (2001) *Report on Evaluation of CAMHS Innovation Projects* (unpublished). London: Young Minds.

Kurtz, Z., Thornes, R. and Wolind, S. (1994) *Services for the Mental Health of Children and Young People in England*. London: Maudsley Hospital/SWTRHA.

Kurtz, Z., Thornes, R. and Wolkind, S. (1995) *Services for the Mental Health of Children and Young People in England: Assessment of Needs and Unmet Need*. London: HMSO.

Landgraf, J.M., Abetz, L. and Ware, J.E. (1996) *The CHQ User's Manual*, 1st edn. Boston, MA: The Health Institute, New England Medical Centre.

Lane, M. (1997) 'Community work, social work: Green and postmodern?' *British Journal of Social Work 27*, 319–341.

Larsen, L. and Plesner, I.T. (eds) (2002) *Teaching for Tolerance and Freedom of Religion and Belief*. Oslo: Oslo Coalition on Freedom of Religion and Belief, University of Oslo.

Lask, J. and Lask, B. (1981) *Child Psychiatry and Social Work*. London: Tavistock.

Leathard, A. (1994) *Going Inter-professional*. London: Routledge.

Leganger-Krogstad, H. (2000) 'Developing a contextual theory and practice of religious education.' *Panorama: International Journal of Comparative Religious Education and Values 12*, 1, 94–104

Leighton, A.H. (1981) 'Culture and psychiatry.' *Canadian Journal of Psychiatry 26*, 8, 522–529.

Leonard, P. (1994) 'Knowledge/power and postmodern implications for the practice of critical social work education.' *Canadian Social Work Review 11*, 1, 11–26.

Leonard, P. (1997) *Postmodern Welfare: Reconstructing an Emancipatory Project*. London: Sage.

Lindon, J. (2003) *Child Protection*, 2nd edn. London: Hodder-Stoughton.

Lindsey, C. (2005) 'Some implications of the Children's National Service Framework for Social Work Practice with regard to Child Mental Health.' *Journal of Social Work Practice 19*, 3, 225–234.

Lorenz, W. (2005) 'Social work and a new social order – challenging neo-liberalism's erosion of solidarity.' *Social Work and Society 3*, 1, 93–101.

Lynch, M. (2004) 'Assessment skills: An inexact science.' *Professional Social Work*, October, 10–11.

Madge, N. (2001) *Understanding Difference – the Meaning of Ethnicity for Young Lives*. London: National Children's Bureau.

Magrab, P., Evans, P. and Hurrell, P. (1997) 'Integrated services for children and youth at risk: An international study of multidisciplinary training.' *Journal of Interprofessional Care 11*, 1, 99–108.

Malek, M. (1993) *Passing the Buck: Institutional Responses to Children with Difficult Behaviour*. London: Children's Society.

Malek, M. and Joughin, C. (2004) *Mental Health Services for Minority Ethnic Children and Adolescents*. London: Jessica Kingsley Publishers.

Marfe, E. (2003) 'Assessing risk following deliberate self-harm.' *Paediatric Nursing 15*, 8, 32–34

Marsh, P. (1997) 'Task-centred Work.' In M. Davies (ed.) *The Blackwell Companion to Social Work*. Oxford: Blackwell.

Martin, G., Rozanes, P., Pearce, C. and Alison, S. (1995) 'Adolescent suicide, depression and family dysfunction.' *Acta Psychiatrica Scandinavica 92*, 336–344.

Martslof, D. and Mickley, J.R. (1998) 'The concept of spirituality in nursing theories: Differing world-views and extent focus.' *Journal of Advanced Nursing 27*, 294–303.

Masson, J. (1988) *Against Therapy*. London: Collins.

Maughan, D. (2005) 'Perspectives on the causes of mental health problems in children and adolescents.' Young Minds Symposium, London: Institute for Public Policy Research.

McClure, G. (2001) 'Suicide in children and adolescents in England and Wales.' *British Journal of Psychiatry 178*, 469–474.

McGuire, J.B., Stein, A. and Rosenberry, W. (1997) 'Evidence-based medicine and child mental health services.' *Children and Society 11*, 2, 89–96.

Meltzer, H., Gatward, R., Goodman, R. and Ford, T. (2000) *Mental Health of Children and Adolescents in Great Britain*. London: HMSO.

Mental Health Act Commission (2004) *Safeguarding Children and Adolescents Detained under the Mental Health Act 1983 on Adult Psychiatric Wards*. London: TSO.

Mental Health Foundation (1993) *Mental Illness: The Fundamental Facts*. London: Mental Health Foundation.

Mental Health Foundation (1999) *The Big Picture: A National Survey of Child Mental Health in Britain*. London: Mental Health Foundation.

Mental Health Foundation (2001) *Turned Upside Down*. London: Mental Health Foundation.

Mental Health Foundation (2006) *Truth Hurts: Report of the National Inquiry into Self-harm among Young People*. London: Mental Health Foundation.

Micklewright, J. and Stewart, K. (2000) 'Well Being of Children in the European Union.' London: Institute for Public Policy Research.

Middleton, L. (1997) *The Art of Assessment*. Birmingham: Venture Press.

Midgley, J. (2001) 'Issues in international social work – resolving critical issues in the profession.' *Journal of Social Work 1*, 1, 21–35.

Mills, R. and Duck, S. (2000) *The Developmental Psychology of Personal Relationships*. Chichester: Wiley.

Milner, J. and O'Byrne, P. (1998) *Assessment in Social Work Practice*. London: Macmillan.

Minnis, H., Rabe-Hesketh, S. and Wolkind, S. (2002) 'Development of a brief, clinically effective scale for measuring attachment disorders.' *International Journal of Methods in Psychiatric Research 11*, 2, 90–98.

Mishra, R. (1999) *Globalization and the Welfare State*. Northampton, MA: Edward Elgar.

Morris, J. (2000) *Having Someone Who Cares – Barriers to Change in the Public Care of Children*. London: NCB.

Morrison, L. and L'Heureux, J. (2001) 'Suicide and gay/lesbian/bisexual youth: Implications for clinicians.' *Journal of Adolescence 24*, 39–49.

Morrissey, J., Johnsen, M. and Calloway, M. (1997) 'Evaluating performance and change in mental health systems serving children and youth: An interorganizational network approach.' *Journal of Mental Health Administration 24*, 1, 4–22.

Morton-Cooper, A. (1988) *Health Care and the Autism Spectrum*. London: Jessica Kingsley Publishers.

Moules, N. (2000) 'Postmodernism and the sacred: Reclaiming connection in our greater-than-human worlds.' *Journal of Marital and Family Therapy 26*, 229–240.

Moules, T. and Ramsay, J. (1998) *The Textbook of Children's Nursing.* Cheltenham: Stanley Thornes.

Mun, E., Fitzgerald, H., Von Eye, A., Puttler, L. and Zucker, R. (2001) 'Temperamental characteristics as predictors of externalising and internalising child behaviour problems in the contexts of high and low parental psychpathology.' *Infant Mental Health Journal 22,* 3, 393–415.

Muncie, J., Wetherell, M., Dallos, R. and Cochrane, A. (eds) (1997) *Understanding the Family.* London: Sage.

Munley, A., Powers, C.S. and Williamson, J.B. (1982) 'Humanising nursing home environments: The relevance of hospice principles.' *International Journal of Ageing and Human Development 15,* 263–284.

Munro, E. (2002) *Effective Child Protection.* London: Sage.

Nash, M. and Stewart, B. (2002) *Spirituality and Social Care: Contributing to Personal and Community Well-being.* London: Jessica Kingsley Publishers.

Newman, T. (2002) *Promoting Resilience: A Review of Effective Strategies for Child Care Services.* Barkingside: Barnardos.

National CAMHS Support Service. *CAMH Service Guidelines.* London: Care Services Improvement Partnership/ HMSO. 29 July 2009

NCH Action for Children (2007) *Fact File.* London: NCH.

National CAMHS Support Service. *CAMH Service Guidelines.* London: Care Services Improvement Partnership/ HMSO.

NCH Action for Children (2007) *Fact File.* London: NCH.

NHS Advisory Service (1995) *Together We Stand: Child and Adolescent Mental Health Services.* London: HMSO.

NICE (2002) *Schizophrenia – Core Interventions in the Treatment and Management of Schizophrenia in Primary and Secondary Care.* London: HMSO.

NICE (2004) *Eating Disorders, Core Interventions in the Treatment and Management of Anorexia Nervosa, Bulimia Nervosa and Related Eating Disorders.* London: HMSO.

NICE (2005) *Depression in Children and Young People: Identification and Management in Primary, Community and Secondary Care.* London: HMSO.

NICE (2008) *Attention Deficit Hyperactivity Disorder: Diagnosis and Management.* London: HMSO.

NISW/DoH Barclay Report (1982) *Social Workers: Their Role and Task.* London: Bedford Square Press.

Nixon, C. and Northrup, D. (1997) *Evaluating Mental Health Services. How Do Programmes for Children Work in the Real World?* Thousand Oaks, CA: Sage.

O'Donnell, G. (2002) *Mastering Sociology.* London: Palgrave.

O'Hagan, K. (1996) *Competence in Social Work Practice. A Practical Guide for Professionals.* London. Jessica Kingsley Publishers.

Oberheumer, P. (1998) 'A European Perspective on Early Years Training.' In L. Abbott and G. Pugh (eds) *Training to Work in Early Years – Developing the Climbing Frame.* Buckingham: Open University Press.

Office for National Statistics (2004) *Child and Adolescent Mental Health Statistics.* London: HMSO.

Office for National Statistics (2006) *Social Trends.* London: HMSO.

Onyet, S., Heppleston, T. and Bushnell, N. (1994) *A National Survey of Community Mental Health Teams: 1 Team Structure.* London: Sainsbury Centre for Mental Health.

Otikikpi, T. (1999) 'Educational Needs of Black Children in Care.' In R. Barn (ed.) *Working With Black Children and Adolescents in Need.* London: BAAF.

Oullette, P., Lazear, K. and Chambers, K. (1999) 'Action leadership: The development of an approach to leadership enhancement for grassroots community leaders in children's mental health.' *Journal of Behavioural Health Services and Research 26,* 2, 171–185.

Ovretveit, J. (1996) 'Five ways to describe a multidisciplinary team.' *Journal of Interprofessional Care 10,* 2, 163–171.

Paloutzian, R.F. (1996) *Invitation to the Psychology of Religion,* 2nd edn. London: Allyn and Bacon.

Papadopoulos, R. (2001) 'Refugee families: issues of systemic supervision.' *Journal of Family Therapy 23,* 405–422.

Parekh, B. (2000) *Rethinking Multiculturalism: Cultural Diversity and Political Theory.* Basingstoke: Palgrave

Parton, N. (1994) 'The nature of social work under conditions of (post) modernity.' *Social Work and Social Sciences Review 5,* 2, 93–112.

Parton, N. (1999) 'Reconfiguring Child Welfare Practices: Risk, Advanced Liberalism and the Government of Freedom.' In A.S. Chambon, A. Irving and L. Epstein (eds) *Reading Foucault for Social Work.* Chichester: Columbia Press.

Payne, M. (1997) *Modern Social Work Theory.* London: Macmillan.

Payne, M. (2002) 'Management.' In R. Adams, L. Dominelli and M. Payne (eds) *Critical Practice in Social Work.* Basingstoke: Macmillan.

Pearce, J.B. (1999) 'Collaboration between the NHS and Social Services in the provision of child and adolescent mental health services: A personal view.' *Child Psychology and Psychiatry Review 4*, 4, 150–152.

Pease, B. and Fook, J. (eds) (1999) *Transforming Social Work Practice: The Challenge of Postmodernism*. London: Routledge.

Pickles, A., Rowe, R., Simonoff, E., Foley, D., Rutter, M. and Silberg, J. (2001) 'Child psychiatric symptoms and psychosocial impairment – relationship and prognostic significance.' *British Journal of Psychiatry 179*, 230–235.

Pieterse, J. N. (2004) *Globalization and Culture*. Oxford: Rowman and Littlefield.

Pinkerton, J., Higgins, K. and Devine, P. (2000) *Family Support: Linking Project Evaluation to Policy Analysis*. Aldershot: Ashgate.

Prince's Trust YouGov Youth Index (2008) *Hold Your Head Up*. London: Princes Trust.

Raval, H. (1996) 'A systematic perspective on working with interpreters.' *Child Clinical Psychology and Psychiatry 1*, 29–43.

Ravazzola, M.C. (1997) *Historia Infames: Los Milagros en las Relaciones*. Buenos Aires: Ediciones Paidos, Terapia Familiar.

Rawson, D. (1994) 'Models of Interprofessional Work: Likely Theories and Possibilities.' In A. Leathard (ed.) *Going Interprofessional: Working Together for Health and Welfare*. London: Routledge.

Read, J. and Barker, S. (1996) *Not Just Sticks and Stones. A Survey of the Stigma, Taboo and Discrimination Experienced by People with Mental Health Problems*. London: MIND.

Reder, P. and Duncan, S. (2004) 'Making the most of the Victoria Inquiry Report.' *Child Abuse Review 13*, 95–114.

Reed, A.W. (2002) *Aboriginal Stories*. Sydney: New Holland Publishers.

Reimers, A. and Treacher, A. (1995) *Introducing User-Friendly Family Therapy*. London: Routledge.

Remschmidt, H. (2001) (ed.) *Schizophrenia in Children and Adolescents*. Cambridge: Cambridge University Press.

Repper, J., Sayce, L., Strong, S., Wilmot, J. and Haines, M. (1997) *Tall Stories from the Back Yard*. London: MIND.

Resnik, M.D., Harris, L.J. and Blum, R.W. (1993) 'The impact of caring and connectedness on adolescent health and wellbeing.' *Journal of Paediatrics and Child Health 14*, 254–269.

Reynolds, A.J. (1998) 'Resilience among black urban youth: Intervention effects and mechanisms of influence.' *American Journal of Orthopsychiatry 68*, 1, 84–100.

Richardson, J. and Joughin, C. (2000) *The Mental Health Needs of Looked After Children*. London: Gaskell.

Richmond, M. (1922) *What Is Social Casework?* New York: Russell Sage.

Robinson, L. (1995) *Psychology for Social Workers: Black Perspectives*. London: Routledge.

Rodney, C. (2000) 'Pathways: A Model Service Delivery System.' In N.N. Singh, J.P. Leung and A.N. Singh (eds) (2000) *International Perspectives on Child and Adolescent Mental Health*. London: Elsevier.

Ruch, G. (ed.) (2009) *Post Qualifying Child Care Social Work – Developing Reflective Practice*. London: Sage.

Rutter, M. (1985) 'Resilience in the face of adversity.' *British Journal of Psychiatry 147*, 598–611.

Rutter, M. (1991) 'Services for Children with Emotional Disorders.' *Young Minds Newsletter 9*, 1–5.

Rutter M. (ed.) (1995) *Psychosocial Disturbances in Young People: Challenges for Prevention*. Cambridge: Cambridge University Press.

Rutter, M. (1999) 'Preventing Anti-Social Behaviour in Young People: The Contribution of Early Intervention.' In R. Bayley (ed.) *Transforming Children's Lives: The Importance of Early Intervention*. London: Family Policy Studies Centre.

Rutter, M. (2005) 'Perspectives on the causes of mental health problems in children and adolescents.' Young Minds Symposium, London: Institute for Public Policy Research.

Rutter, M. and Smith, D. (1995) *Psychosocial Disorders in Young People*. London: Wiley.

Ryan, M. (1999) *The Children Act 1989: Putting It Into Practice*. Aldershot: Ashgate.

Salzberger-Wittenberg, I. (1981) *Psycho Analytic Insight and Relationships: A Kleinian Approach*. London: Routledge.

Savin-Williams, R. (2001) 'A critique of research on sexual minority youth.' *Journal of Adolescence 24*, 5–13.

Sawyer, M.G., Arney, F.M., Baghurst, P.A. *et al.* (2000) *Child and Adolescent Component of the National Survey of Mental Health and Well-Being*. Canberra: Dept Health and Aged Care.

Schaffer, D., Gould, M.S., Brasic, J. *et al.* (1983) 'Child Global Assessment Scale.' *Archives of General Psychiatry 40*, 1228–1231.

Schoon, I., Wiggins, R.D., Bynner, J., Joshi, H. and Parsons, S. (2002) *The Accumulation of Risk in the Life Course from Birth to Young Adulthood*. Brighton: Trust for Study of Adolescence/ESCR.

Scott, S., Knapp, M., Henderson, J. and Maughan, B. (2001) 'Financial cost of social exclusion: Follow-up study of antisocial children into adulthood.' *British Medical Journal 323*, 191–194.

Sebuliba, D. and Vostanis, P. (2001) 'Child and adolescent mental health training for primary care staff.' *Clinical Child Psychology and Psychiatry 6*, 2, 191–204.

Shadish, W.R., Ragsdale, K., Glaser, R.R. and Montgomery, L.M. (1995) 'The efficacy and effectiveness of marital and family therapy: A perspective from meta-analysis.' *Journal of Marital and Family Therapy 21*, 345–360.

Singh, N., Leung, J. and Singh, A. (2000) *International Perspectives on Child and Adolescent Mental Health.* Oxford: Elsevier.

Sinha, C. (1998) *Language and Representation: A Socio-Naturalistic Approach to Human Development.* London: Harvester Wheatsheaf.

Smaje, C. (1995) *Health, Race and Ethnicity: Making Sense of the Evidence.* London: Kings Fund Institute.

Snelgrove, S. and Hughes, D. (2000) 'Interprofessional relations between doctors and nurses: Perspectives from South Wales.' *Journal of Advanced Nursing 31*, 3, 661–667.

Social Care Institute for Excellence (2005) *Knowledge Review – Learning and Teaching in Social Work Education – Assessment.* London: Social Care Institute for Excellence.

Solomos, J. (1999) *Race and Racism in Contemporary Britain,* 3rd edn. Basingstoke: Macmillan.

Spence, S.H., Barrett, P.M. and Turner, C.M. (2003) 'Psychometric properties of the Spence Children's Anxiety Scale with young adolescents.' *Journal of Anxiety Disorders 17*, 6, 605–625.

Spencer, N. (1996) 'Race and ethnicity as determinants of child health: A personal view.' *Child Health and Development 22*, 5, 327–345.

Spender, Q., Salt, N., Dawkins, J., Kendrick, T. and Hill, P. (2001) *Child Mental Health in Primary Care.* London: Radcliffe Medical Press.

Stanley, K. (2001) *Cold Comfort: Young Separated Refugees in England.* London: Save the Children.

Statham, J. (2000) *Outcomes and Effectiveness of Family Support Services: A Research Review.* London: Institute of Education.

Stepney, R. and Ford, S. (2000) *Social Work Models, Methods, and Theories.* Lyme Regis: Russell House.

Sue, D., Ivey, A. and Penderson, P. (1996) *A Theory of Multicultural Counselling and Therapy.* New York: Brooks/Cole Publishing.

Sutton, C. (2000) *Helping Families with Troubled Children.* London: Wiley.

Suwa, M., Suzuki, K., Hara, K., Watanabe, H. and Takahashi, T. (2003) 'Family features in primary social withdrawal among young adults.' *Psychiatry and Clinical Neurosciences 57*, 586–594.

Sveaass, N. and Reichelt, S. (2001) 'Refugee families in therapy: From referrals to therapeutic conversations.' *Journal of Family Therapy 23*, 2, 119–136.

Swinton, J. (2003) *Spirituality and Mental Health Care.* London: Jessica Kingsley Publishers.

Sylva, K. (1994) 'School influences on children's development.' *Journal of Child Psychology and Psychiatry and Allied Professions 35*, 1, 135–170.

Taylor, B. and Devine, D. (1993) *Assessing Needs and Planning Care in Social Work.* London: Arena.

Taylor, C. and White, S. (2000) *Practising Reflexivity in Health and Welfare.* Buckingham: Open University Press.

Thoburn, J., Wilding, J. and Watson, J. (1998) *Children in Need. A Review of Family Support Work in Three Local Authorities.* Norwich: University of East Anglia/Dept of Health.

Thompson, N. and Thompson, S. (2002) *Understanding Social Care.* Lyme Regis: Russell House.

Tillich, P. (1963) *Christianity and the Encounter of the World Religions.* Washington, DC: Columbia University Press.

Timimi, S. and Maitra, B. (2005) *Critical Voices in Child and Adolescent Mental Health.* London: Free Association Books.

Titmuss, R.M. (1958) *Essays on the Welfare State.* London: George Allen and Unwin.

Tovey, W. (ed.) (2007) *The Post Qualifying Handbook for Social Workers.* London: Jessica Kingsley Publishers.

Treacher, A. (1995) *Reviewing Consumer Studies of Family Therapy.* In A. Treacher and S. Reimers *Introducing User-Friendly Family Therapy.* London: Routledge.

Treseder, P. (1997) *Empowering Children and Young People: A Training Manual for Promoting Involvement in Decision-Making.* London: Save the Children.

Trevithick, P. (2000) *Social Work Skills.* Buckingham: Open University Press.

Trotter, J. (2000) 'Lesbian and gay issues in social work with young people: Resilience and success through confronting, conforming and escaping.' *British Journal of Social Work 30*, 1, 115–123.

Tseng Yueh-Hung (2002) 'A lesson in culture.' *ELT Journal 56*, 1, 11–21.

Tucker, N. and Gamble, N. (eds) (2001) *Family Fictions.* London: Continuum.

Tucker, S., Strange, C., Cordeaux, C., Moules, T. and Torrance, N. (1999) 'Developing an interdisciplinary framework for the education and training of those working with children and young people.' *Journal of Interprofessional Care 13*, 3, 261–270.

Tunstill, J. (1996) 'Family support: Past, present and future challenges.' *Child and Family Social Work 1*, 151–158.

Valentine, C.A. (1976) 'Poverty and Culture.' In P. Worsley (ed.) *Problems of Modern Society*. London: Penguin.

Valentine, L. and Feinauer, L.L. (1993) 'Resilience factors associated with female survivors of childhood sexual abuse.' *American Journal of Family Therapy 21*, 3, 216–224.

VanDenBerg, J. and Grealish, M. (1999) 'Individualized services and supports through the wraparound process – philosophy and procedures.' *Journal of Child and Family Studies 5*, 7–21.

Vostanis, P. (2007) *Mental Health Interventions and Services for Vulnerable Children and Young People*. London: Jessica Kingsley Publishers.

Vincent, J. and Jouriles, E. (eds) (2000) *Domestic Violence: Guidelines for Research Informed Practice*. London: Jessica Kingsley Publishers.

Walker, S. (2001a) 'Developing child and adolescent mental health services.' *Journal of Child Health Care 5*, 2, 71–76.

Walker, S. (2001b) 'Consulting with children and young people.' *International Journal of Children's Rights 9*, 45–56.

Walker, S. (2001c) 'Tracing the contours of postmodern social work.' *British Journal of Social Work 31*, 29–39.

Walker, S. (2002) 'Family support and social work practice: Renaissance or retrenchment?' *European Journal of Social Work 5*, 1, 43–54.

Walker, S. (2003a) *Social Work and Child and Adolescent Mental Health*. Lyme Regis: Russell House Publishers.

Walker, S. (2003b) 'Social work and child mental health – psycho social principles in community practice.' *British Journal of Social Work 33*, 673–687.

Walker, S. (2003c) 'Interprofessional work in child and adolescent mental health services.' *Emotional and Behavioural Difficulties 8*, 3, 189–204.

Walker, S. (2004) 'Community work and psychosocial practice – chalk and cheese or birds of a feather?' *Journal of Social Work Practice 18*, 2, 161–175.

Walker, S. (2005) *Culturally Competent Therapy: Working with Children and Young People*. Basingstoke: Palgrave.

Walker, S. and Akister, J. (2004) *Applying Family Therapy – A Guide for Caring Professionals in the Community*. Lyme Regis: Russell House Publishers.

Walker, S. and Beckett, C. (2003) *Social Work Assessment and Intervention*. Lyme Regis: Russell House Publishers.

Walker, S. and Thurston, C. (2006) *Safeguarding Children and Young People – A Guide to Integrated Practice*. Lyme Regis: Russell House Publishers.

Warnick, E.M., Bracken, M.B. and Kasl, S. (2008) 'Screening efficiency of the child behaviour checklist and strengths and difficulties questionnaire: A systematic review.' *Child and Adolescent Mental Health 13*, 3, 140–147.

Waterhouse, S. (2000) *A Positive Approach to Autism*. London: Jessica Kingsley Publishers.

Watkins, D. and Gerong, A. (1997) 'Culture and spontaneous self-concepts among Filipino college students.' *Journal of Social Psychology 137*, 480–488.

Weaver, H. and Burns, B. (2001) 'I shout with fear at night – understanding the traumatic experiences of refugee and asylum seekers.' *Journal of Social Work 1*, 2, 147–164.

Webb, S. (2001) 'Some considerations on the validity of evidence-based practice in social work.' *British Journal of Social Work 31*, 57–79.

Webster-Stratton, C. (1999) *How to Promote Children's Social and Emotional Competence*. London: Sage.

White, M. and Epston, D. (1990) *Narrative Means to Therapeutic Ends*. New York: W.W. Norton.

White, K. and Grove, M. (2003) *Towards an Understanding of Partnership*. London: NCCVCO.

Whiting, L. (1999) 'Caring for children of differing cultures.' *Journal of Child Health Care 3*, 4, 33–38.

Whyte, B. (2007) 'Developments in Youth Justice in Scotland for the 21st Century.' In P. Raynor and G. McIvor (eds) *Developments in Social Work with Offenders*. Research Highlights. London: Jessica Kingsley Publishers.

Williams, B., Catell, D., Greenwood, M., LeFevre, S., Murray, I. and Thomas, P. (1999) 'Exploring person centredness: User perspectives on a model of social psychiatry.' *Health and Social Care in the Community 7*, 6, 475–482.

Williams, R. (1997) *The Barefoot Book of Fairies*. Bath: Barefoot Books.

Wilson, J. (1999) *Child Focused Practice*. London: Karnac Books.

Wilson, K. and James, A. (2002) *The Child Protection Handbook*. London: Balliere Tindall.

Wong, V. (2009) 'Youth locked in time and space? Defining features of social withdrawal and practice implications.' *Journal of Social Work Practice 23*, 3, 337–352.

Wong, V. and Ying, W. (2006) 'Social withdrawal of young people in Hong Kong: A social exclusion perspective.' *Hong Kong Journal of Social Work 40*, 1/2, 61–92.

Woodhead, M. (1998) 'Understanding Child Development in the Context of Children's Rights.' In C. Cunninghame (ed.) *Realising Children's Rights*. London: Save the Children.

Woods, M. and Hollis, F. (1990) *Casework: A Psychological Process*, 2nd edn. New York: Random House.

World Health Organization (1992) *International Classification of Diseases (ICD 10)*. New York: World Health Organization.

World Health Organization (2005) *Mental Health Policy and Service Guidelines: Child and Adolescent Mental Health Policy and Plans*. Geneva: World Health Organization.

Yelloly, M. (1980) *Social Work Theory and Psychoanalysis*. New York: Van Nostrand.

Yeo, S. (2003) 'Bonding and attachment of Australian Aboriginal children.' *Child Abuse Review 12*, 292–304.

Young Minds (2003) Conference on Child and Adolescent Mental Health, London.

Young, K. and Haynes, R. (1993) 'Assessing population needs in primary health care: The problem of GOP attachments.' *Journal of Interprofessional Care 7*, 1, 15–27.

Youth Justice Board (2002) *Building on Success – YJB Annual Review*. London: HMSO.

Subject Index

Italic page numbers indicate tables and figures

Aboriginal peoples 242, 247–8
abuse 166, 196, 211, 247, 259–60
  racist 205–6
Access to Personal Files Act 1987 195
accessible services 34
accommodation centres 162
adaptation, to needs of child 207
adaptiveness 56
adolescence 218–19
adolescents see young people
adult mental health problems, childhood origins 26–7
adults
  attachment 64
  behaviour towards children 54
  construction of childhood 66–7
adversity, impact of 133
advocacy 136, 195, 199, 202
African cultures, religion and spirituality 241
Afro-Caribbean children and young people 206
afterlife 239
age-appropriate services 195
agencies
  relationships between 177
  variety 142
  varying responses 192
agency culture 225
agency, sense of 257
agreements 166
alcohol addiction, of parents 23
alcohol misuse 80–1, 91
Anglo-Saxon monoculture 214
anorexia nervosa 92
  treatments 117–18
anti-discriminatory practice 224
anti-racism 206
anti-social behaviour 89–91
anxiety 75–6, 237
  treatments 116

Approved Mental Health Practitioner (AMHP) 24
archetypes 233
arranged marriages 220
Asian children and young people, cultural identities 206
Asian girls, competing cultures 220
Asperger syndrome (AS) 78–9
  case illustration 79–80
assessment 105–6
  attention deficit hyperactivity disorder (ADHD) 97–8
  autism 79, 102
  black and ethnic minority communities 107
  Common Assessment Framework see separate heading
  eating disorders 91–2, 102
  Framework for the Assessment of Children in Need 111–12
  importance of 106–7
  inadequate 191
  needs-led 197
  parental satisfaction 112
  principles of 106
  psychiatric 198
  psychosocial methods 39–40
  refining and developing 212
  schizophrenia 94–5
  standardisation 64
  theoretical frameworks 216–17
  therapeutic element 174
  variation in 106
assessment tools 71–2, 100–1, 102, 106
asylum seekers 161, 162, 170, 196, 200, 206, 210, 211, 214, 220
at risk labels 35
attachment 257–8
  Aboriginal societies 242
  adults 64
  ambivalent-preoccupied-entangled patterns 62–3
  avoidant-dismissing patterns 61
  behaviours and patters 59

and brain development 260
  complexity 63
  secure and autonomous patterns 59–60
  single parent households 242
attachment theory 56–64
attention deficit hyperactivity disorder (ADHD) 97–9, 102
  treatments 117
attitudes, ambivalence 52–3
Australia 136, 247–8
authoritarianism 242
autism 76–8, 102
autonomy 140

Bangladeshi young people 206
Barclay Report 27–8
barriers
  cultural and practice 28
  to effective multi-agency working 40–1, 137, 141
  overcoming 150
becoming, and spirituality 232
behaviour therapy 118
behavioural disturbance, prevalence and complexity 22–3
behavioural management, as media focus 29
behavioural problems, in autism 77
behavioural therapies 116
belief, and religion 234–6
beliefs
  acceptance of 246
  pathologising 237
  traditional 238–9
  see also faith; religion; spirituality
Bible 239
bipolar disorder, treatments 117
bisexuality, risk of suicide 75
Black children and young people
  cultural identities 206
  stereotypes 220
Black clients 38, 39
  assessment 107
  disproportionate diagnoses 40

Black immigrants 161
'black', use of term 18
body dysmorphic disorder, treatments
    116
boundaries 129
    professional 143–4
Bowlby, John 216
British Association of Social Workers
    (BASW), code of ethics 21
British Nationality Act 1948 161
budgets 184
bulimia nervosa 93
    treatments 118
bullying 23

CAMHS
    focus 136
    four tier structure 34, 34–5
    renaissance 27
Canada 210, 242
capitalism 219–20
carers
    Common Assessment Framework
        110
    schizophrenia 95
Catholicism 232, 242
causal explanations 40
causality 178
causation, factors to consider 254
census data 213
change
    potential for 134
    social 212
Change for Children 30
changes
    disadvantages of 178
    genetic 212
    resistance to 164
    structural 30, 168
charitable support, pressure on, 26
Child Behaviour Checklist (CBCL)
    71–2, 72, 100
child-centred services 184
child development 56
    central processes 67
    effect of attachment 260
    effect of neglect 260
    social policy perspectives 66–7
    within social work 47
Child Global Assessment Scale 100
child guidance 25–6, 137
Child Health Questionnaire 52–3, 53
child poverty 166
childhood
    child's perspective 263–4
    normative model 215
children
    as active participants 15–16, 32
    attachment 60, 61, 62
    as consumers 208
    empowering 43–5
    heterogeneity 16
    participation in research 43–4
    right to make decisions 202
    role in defining mental health 54
    silencing 134
    support for those without families
        202

use of term 18
Children Act 1989 92, 111, 141,
    192, 196–9
Children Act 2004 28, 30, 42, 152,
    188
    guidance for NHS 153
Children and Young people's Plans
    189
Children's Depression Inventory 100
Children's Legal Centre 190, 201–2
children's perspectives 169
Children's Plan 28
children's rights 43, 190
children's services reorganisation,
    1970 25–6
Children's Trusts 28, 30, 187–90
citizenship 161
code of ethics (BASW) 21
cognitive behavioural practice 122–3
cognitive behavioural therapy 116,
    117, 118
    attention deficit hyperactivity
        disorder (ADHD) 99
    bulimia nervosa 93
    schizophrenia 96
collaboration, co-operation and co-
        ordination 139
collaborative working 157
    defining 135–6
    difficulties 186
    see also multi-disciplinary working;
        partnership working
collectivism 242
colonialism 209
Commission for Health Improvement
    (CHI) 146
commissioners, relationship with 184
commissioning 253
Common Assessment Framework 28,
    52, 100, 108–11, 198
    development of child 109–10
    elements 109–11
    family and environmental factors
        110
    parents and carers 110
    process 108–9
    social and community resources 111
common assessment tools 100–1
Common Core Skills and Knowledge
    28
'common' problems 69–70
communication 142, 150–1, 157
    in context of beliefs 246
    cultural styles 225
    strategies for improvement 153–6
    through stories 241–2
community developments 160–2
community resources, Common
        Assessment Framework 111
community treatment, supervised 196
community work practice 120
comparative perspective 66
competence 194
    cultural 211–12, 217, 220–2,
        228, 242
complaints procedure 199
complex needs 70, 102
complexity

of needs 136
    organisational 191–2
compulsory admissions 193
conduct problems 64–5
    cost 90
    treatments 116–17
confidentiality 150–1, 184, 190,
    194–6
conflict, dealing with 150
connecting, and spirituality 232
Conners' Rating Scale Revised 100
consent 190, 193–4
constructionism, view of mental
        health 66
consultation
    with children and young people
        15–16, 189
    understanding of term 31
consumers, children and young people
        as 208
contemporary practice model 37–8
contemporary society, character of 40
context
    changing 21–2
    client's 128–9
    organisational 137–9, 172
    policy and professional 202
    social policy 160
control, and self-harm 87
cost-effectiveness 26
cost, of anti-social behaviour 90–1
creationism 235
crime 23, 89–91
Crime and Disorder Act 1998 192
crisis intervention 119–20, 168, 220
critical period 56
critical thinking 106
cross-cultural services 223
cross-cultural studies 210–11
cultural belief, and therapy 245–50
cultural competence 211–12, 217,
        220–2, 222–6, 228, 242
    case illustration 225–6
    religion and spirituality 234
    and systemic theory 223–4
cultural difference 227
cultural diversity 127–8
cultural identities 206, 237
cultural influences 172
cultural models, of illness 107
cultural values, sensitivity to 225
culture
    characteristics 218
    conceptualising 211–12
    defining 208–10, 223
    diversity and difference 217–19
    and emotional well-being 214–17
    evolution of 227, 228
    globalisation 220
    large and small 212
    maintaining 228
    minority ethnic 206, 228
    as organic and dynamic 218, 227
    organisational 221
    safeguarding 210–11
    and spirituality 236–8
    theoretical concepts 228
custodial sentencing 75

daily living 51
dangerousness 126–7
Data Protection Act 1984 152, 195
debates
    importance of 221
    moving away from polarity 255
    within social work 22
demonic possession 246
depression 72–3, 237
    and suicide 74
    treatments *116*
deprivation 23
detention 192, 200
developmental concepts *57–8*
developmental group psychotherapy
    118
diagnosis, limitations of 50
diet 258–9
    attention deficit hyperactivity
        disorder (ADHD) *117*
difference
    cultural 227
    and diversity 217–19
    fear of 209
    and globalisation 220
    signifiers of 214
differences
    individual and group 254
    in mental health problems 69
    between team members 41
differentials, pay and conditions 175
dignity 21
direct work, skills in 115–18
disability, definition 197
discourses, professional 44–5, 50
discrimination 143, 190, 205, 214
    disempowerment 164
disorders
    eating disorders 40, 75, 91, 102,
        117–18
    spiritual 247
disruption, of attachment 59
diversity
    of children and young people 16
    and difference 217–19
domestic violence 166
dowries 220
drug dependency, of parents 23
drug misuse 80–1
    and offending 91
Durkheim, Emile 217
dynamics, emotional 174

early childhood studies 67, 68
early intervention 147–8, 166–7, 179
Eastern cultures, religion and
    spirituality 241
Eating Attitudes Test *100*
eating disorders 40, 75, 91, 102
    treatments *117–18*
economics 81
education
    early intervention 166–7
    expectations 254
    failure in 23
    low achievement 258
    segregation 162
eligibility criteria 220

emancipatory practice 221–2
emotional disturbance, prevalence and
    complexity 22–3
emotional dynamics 174
emotional illiteracy 40, 75
emotional literacy 49–50
emotional problems, in autism 77
emotional well-being 49–50
    and culture 214–17
    use of term 18
empathy 129
empowerment 54, 155, 202, 224
    of children and young people 43–5
    of women 75
enlightenment 235
environment
    Common Assessment Framework
        110
    impoverished 258
    interplay with nature 215
    religion and spirituality 245
environmental factors 255
epidemiological studies 31, 246–7
Eriksen, Erik 216
ethics 190
    of young people's participation 32
ethnic conflicts 211
ethnic diversity 161
ethnic focused theory *223*
ethnic identity, and inequality 214
ethnic rivalry 221
ethnicity, understanding 212–14
ethnocentrism 224, 229
eugenics 213
Eurocentrism 39, 224, 229
European Parliament 27
European Union 160–1
evaluation 172
evaluation tools 144–8
Every Child Matters 22
Every Child Matters: Change for Children
    22
Every Child Matters policy 28, 30
evidence base 134
evolutionism 235
expansionism 209
expenditure *184*
experience 59
Experience of Service Questionnaire
    146–7, *147*
explanations, seeking 234–5
exploitation 219
exposure and response prevention *117*
externalisation 125
externalised families 80–1
extrinsic religiousness 239
eye movement desensitisation and
    reprocessing (EMDR) *116*

fairies 238–9
fairy tales 233, 238
faith 233
    stages of development *241*
    see also beliefs; religion; spirituality
families
    case illustration 165
    change in perceptions of 212

Common Assessment Framework
    110
    defining 162–3
    disruption 254
    externalised and internalised 80–1
    and gender 163
    response to therapy 174, 175
    schizophrenia 95, 96
    and social workers 163–6
family breakdown, and suicide 74
family centres 165
Family Group Conference 237–8
family life
    problems and risks 23–4
    right to 200
family support 159–60, 168–72,
    179, 202
family therapy *116, 118*
    and/or support 175–6
    consumer studies 171
    learning from families 179
    research evidence 173–4
    value of 163–4
family, use of term 18
fear, neutralising 259
flexibility, of approach 170
food 258–9
forced marriages 220
foster care, therapeutic *117*
four tier pyramidal structure 137–8,
    186–7
Framework for the Assessment of
    Children in Need *100*, 111–15
    case illustration 113–15
France 237
Fraser competence 194
freedom of expression 201
Freud, Sigmund 216, 239
funding 168

gay young men 206
    risk of suicide 75
gender
    and Asperger syndrome (AS) 78
    and autism 77
    and families 163
    and suicide 74–5
General Practitioners 52, 68
General Social Care Council (GSCC)
    Specialist Standards and
        Requirements 36–7
    user-focused values 37
generalised anxiety disorder 76
generic social work 25
genital mutilation 220–1
geographical boundaries, of different
    agencies 40–1
Gillick competence 194
globalisation 209–10, 219–20, 228
goals 178
government initiatives 30, 35
Great Britain 210
group parent-training programmes
    116, 117
guidelines, for extreme situations 191
guilt 244, 245, 261
    parents feeling 143
    self-harm 88

Habermas, Jurgen 217
harm, duty to investigate 198
Harter's Self Perception Profile for
    Adolescents *101*
Harter's Self Perception Profile for
    Children *101*
Health Act 1999 28, 42
Health of the Nation Outcome Scales
    for Children and Adolescents
    (HoNOSCA) *100*, 144–6, *145*
Health of the Nation Outcome Scales
    (HoNOS) 144
Health of the Nation Strategy 144
health services, focus 136
heritage 234
heterogeneity, of children and young
    people 16
heterosexism 75
higher education 33
hijab bans 237
hikikomori (social withdrawal) 216
HMSO 45
holism 38–9, 46, 54, 70
Home Office 23
homophobia 75
Hong Kong 210, 215–16
House of Commons Health
    Committee, report on CAMHS
    183
Human Rights Act 1998 161, 192,
    200–1
human rights, and service provision
    201
hybridisation
    developing new practitioner 140–1
    of roles and identities 42–3, 46

identities
    cultural 206, 237
    and globalisation 219–20
identity
    effect of neglect 259–60
    national 221
illness, cultural models of 107
immigration 161
imperialism 209
'in need', definition 197–8
India 210
indigenous healing 224
individualism 40, 242
individuation 233, 259–60
inequality 179
    biological basis 213
    race and ethnic identity 214
    of wealth 209–10
infant, use of term 18
infants, attachment 59–60, 61, 62
information
    for child 201
    control and manipulation 208
    disclosure 195
    dissemination 142
    sharing 151–2, 177–8
inner worlds 244–5
inpatient care *118*
institutional racism 161
Integrated Children's System 28
intellectual modesty 67

inter-agency co-operation 34
inter-agency mind-set 150
internal working model 59
internalisation 125
internalised families 80–1
International Federation of Social
    Workers 14
interpersonal psychotherapy *118*
interplay, nature and environment 215
interpreters 226
intervention
    autism 79–80
    early 147–8, 166–7, 179
    least restrictive 202
    linking to outcomes 35
    opportunities 255
    purpose of 167–8
    refining and developing 212
    role of PMHWs 31–2
    self-harm 84
intrinsic religiousness 239
Islam 232

Japan, *hikikomori* (social withdrawal)
    216
joined up thinking 15
joined up working 40–1, 143
joint working 31–2
judicial review 199
Jung, C.G. 233, 239

key purpose, of social work 13–14
keyworkers 136
Klein, Melanie 216
knowledge 106
    of difference and cultural diversity
        211
    dissemination 150
Krishna 244

labelling 29, 35, 38, 52, 128, 164–5,
    192
Labour government, NHS pledge 183
language 48, 214
    religious 240
large culture 212
legal framework 190–1, 203
legal system, stereotyping 214
legends 233, 238
lesbian girls 206
    risk of suicide 75
Liberation Theology 232, 242
liberty 191, 200
listening 225
live supervision 176
local authorities
    Children's Trusts 189, 190
    duties 198
loss 206

machismo 242
Malaysia 210
management 140
managerialism 26
Maori 237–8
marginalisation, risk of suicide 75
marriages, forced/arranged 220
Marx, Karl 217

meaning
    search for 233
    and spirituality 232
media representations 29–30, 48, 52
    racist 214
medical model 50, 236–7
medication *116*, *117*, *118*, 191
menarche 219
mental disorders, prevalence *55*
mental health
    defining 50–1
    as global issue 27
    orthodox evidence 214–16
    prospects 262–4
    social model 202
    young people 64–5
Mental Health Act 1983 92, 192–3
Mental Health Act 2007 195
    requirements 24
Mental Health (Approval of Persons
        to be Approved Mental Health
        Professionals) (England)
        Regulations (2007), requirements
        24–5
mental health disorder, use of term 49
mental health problems
    in context of offending 89
    defined by adults 54
    differences in 69
    early identification 42
    increase 203
    possible causes 254–5
    possible consensus on causes 255–6
    predictive factors 211
    recognition 52–4
    sociological explanations 66
    time trends and vulnerability 256–7
    use of term 18, 49
    and well-being 261–2
Mental Health Tribunal 196
mental illness
    construction of 50
    lack of legal definition 190
    use of term 49
mentalisation 259–60
method, model and focus *171*
migrant cultures 206, 228
migration 160–1
Mills, C. Wright 217
minority ethnic communities 161
    assessment 107
    culture 206
minority ethnic cultures 228
model of contemporary practice 37–8
models of practice 118–26
    cognitive behavioural practice
        122–3
    community work practice 120
    crisis intervention 119–20
    narrative therapeutic practice 124–6
    psychodynamic practice 121–2
    systemic practice 120–1
    task-centred practice 123–4
modesty 67
monoculture 214
monotropy 59
Moods and Feelings Questionnaire
    101

moral awareness 261
motivational interviewing *118*
multi-agency partnerships 15
multi-cultural societies 222
multi-cultural therapy 249
multi-dimensional theory 224
multi-disciplinary teams 41
multi-disciplinary working 28, 29–30,
    46, 148–9, *184*
    barriers to 137
    challenge of 40–3
    challenges of 141–4
    communication 150–1
    dealing with conflict 150–1Furniss
    defining 136
    family support and therapy 171
    interprofessional training 42
    offending 91
    working and learning 222–6
    see also collaborative working;
        partnership working
multiple caregiving 242
multisystemic therapy *117, 118*
myths 233, 238

narrative therapeutic practice 124–6
National Advisory Council 253
National Children's Commissioners 30
national identity 221
National Priorities Guidance, Modernising
    Health and Social Services 29,
    185–6
National Service Framework for
    Children, Young People and
    Maternity Services 22, 30, 32
National Service Framework for
    Mental Health 107
national strategy, lack of 15
nationality 161
Nationality, Immigration and Asylum
    Bill 2002 162
Native American cultures, religion and
    spirituality 241
nature and environment, interplay 215
needs
    complex 70, 136
    defining 197–8
    spiritual and psychological 232–3
needs assessment, difficulty of 32
'NEET' 71
neglect 196, 247, 259–60
neo-racism 205–6
networking 226
networks
    challenges of 141–4
    professional 177–8
neutrality 177
new practitioner 140–1
New Zealand 237–8
'normal', defining 47–8
not believing 234
Nuffield Foundation 64
nutrition, attention deficit
    hyperactivity disorder (ADHD)
    117

obsessive-compulsive disorder 52, 76
    treatments *116*

Oedipus 238
operations *184*
organisation, structural changes in 168
organisational complexity 191–2
    case illustration 191–2
organisational context 137–9, 172
organisational culture 221
organisational structure *186–7*
orthodoxy, theoretical 214–16
other, fear of 220, 235
outcome evaluation, difficulty of 26
outcome research 254

parables 239
paradigms
    competing 44–5, 50
    scientific 235
parasuicide 74, 206
parent training *116, 117*
parental conflict 258
parenting programmes 90
    attention deficit hyperactivity
        disorder (ADHD) 99
parents
    Common Assessment Framework
        110
    drug and alcohol problems 23
    satisfaction with assessment 112
Parsons, Talcott 217
participation, service users 144
particularist theory 223
partnership working 106, 127
    defining 135–6
    essential elements 156
    see also collaborative working; multi-
        disciplinary working
paternalism 169
pathologising, beliefs 237
persecution, religious 235
personal growth 231
perspectives
    children's 169
    professional 191
    seeing others' 225
    understanding and valuing 149
Philippines 210
physical punishment 220
place of safety 259
places, special 247, 251
polarisation, social 133
police, stereotyping 214
policy
    'race'-related 213
    response to childhood and adoles-
        cent experience 52–3, 54
    young people as centre 89
policy changes 27, 33–4, 168
policy shift 44–5
political parties, xenophobia and
    racism 214
Popper, Karl 217
popular culture 208
population changes 211
positive factors 44
possession 246
Post Qualifying Award in Social Work
    (PQSW) 33

post-traumatic stress disorder (PTSD)
    116
post-traumatic stress syndrome 210
postmodernism 248
poverty 40, 166, 211, 242, 258
power differentials 224
practice
    cognitive behavioural practice
        122–3
    community work practice 120
    crisis intervention 119–20
    culturally aware 206–7
    culturally competent 220–6
    emancipatory 221–2
    models and methods 118–26
    narrative therapeutic practice 124–6
    psychodynamic practice 121–2
    reflective 217, 222–3, 228
    systemic practice 120–1
    taking account of religion and
        spirituality 248
    task-centred practice 123–4
practice changes, need for 33–4
practitioner, developing new 140–1
prevalence 54–6
    Asperger syndrome (AS) 78
    autism 77
    self-harm 81, 102
preventive focus 15
primary mental health workers
    (PMHW) 30–3
Prince's Trust, survey of young people
    70–1
prioritising 35
privacy 200
problem solving *116*
professional development 22
professional discourses 44
professional identities, blurring of
    42–3, 46
protective factors 23
proverbs 239
proximity 177
psychiatric admissions 192–3
psychiatric assessment 198
psychiatric terminology 18
psychiatry, as dominant discourse
    44, 50
psychodynamic practice 121–2
psychological problems, use of term 18
psychological therapies *117*
psychology, religion and spirituality
    241–3
psychosis, and suicide 75
psychosocial model 38–9
    holism 54
psychosocial practice, and spirituality
    245
psychotherapy *116*
puberty 219
public authorities, definition and
    duties 161
punishment 89, 220
purpose 233

qualitative measures 146
Quality Protects 44
quantification, of outcomes 26

quantitative measures 146
questions, willingness to ask 149
Qur'an 232, 239

'race' 213, 214
Race Relations Act 1976 161
Race Relations (Amendment) Act 2000 161
racism 51, 113–14, 143, 160–1, 205, 220, 224
rationalism 235
reactive provision 15
realism 156
reciprocity 156
recognition, mental health problems 52–4
record keeping 176
referrals 73
reflection 154, 255
  and mental health 261–2
  on personal attitudes and bias 215
reflective practice 217, 222–3, 228
refocusing 44
refugees 161, 170, 200, 206, 210, 211, 214, 220
Relationship Problems Questionnaire 101
relationship with commissioners 184
relativity 51
religion
  assessing relevance 240–1
  and belief 234–6
  decline of organised 236
  inner world of child 244–5
  overview 231–4
  and psychology 241–3
  as psychotherapeutic 233
  recognising importance 251
  and social development 235
  threats from environment and conflict 245
  viewed as oppressive 232
  see also beliefs; faith; spirituality
religious education 240
religiousness, intrinsic and extrinsic 239
research
  care in interpretation 254
  flaws in 43
  national programme 35
  outcome research 254
  participation in 43–4
research and development, role of PMHWs 32
research evidence, family therapy 173–4
resentment 211
resilience 23, 39, 44, 68, 206, 257–8
  and spirituality 234
resources
  constraints 168
  theoretical 216–17
respect 156, 202
responsibility 15
  individual 89–90
  for well-being 16
revelation, of self 233

risk
  competent practice 133
  defining 130–3
  guidance and legislation 132–3
  to social workers 128
  taking holistic view 130
risk assessment
  and management 126, 134
  self-harm 83–4, 86
risk control perspective 130–1
risk factors 23, 39, 46, 255, 257–8
  inequality 214
  interplay 254
  new 212
  offending 90–1
  schizophrenia 94
  suicide 74
risk management perspective 131–2
risk taking 130, 156
robustness 59
roles
  blurring of 42–3, 46
  changing 30
  expansion of 143
Royal College of Psychiatrists 144, 207
running away 23

safeguarding children boards 30
safeguards 191, 196
safety, place of 259
scapegoating 129
schizophrenia 93–6, 102
  assessment 94–5
  care 94
  case illustration 95–6
  and ethnic origin 40
  service users and carers 95
  treatments 117
school exclusion 54–5, 206
school phobia 76
schools, duty to co-operate 189
science 235
Seebohm Report 45
self
  individuation and revelation 233
  sense of 259
self-harm 54, 74, 81–9, 102
  child and family resources 85
  control 87
  initial intervention 84
  levels of risk 86
  moving forward 88
  other problems 84
  prevention 85–6
  risk assessment 83–4, 86
  treatments 118
self-help, bulimia nervosa 93, 118
self identity 39
self-management, of self harm 118
sensitivity, to cultural values 225
separation anxiety disorder 76
service development 27–8
service evaluation tools 144–8
service-level agreements 184
service provider guidelines 184, 185–6
service provision

  broader context 33–6
  development of 137–8
  fragmentation 135
  and human rights 201
  problems with 253
  uneven 185–6, 203
service users
  empowerment 43–5
  participation 144
  schizophrenia 95
services
  age-appropriate 195
  aims 185
  cross-cultural 223
sex, decision making 255
shame 244
  self-harm 88
similarities, between team members 41
sin 244, 245–6
single parent households 242
Sioux 217–19
skills base
  improving 34
  reduction of 26
skills, in direct work 115–18
skills training 105, 176
  see also training
skin colour 214
Skinner, B.F. 216
small culture 212
social care, adopting business characteristics 219
social change 168, 212
social class, and mental health problems 40
social conditions, pathologising 91
social construction, view of mental health 66
social disability 73
social exclusion 34, 40, 90–1, 179
social justice 231
social policy context 160
social policy perspectives, child development 66–7
social resources, Common Assessment Framework 111
social skills training 116
social welfare, effects of globalisation 219–20
social withdrawal 215–16
social work
  changes in focus and practice 27
  changing context 21–2
  debates 27–8
  evolution of 22
  generic 25
  key purpose of 13–14
  lack of attention to 46
  perceptions of 199
  principles of 203
  skills 105
social work role 36–40, 201–3
social workers
  and families 163–6
  risk to 128
sociological explanations, mental health problems 66–7

sociology, as theoretical resource 217
South America 242
special educational needs 192
Special Educational Needs and
    Disability Act 2001 192
special places 247, 251
specialist care, schizophrenia *117*
specialist social workers, changing role
    and function 25–7
speech, in autism 77
Spence Children's Anxiety Scale *101*
spiritual development 240
spiritual disorder 247
spirituality
    Aboriginal peoples 247–8
    assessing relevance 240–1
    and child development 238–41
    core qualities 244
    cross-cultural studies 240
    and culture 236–8
    defining 232
    inner world of child 244–5
    overview 231–4
    and psychology 241–3
    and psychosocial practice 245
    qualities of 251
    recognising importance 251
    and resilience 234
    threats from environment and
        conflict 245
    see also beliefs; faith; religion
standardisation, of assessment 64
statutory power, of social workers 202
stereotypes 48, 75, 114, 163, 207,
    214, 220, 224
stigma, 48, 52, 143, 175, 199
stories 238, 241–2, 246
storytelling 124–6
strategic planning, role of PMHWs 32
Strengths and Difficulties
    Questionnaire (SDQ) 71–2, *101*
stress 259
    cross-cultural studies 210–11
    within families 211
structural changes 30
subculture 212
substance misuse 80–1, 255
    and offending 91
    and suicide 74
suicidal thoughts 73
suicide 54–5, 74–5, 206
supervised community treatment 196
supervision 176
surah 239
synthesis, between methods and
    models 224
systemic practice 120–1, 165, 179
systemic theory 63–4
    and cultural competence 223–4
systemic therapy 173

task-centred practice 123–4
teachers, stereotyping 214
team management 140
technique 176
terminology 18, 48, 68
    definitions and distinctions 48–9, *49*

The Arabian Nights 246
'The Fisherman and the Jinny' 246
The Next Steps 30
theo-politics 236
theonomy 249
theoretical understanding, importance
    of 68
theories, linking 68
therapeutic foster care *117*
therapy
    and cultural belief 245–50
    multi-cultural 249
therapy culture 208
threat
    sense of 259
    social workers as 164
Tillich, Paul 249
timing 177
Together we Stand 41
top-level trust planning *184*
Torah 239
tradition, in methods and models
    224–5
training 22, 32–3
    core programme 138–9
    cultural competence 207
    focus of role 202
    initial 253
    interprofessional 42, 141
    role of PMHWs 31
    see also skills training
transcendence 232, 233
transition
    to adult services 253
    childhood to adolescence 218–19
translators 226
trauma 170, 206, 210, 260
Trauma Symptom Checklist for
    Children *101*
treatments *116–18*
trust 247

ultra vires 199
UN Convention on the Rights of the
    Child 90, 196
unemployment 206
unfairness, of decisions 199
United Kingdom Council for
    Psychotherapy 167
United States 206, 208, 210
universal services 32
universalist theory 223
unqualified support 35
unreasonableness, of decisions 199

value, and spirituality 232
values 37
victimisation, risk of suicide 75
violence 91
voluntary agencies 35
voluntary support, pressure on 26
vulnerable children 70, 102
vulnerable groups *14*

waiting times 14
Wally Feelings Game *101*

Wally Social Skills and Problem
    Solving Game *101*
war 206
    religion and spirituality 245
watchful waiting *116*
wealth inequalities 209–10
welfare context 28–30
welfare state, changing 22
well-being 49–50, 188, 261–2
    in context of offending 89
    importance of promotion 65–6
    religion and spirituality 241, 251
    responsibility for 16
    young people 64–5
what works 172
white superiority 214
women, empowerment of 75
workforce 23–7, 24, 30–1, 33
working class clients 38
workloads 155
worth 21

xenophobia 160–1, 214

young people
    as active participants 15–16, 32
    attachment 60, 61, 62–3
    as centre of policy 89
    as consumers 208
    control 87
    empowering 43–5
    explanations of self-harm 82–3
    heterogeneity 16
    media representations 29–30
    mental health 64–5
    offending 89–91
    participation in research 43–4
    promoting well-being 65–6
    role in defining mental health 54
    use of term 18
    well-being 64–5
youth justice 89–91, 192

Author Index

Italic page numbers indicate tables and figures.

Achenbach, T.M. 71–2, *100*
Ackroyd, J. 206, 211
Adams, R. 24, 27
Aggleton, P. 74
Ainsworth, M. 56, 59
Akister, J. 162, 163, 173, 175
Alderson, P. 43, 66, 143
Alihbai-Brown, Y. 227
Allan, W. 211
Alvarez, A. 78
American Psychiatric Association 50
Amin, K. 213
Amos, T. 74
Anderson, K. 51
Anderson, L. 51
Angold, M. *101*
Appleby, L. 74
Arcelus, J. 34
Audit Commission 22, 33, 54, 167, 168–9, 183

Bagley, C. 210, 211
Bahl, V. 223
Bailey, R. 219
Baistow, R. 142
Baldwin, M. 221
Barclay, P. 24
Barker, S. 142
Barnes, M. 143
Barter, C. 210
Baumann, G. 227
Bayley, R. 42, 141, 166
Beatch, R. 242
Beckett, C. 40, 118, 216, 219
Bellerby, T. 34
Berger, M. 170
Bhugra, D. 223
Bhui, K. 143
Bilton, T. 66, 214
Birchall, E. 114
Blackwell, D. 210
Blum, R.W. 234

Bochner, S. 210
Borland, M. 43
Bowlby, John 56, *58*
Bracken, M.B. 71
Bradshaw, J. 40
Brake, B. 219
Brammer, A. 194, 197
Brearley, J. 24, 132
Briere, J. *101*
Briggs, S. 29, 75, 220
Broidy, L.M. 91
Brown, B. 143, 175
Burnham, J. 175
Burns, B. 210
Bushnell, N. 140
Butrym, Z. 24

Campbell, D. 170
Caplan, G. 119
Carmel, F. 40
Carr, A. 23, 144, 210
Carroll, M. 232
Central Council for the Education and Training of Social Workers (CCETSW) 24, 27–8
Chalmers, I. 174
Chambers, K. 35
Chand, A. 210
Christiansen, E. 44
Clarke, L. 40
Cobb, M. 236
Coles, R. 240
Colton, M. 168
Conners, C.K. *100*
Cook, W.L. 64
Cooper, J. 74
Cooper, P. 23
Copley, B. 24
Corby, B. 112
Corrigan, P. 28, 219
Costello, P. *101*
Coulshed, V. 44, 118
Crawford, P. 143
Crisp, B. 247

Crittenden, P.M. 59
Crompton, M. 244, 247

Dallos, R. 169
Darongkamas, J. 143
Davies, M. 24
Davis, H. 26, 34, 35, 39, 140
Davis, J. 43
Daycare Trust 242
DeBell, D. 138
Dennis, J. 162
Department for Children, Schools and Families 28, *100*, 185, 253
Department for Education and Employment 42, 141
Department for Education and Skills (DfES) 22, 30, 108, 151, 152
Department of Health 22, 26, 27, 28, 29, 30, 35, 42, 44, 45, *100*, 107, 111, 141, 143, 144, 146, 153, 167, 183, 185
Department of Health and Social Security 199
Devine, D. 39, 106
Devine, P. 169
Dimigen, G. 141
Doel, M. 118
Dogra, N. 206
Dominelli, L. 24, 28, 38, 160, 219, 223
Draper, R. 169, 170
Duck, S. 216
Dulmus, C. 23, 35
Duncan, S. 150
Dundes, A. 239
Durlak, J. 35, 167
Dwivedi, K.N. 205
Dyer, M. 42

Early Childhood Education Forum 67
Eayrs, C. 166
Eber, L. 222
Egan, G. 28
Elliot, V. 226
Epston, D. 125

Erikson, Erik 57
Evans, P. 42

Fadden, G. 148
Fagin, C.M. 42, 141
Falicov, C. 224
Falloon, I. 148
Feeney, J.A. 64
Feinauer, L.L. 234
Ferguson, H. 33
Fernando, S. 241
Fieldhouse, R. 33
Firth, M. 42, 141
Fombonne, E. 40
Fonagy, A. 210
Fonagy, P. 48, 70, 260, 261
Fook, J. 26, 221
Forryan, B. 24
Fortune, S. 83, 88
Frankel, S. 74
Freeman, I. 43
Freud, Sigmund 57
Friedlander, M.L. 173
Fulcher, L.C. 237
Furedi, F. 208
Furlong, A. 40
Furniss, T. 150

Gale, F. 30, 31, 140
Galpin, D. 33
Gamble, N. 212
Garner, D.M. 100
General Social Care Council (GSCC)
    22, 24, 36–7
George, C. 59
Gerong, A. 210
Ghaziuddin, M. 77
Ghuman, P. 237
Gibson-Cline, J. 210
Giddings, F.H. 24
Gillick, V. 151
Glaser, D. 260
Goldenberg, H. 173
Goldenberg, I. 173
Goodman, R. 29, 33, 71, 101
Gordon, G. 43, 169
Gorell Barnes, G. 163, 164, 169
Gowers, S. 100, 145
Grant, R. 43, 169
Grealish, M. 223
Grove, M. 156
Guerin, S. 232
Gunnell, D. 74

Hacking, I. 44
Hadfield, J. 51
Hagel, A. 64
Hagell, A. 90
Hall, S. 208
Hallett, C. 114
Haralambos, M. 209
Harris, L.J. 234
Harris, P. 80, 81
Harrison, R. 156
Harter, S. 101
Hartley, J. 207
Hassett, A. 30

Hawton, K. 83
Hay, D. 240, 244
Health Advisory Service 27, 50, 138,
    183, 185
Healy, K. 222
Hellinckx, W. 168
Hendrick, H. 66, 152
Hennessey, E. 43
Heppleston, T. 140
Herington, S. 26
Hetherington, J. 142
Heyman, L. 52
Higgins, K. 169
Higham, P. 24
Hill, M. 43, 169
Hodes, M. 245
Holliday, A. 212, 227
Hollis, E. 38
Howarth, J. 112
Howe, D. 24, 28, 39, 59, 171, 174
Howe, G. 26
Howlin, P. 78
Hughes, D. 143
Human Rights Commission 248
Hurrell, P. 42
Hurry, J. 74
Hutchings, J. 39

International Association of Schools of
    Social Work 14
Ivey, A. 224

Jackson, R. 240
James, A. 151
James, G. 44
Jayajaran, U. 248
Jenkins, R. 209, 218
Jensen, A.L. 71
Jezzard, B. 255
Joint Council for the Welfare of
    Immigrants (JCWI) 162
Jones, R. 166
Jones, T. 206
Jordan, B. 28, 38
Joughin, C. 23, 142, 207
Jouriles, E. 211
Joy, I. 90, 117–18
Jurkovic, G. 170

Kanner, L. 76
Kashani, J. 211
Kasl, S. 71
Kearney, P. 149
Kehily, J. 207
Kemps, C. 263
Kemshall, H. 24
Kendall, P. 76
Klineberg, O. 217
Kohn, M. 213
Kovacs, M. 100
Kurtz, Z. 15, 33, 35, 137, 141, 183

Lane, M. 45
Larkin, Philip 162
Larsen, L. 240
Lask, B. 25
Lask, J. 25

Lavalette, M. 33
Laybourn, A. 43
Lazear, K. 35
Leathard, A. 148, 152
Leganger-Krogstad, H. 240
Leighton, A.H. 223
Leonard, P. 26, 28, 219
Leung, J. 22
Levin, E. 149
L'Heureux, J. 75
Lindon, J. 152
Lorenz, W. 33
Lynch, M. 106

McClure, G. 54–5
McGuire, J.B. 26
Madge, N. 212
Magrab, P. 42, 141, 222
Maitra, B. 97
Malek, M. 207
Mallick, A. 210, 211
Marsh, P. 38, 118
Martin, G. 210
Marx, Karl 162
Mason, Julia 262
Masson, J. 208
Maughan, D. 261
Meltzer, H. 40
Melzak, S. 210
Mental Health Act Commission 192
Mental Health Foundation 22, 26, 33,
    51, 52, 81, 82, 87, 167
Micklewright, J. 22, 166, 167
Middleton, L. 40
Midgeley, J. 219, 221
Millar, M. 112
Mills, R. 216
Milner, J. 40, 118
Minnis, H. 101
Mishra, R. 219
Morrison, L. 75
Morton-Cooper, A. 77
Moules, N. 151, 248
Mun, E. 141
Muncie, J. 163
Munley, A. 143

Nash, M. 233
National CAMH Support Service 31
National Institiute for Health and
    Clinical Excellence 92, 94, 97
National Institute for Health and
    Clinical Excellence 72
NCH Action for Children 23
Newman, T. 90, 206
NHS Advisory Service 41
NISW 143

Oberheumer, P. 222
O'Byrne, P. 40, 118
O'Donnell, G. 217
Office for National Statistics 54
O'Hagan, K. 24, 199
Olajide, D. 143
Onyet, S. 140
Orme, J. 44, 118
Osuch, R. 222

Otikikpi, T. 206
Oullette, P. 35
Ovretveit, J. 41

Paloutzian, R.F. 239
Papadopoulos, R. 170
Parekh, B. 207
Parton, N. 26, 39
Payne, M. 24, 26, 27, 118
Pearce, J.B. 33, 143, 186
Pease, B. 26
Penderson, P. 224
Piaget, Jean 58
Pickles, A. 50
Pieterse, J. N. 219
Pilkington, A. 206, 211
Pinkerton, J. 169
Plesner, I.T. 240
Pope, A. 112
Powers, C.S. 143
Prince's Trust 70–1

Rabe-Hesketh, S. 101
Ramsay, J. 151
Rapp-Paglicci, L. 23, 35
Raval, H. 249
Ravazzola, M.C. 242
Rawson, D. 42, 141
Read, J. 142
Redditt, C. 222
Reder, P. 150
Reed, A.W. 239
Reichelt, S. 170
Reimers, A. 165
Remschmidt, H. 142
Rendell, P. 43
Repper, J. 143
Resnik, M.D. 234
Reynolds, A.J. 206
Richardson, J. 23, 142
Richmond, M. 24
Robshaw, V. 236
Rodney, C. 146
Rosen, G. 149
Rosenberry, W. 26
Roth, A. 210
Ruch, G. 24
Rutter, M. 22, 23, 29, 39, 40, 78, 90,
    167, 219, 254, 257, 262–3

Salzberger-Wittenberg, I. 29
Savin-Williams, R. 75
Sawyer, M.G. 136
Schaffer, D. 100
Schoon, L. 133
Scott, S. 29, 65
Sebuliba, D. 30, 42, 141
Shadish, W.R. 173
Sims, D. 43
Sinclair, J. 83
Singh, A. 22
Singh, N. 22, 29, 167
Sinha, C. 232
Smaje, C. 40
Smith, D. 22, 40
Smith, T. 162
Snelgrove, S. 143

Social Care Institute for Excellence
    (SCIE) 106, 134
Solomon, J. 59
Solomos, J. 161
Spence, S.H. 101
Spencer, N. 206
Spender, Q. 77, 97
Spurr, P. 26, 39
Stanley, K. 210
Statham, J. 45, 163, 168
Stein, A. 26
Stepney, R. 27
Stewart, B. 233, 242
Stewart, K. 22, 166, 167
Sue, D. 224, 249
Sutton, C. 23, 169, 223
Suwa, M. 216
Sveaass, N. 170
Swann, J. 207
Swinton, J. 236, 237
Sylva, K. 167

Taylor, B. 39, 106
Taylor, C. 44, 222
Thoburn, J. 45, 168
Thompson, N. 217
Thompson, S. 217
Thornes, R. 15
Thurston, C. 149
Timini, S. 97
Titmuss, R.M. 24
Tovey, W. 24
Treacher, A. 165, 170, 171, 173
Treseder, P. 143
Trevithick, P. 24, 27, 105, 119
Tseng Yueh Hung 227
Tucker, N. 212
Tucker, S. 146, 222
Tunstill, J. 168

Valentine, C.A. 209
Valentine, L. 234
VanDenBerg, J. 223
Vincent, J. 211
Vostanis, P. 23, 42, 70, 141, 205
Vostanis, V. 34

Walker, S. 22, 23, 26, 28, 38, 39, 40,
    43, 44, 45, 118, 138, 142, 143,
    149, 161, 162, 163, 166, 167,
    169, 173, 175, 193, 194, 206,
    207, 208, 209, 213, 217, 219,
    222, 224, 234, 235, 246, 263
Warnick, E.M. 71
Warren, L. 143
Warwick, I. 74
Waterhouse, S. 77
Watkins, D. 210
Watson, J. 45
Weaver, H. 210
Webb, S. 172, 174
Webster-Stratton, C. 101
Weherner, H. 74
Weisz, J.R. 71
Wells, A. 35
White, K. 156
White, M. 125

White, S. 44, 222
Whiting, L. 225
Whyte, B. 89, 91
Wilding, J. 45
Wilkes, J. 42
Williams, B. 143
Williams, J. 40
Williams, M. 168
Williams, R. 238
Williamson, J.B. 143
Wilson, J. 43
Wilson, K. 151
Wisbech and West Norfolk AHA 151
Wolkind, S. 15, 101
Wong, V. 215–16
Woods, M. 38
World Health Organization 23, 27,
    29, 50
www.rip.org.uk 14

Yelloly, M. 29
Yeo, S. 242, 248
Ying, W. 216
Young, L. 211
Young Minds 262
Youth Justice Board 75